Entrepreneurial Values and Strategic Management

Bocconi on Management Series

Series Editor: **Robert Grant**, Eni Professor of Strategic Management, Department of Management, Università Commerciale Luigi Bocconi, Italy.

The *Bocconi on Management* series addresses a broad range of contemporary and cutting-edge issues relating to the management of organizations and the environment in which they operate. Consistent with Bocconi University's ongoing mission to link good science with practical usefulness, the series is characterized by its integration of relevance, accessibility and rigor. It showcases the work of scholars from all over the world, who have produced contributions to the advancement of knowledge building on theoretical, disciplinary, cultural or methodological traditions with the potential to improve management practice.

The series is edited by the Center for Research in Organization and Management (CROMA) at Bocconi University, and is published through an agreement between Palgrave Macmillan and Bocconi University Press, an imprint of Egea.

For information about submissions of book proposals or the series in general, please contact Maurizio Zollo at maurizio.zollo@unibocconi.it or Robert Grant at grant@unibocconi.it.

Titles include:

Massimo Amato, Luigi Doria and Luca Fantacci (*editors*)
MONEY AND CALCULATION
Economic and Sociological Perspectives

Vittorio Coda
ENTREPRENEURIAL VALUES AND STRATEGIC MANAGEMENT
Essays in Management Theory

Bocconi on Management Series
Series Standing Order ISBN 978–0–230–27766–3

You can receive future title in this series as they are published by placing a standing order. Please contact your bookseller or, in case of difficulty, write to us at the address below with your name and address, the title of the series and the ISBN quoted above.

Customer Services Department, Macmillan Distribution Ltd, Houndmills, Basingstoke, Hampshire RG21 6XS, England.

Entrepreneurial Values and Strategic Management

Essays in Management Theory

Vittorio Coda

First published 2010 by
PALGRAVE MACMILLAN

Palgrave Macmillan in the UK is an imprint of Macmillan Publishers Limited,
registered in England, company number 785998, of Houndmills, Basingstoke,
Hampshire RG21 6XS.

Palgrave Macmillan in the US is a division of St Martin's Press LLC,
175 Fifth Avenue, New York, NY 10010.

Palgrave Macmillan is the global academic imprint of the above companies
and has companies and representatives throughout the world.

Palgrave® and Macmillan® are registered trademarks in the United States,
the United Kingdom, Europe and other countries.

ISBN: 978–0–230–25016–1 hardback

This book is printed on paper suitable for recycling and made from fully
managed and sustained forest sources. Logging, pulping and manufacturing
processes are expected to conform to the environmental regulations of the
country of origin.

A catalogue record for this book is available from the British Library.

Library of Congress Cataloging-in-Publication Data

Coda, Vittorio.
    Entrepreneurial values and strategic management : essays in
management theory / Vittorio Coda.
        p. cm.—(Bocconi on management series)
        ISBN 978–0–230–25016–1
            1. Industrial management. 2. Strategic planning. 3. Entrepreneurship. I. Title.

HD31.C578 2010
658.4'012—dc22   2010023770

10 9 8 7 6 5 4 3 2 1
19 18 17 16 15 14 13 12 11 10

Printed and bound in Great Britain by
CPI Antony Rowe, Chippenham and Eastbourne

To all those who passionately pursue management studies in order to contribute to the common good

Contents

Acknowledgments

First of all, my thanks go to my dear colleagues in the Strategic and Entrepreneurial Management area at Bocconi University; their initiative is what led to the creation of this book. In particular, thanks to Giorgio Brunetti, who selected the writings included in this volume; Carlo Salvato, who took on the task of editing the excellent translations by Jill Connelly; and Robert Grant, who willingly accepted the invitation of his colleagues and wrote the Introduction as only he could.

As for this collection of writings, for anything of value in them I am indebted to so many people in the academic and business worlds for their ideas and input that I cannot possibly list them all without some unforgivable omissions. So, I will name only a few here: Carlo Masini, who gave me my grounding in Italian economic and management inquiry; my colleagues at SDA Bocconi School of Management, who share my passion for management and the ideal of contributing to improving organizations; the people involved in the two studies that substantially enriched the empirical foundations on which I developed my view, one on corporate crises in the late 1970s, and one on entrepreneurial values and strategic behavior in the 1980s, conducted in conjunction with a related course given with Professor Marco Vitale; friend and management consultant Andrés Breiter, who initiated me into system dynamics for a deeper understanding of the complexity and dynamism of organizational systems; and my students, who gradually found themselves involved in the specific research needed for some of these papers. To everyone my profound gratitude. Naturally, for the content of these writings, I alone am responsible for any shortcomings, for which I sincerely apologize.

The author and publishers are grateful to the following publishers for permission to publish these new English translations of Professor Coda's original Italian essays:

Chapter 1: "L'economia aziendale: contenuti, specificità e ruolo," in AA.VV., *Scritti in onore di Francesco Brambilla*, vol. 1, Milan: Edizioni Bocconi Comunicazione, 1986.

Chapter 2: "L'economia aziendale nella seconda metà degli anni '50: una rivisitazione delle 'produzioni' e dell'opera postuma di Gino Zappa," *Rivista di contabilità e cultura aziendale* 2 (2), 2002.

Chapter 3: "La valutazione della formula imprenditoriale," *Sviluppo & Organizzazione* 82 (March–April), Milan: Este, 1984.

Chapter 4: "Finalismo dell'impresa: fisiologia e patologia," *Aggiornamenti sociali*, 39 (2–3), Milan, 1988.

Chapter 5: "Il governo della dinamica della strategia," by Vittorio Coda and Edoardo Mollona, *Finanza, Marketing e Produzione* 4, Milan: Egea, 2002.

Chapter 6: "Strategie d'impresa e comunicazione, il legame mancante," *Finanza, Marketing e Produzione*, 1, Milan: Egea, 1990.

Chapter 7: "Ruolo della proprietà nei risanamenti di imprese," in AA.VV., *Finanza aziendale e mercato finanziario. Scritti in onore di Giorgio Pivato*, vol. 2, pp. 681–90, Milan: Giuffrè, 1982.

Chapter 8: "Il rapporto tra impresa e lavoro: prospettive di evoluzione," in AA.VV., *Scritti in onore di Carlo Masini*, vol. 1: *Istituzioni di economia*, Milan: Egea, 1993.

Chapter 9: "Codici etici e liberazione dell'economia," in *Codici etici e cultura di mercato*, Atti del Workshop ISVI, Milan, 5 November 1993.

Chapter 10: "Da una economia bloccata a una economia imprenditoriale, libera e responsabile," *La società*, Verona: Fondazione Toniolo, 1995.

Illustrations

Figures

Table

Introduction: Some Thoughts on Vittorio Coda's Contributions to Strategic Management

Robert M. Grant,
Eni Professor of Strategic Management in the Energy Sector,
Bocconi University

When I joined Bocconi University at the beginning of 2008, I already knew Vittorio Coda from my previous visits to Bocconi and our joint involvement in Eni's corporate university. Although I was aware of Professor Coda's leading role in the development of strategic management at Bocconi and within Italy, the barrier of language had prevented me from reading all but a few of his writings. These translations of a selection of Professor Coda's papers have offered me a wonderful opportunity to become acquainted with his research.

In this brief introduction, I will not attempt either to summarize Vittorio Coda's papers or to appraise his contribution to the development of the field of strategic management. My goal is more limited and more personal. I will restrict myself to three types of observation on his papers. First, I will identify the ideas, concepts, and theories he has contributed that I have found particularly interesting and thought-provoking. Second, I will attempt to link these developments to parallel and subsequent research that has appeared in English-language journals. Third, I will identify those contributions that have not, in my opinion, received the attention they merit in the Anglo-Saxon world and which have the potential to contribute to the development of our field. It is in this last area that I believe this volume will prove particularly valuable.

I will organize my commentary around five themes: first, Coda's contribution to the debate over the goals of the firm, notably his integrative perspective on shareholder and stakeholder approaches

1

to the firm; second, his conceptualization of firm strategy, concentrating on his "entrepreneurial formula" construct and the overall strategy framework within which it is located; third, his contribution to our understanding of the strategy-making process within firms; fourth, his development of the link between business strategy and management communication; finally, in recognition of the Italian context within which Coda has developed his analysis, the contextual specificity of Coda's management theory. I specifically address whether Coda's socially embedded, systemic view of the firm and the "free and responsible entrepreneurial economy" within which it is located offer a model that is especially relevant to the post-financial-crisis world in which we find ourselves.

1. Firm goals and business purpose

Coda's discussion of the goals and purpose of the business enterprise offers an interesting perspective on the long-running debate over the goals of the firm. His conceptualization of the firm and its relationships within society transcends stale arguments over shareholders versus stakeholders and views the firm less as an agent of individual interests and more as a social and economic institution that unifies the interests of the different participants.

Similar views have been expressed subsequently by several writers. William Allen (1992) contrasts two notions of the public corporation: "the property conception," which views the firm as a set of assets owned by stockholders, and the "social entity conception," which views the firm as a community of individuals sustained by relationships to the firm's social, political, economic, and natural environment. The stakeholder view of the firm can be viewed as a variant of the notion of the firm as property: although customers, employees, and suppliers do not have ownership rights over the firm, the idea that the firm reflects the interests of its individual participants clearly parallels the property conception.

In contrast, the social entity view – which I consider much closer to Coda's conceptualization – regards the firm as possessing aspirations that are not simply the personal interests of its owners, stakeholders, or top management team. One of the most appealing expositions of this view is Arie De Geus's (1997) conception of the "Living Company," which views the company as a purposeful living organism that seeks development and longevity. The firm as social entity concept is also central to Charles Handy's view of the business enterprise. He dismisses "shareholder capitalism" as a hangover from the 19th century: in the 21st century shareholders invest in companies but are not "owners" in any meaningful sense (Handy, 2002).

Core to this debate over different conceptions of the firm is the issue of the appropriate goals for the firm. The appeal of the property conception is that it simplifies management: owners desire profit, and from the principle of profit maximization derives a whole system of management tools ranging from capital budgeting rules to incentive pay for workers. Of course, problems arise – the agency problem in particular. But these problems impose costs and necessitate mechanisms to align the objectives of owners and managers; they do not undermine the viability of the profit-maximizing (or shareholder-value-maximizing) firm. Once we transition from shareholder focus to stakeholder focus, this simplicity is gone. Management becomes lost in quagmire of multiple, conflicting objectives and a near-total absence of the management tools necessary for linking multiple objectives to resource allocation and operating decision making. As a result, we face a dilemma: either we adopt a narrow shareholder focus that is uninspiring for most of the individuals who are actively engaged in the firm or we adopt a more inclusive conception and in doing so lose our capacity to manage the firm.

In "The Purpose of the Firm: Physiology and Pathology," Coda offers us a way out of this dilemma. In seeking a middle way between the dangers of "absolutizing profit" and "downgrading the role of profit" through "misconceived sociality" or the quest for "technical excellence," Coda points to the need for "creatively integrating social needs and market demands in a winning entrepreneurial vision with intrinsic economic validity." There are two components to this integration, both of which anticipate subsequent contributions to the literature on firm objectives and social goals.

The first component is the establishment of commonality among the goals of profit, competitiveness, and social purpose. Coda's "physiological" view of the firm envisages profit as a "key element in the circular movement of other equally important goals and objectives." The result is that "shareholders' prosperity and stakeholders' satisfaction" become "indivisible." What distinguishes this approach from subsequent writings on the compatibility between stakeholder goals and shareholder goals (e.g., Preston and Sapienza, 1990) and between profit performance and corporate social responsibility (e.g.,

Porter and Kramer, 2006) is Coda's articulation of a dynamic relationship between profit and the interests of stakeholders in which the critical linking mechanism is the building of competitive advantages through the development of distinctive competences.

The second component of Coda's integration of profit goals with broader stakeholder and societal objectives is his concept of business purpose. Despite Coda's endorsement of a stakeholder approach to the firm, it is clear that he does not view the firm simply as a vehicle for pursuing the interests of its owners and other stakeholders: it is an institution with purpose. As Coda observes when discussing the "entrepreneurial formula" in Chapter 3: "Continuity leads to a view of the enterprise as an institution which goes beyond the life and interests of those stakeholders who are in charge of it for a brief span of its history and must be maintained and passed on intact to future generations."

Thus, although Coda recognizes the importance of meeting the needs of key stakeholders – providing a return to shareholders, satisfying customers, enhancing the potential of company personnel – the performance goals that most concern him are those that relate directly to the health of enterprise in terms of "profit, efficiency, productivity, profitability, and so forth, which are correlated to the competitive dimension."

The notion of enterprises having a purpose and pursing goals that are not simply amalgams of the individual interests of stakeholders has received increasing recognition from later writers. Jim Collins and Jerry Porras (1995) argue that "core purpose" – the organization's fundamental reason for being – links with "core values" to form the organization's "core ideology," which "defines an organization's timeless character" and is "the glue that holds the organization together" (p. 46). In a similar vein, Lovas and Ghoshal (2000) view the firm's objective function in terms of its strategic intent.

This focus on the goals of enterprises rather than those of the firm's members can also be seen in the entrepreneurial visions that have driven the founders of many of the world's great enterprises. The goal that drove Henry Ford was not the desire for wealth or power but the prospect of extending the freedom of private motoring to the masses. Similarly with Steve Jobs and Steve Wozniak: their driving force was the revolutionary vision of "one person, one computer." For Walt Disney it was enriching people's lives with "the best in family entertainment." Coda's concept of "business purpose" can liberate us from the debate over whether firms should exist to serve their shareholders or a wider coalition of stakeholders. By identifying firm goals with the vision and strategic intent of the enterprise we have the potential to avoid what Charles Handy (2002) views as "the tragic confusion" of regarding profit as the purpose for which companies exist while not falling into the management politicization and paralysis that tend to accompany a commitment to stakeholder interests.

2. The analysis of firm strategy

Vittorio Coda's most important contribution to the analytical framework of strategic management, in my view, is his conceptualization of strategy around what he calls "the entrepreneurial formula." Defining what strategy is has been a critical challenge for scholars. Most approaches to describing firm strategy adopt some variant of Bourgeois's (1980) dichotomization of strategy into "domain selection" and "domain navigation." For example, Markides (2000) defines strategy in terms of the answers to three questions: Who? What? and How? Here, the first two questions correspond to domain selection; the last, to domain navigation. Similarly, Collis and Rukstad (2008) argue that strategy can be articulated in terms of three components: objectives, scope, and competitive advantage.

The entrepreneurial formula is characterized by its breadth: it is the outcome of decisions made in five arenas: the competitive system, the product system, the broader stakeholder system, the firm's understandings with these stakeholders with regard to the implicit contractual arrangements ("prospects offered to/contributions requested from stakeholders"), and the enterprise structure. Coda's argument regarding the coherence among these five systems extends beyond the conventional notions of strategic fit found in the mainstream strategy literature, where the primary emphasis has been the strategy/ structure interface (e.g., Habib and Victor, 1991; Kim and Mauborgne, 2009). It is noteworthy that this broader systemic view of strategy anticipates the work of Teece et al. (1994) on corporate coherence.

These components of the entrepreneurial formula can be categorized into two broad subgroups. The first of these combines the product system, the competitive system, and structure to determine the "competitive formula" of the firm. This competitive formula is concerned with building a lasting competitive advantage, which, in turn, is the result of linking "key success factors" with "distinctive competences." Again, Coda anticipates the basic framework for the analysis of competitive advantage that was to enter the mainstream strategy literature during the late 1980s and early 1990s.

Whereas the competitive formula relates to competitive advantage in the firm's product market, the other subgroup, comprising the stakeholder system, operates at the corporate level and determines the availability of resources to the business units. An interesting distinction between Coda's analysis and the subsequent "resource-based view" of the firm is that the resource-based theorists tended to regard the firm's resources as either exogenous endowments or the result of path-dependent processes. In Coda's system, in contrast, the availability of resources is the outcome of the firm's management of a complex set of relationships with various stakeholders.

3. The strategy-making process

In "Governing Strategy Dynamics," Vittorio Coda and co-author Edoardo Mollona address the challenges to conventional notions of strategy formulation presented by the "process school" led by Henry Mintzberg, which includes the work of Bower, Burgelman, Pascale, and others. The result is a penetrating analysis of the strategy-making process that makes major strides in specifying the central features of strategy-making within firms, clarifying the role of management in the strategy process, and reconciling emergent processes with conscious strategic planning.

The key insights offered by Coda and Mollona are in three areas. The first area is bridging the "strategy as rational design" and "strategy as emergence" conceptions of strategy-making within organizations. The second is recognizing the cognitive and behavioral aspects of strategy. The third is distinguishing static from dynamic aspects of strategy and identifying the processes that constitute and determine these dynamics.

Coda reconciles the design and learning/emergence schools through a consideration of the role of management in the strategy process. In contrast to Mintzberg's view of emergence as an unspecified process that occurs somewhere outside the executive suite, Coda points to feedback mechanisms through which top management both shapes and is shaped by the processes of emergence. Coda argues that the "top executive manipulates the strategic/organizational context so as to induce emerging strategic initiatives." In my own study on strategic planning by large petroleum majors, I show that one mechanism for such manipulation is the strategic planning process itself, a process which I describe as "planned emergence" (Grant, 2003).

There is a further dimension to the distinction between strategy as design and strategy as emergence. Coda and Mollona point to strategy existing within two domains: the cognitive and the behavioral. At the cognitive level, strategy exists as mental models (including a "basic strategic orientation") and strategic intentions, both of which are influenced by deliberation and learning. This corresponds closely to the notion of strategy as rational design. (Such rationality may be both limited and distorted; see Schwenk, 1984; Spender, 1989.) Conversely, the emergent strategy school views the realized strategy that arises from emergent processes as constituting behavior in the form of decisions and actions; it is a "continuous flow of realized managerial actions." These two domains of strategy – "the world of thought and the world of action" – and their interactions are explored in greater depth by Gavetti and Rivkin (2007).

The main contribution of the dynamic model of strategy-making proposed by Coda and Mollona is to specify the processes through which strategy is created – both intended and emergent. These processes comprise

- learning processes through which senior managers revise their mental models and strategic intentions
- strategic planning processes through which strategy intentions are formulated (e.g., goal-setting, environmental assessment, benchmarking)
- strategy implementation processes, including communication processes, structural change processes, project initiation, and budgeting and staffing processes
- innovation processes relating to research projects, new product development, and business development
- selection mechanisms, including project "filtering" and capital budgeting

However, the key to the overall working of the strategy process is the existence of feedback loops within the system. For example, the "strategic control loop" drives actions triggered by performance gaps between goals and results. The "strategic intent formation loop" causes strategic intentions to adjust in response to outcomes. The "entrepreneurial loop" represents the link between realized strategy and the generation of bottom-up strategic initiatives. Through the "learning loop" senior managers' mental models adjust in response to the strategies that are being realized. These loops shape the dynamics of the strategy-making process. The critical requirement for a firm's successful adaptation and development is a balance among these feedback loops.

4. Strategy and management communication

In "Strategy and Communication: The Missing Link," Coda recognizes the role of communication in the implementation of corporate strategy and offers a transformative approach to the management of communication. Conventionally, communication by firms has been a fragmented activity within firms, with responsibility divided among multiple functions: public relations, marketing, human resource management, and shareholder relations. Often, key components of the communications function are outsourced to specialist public relations firms and marketing consultants.

Coda begins by recognizing that communication is central to the existence of the firm: "A firm communicates simply because it exists – it produces and markets certain products or services, and interacts with its myriad audiences." This provides the foundation for a view of communication that lies at the center of management activity: "both an activity that is firmly anchored in business strategy and a powerful lever for implementing this strategy." Once the firm is viewed as a system dependent upon maintaining relationships with consumers and the suppliers of resources, it is "management's responsibility to activate, connect, and maintain the virtuous circles in this model over time. Within this context, communication of all kinds plays a key role."

In addition to the development and reinforcement of these external and internal relationships, communication is directed toward investing in corporate image. In referring to the role of communication in building image – the "perceived identity of the firm" – Coda explicitly anticipates subsequent scholarly interest in the nature and role of corporate identity – in particular, the role of identity as a rationale for the existence of the firm (Kogut and Zander, 1996) and the determinants and consequences of organizational identity (Schultz et al., 2000). Coda also explores the links between communication and the culture of the firm and between communication and the emotional climate of the firm. This last topic anticipates the reviving interest in the role and use of rhetoric in managing organizational cognition, emotion, and behavior.

At the same time, Coda's view of the role of communication extends beyond issues of image and identity. To the extent that Coda conceptualizes the firm as a complex social entity embedded with a network of relationships – not just with suppliers and customers but also with the political and social systems – communication expresses "an underlying, long-term strategic orientation that takes functionality and enduring development of the firm as the primary value, and subordinates every other value to it." To support the functionality and continuous development of the firm communication must be viewed as a long-term strategic investment that is both dispersed across all forms of activities and integrated around consistent themes.

5. The contextuality of Management Theory

The papers in this volume span a period of two decades from the early 1980s to the early 2000s. As would be expected from a scholar who "approaches reality armed with theories that are anchored in what actually happens in the business world" (see Chapter 1, "Management Theory: Its Content, Specificities, and Role"), Coda's work is strongly influenced by the Italian business environment of the period. This raises the issue of the relevance of Coda's work to the international business environment of the second decade of the 21st century.

Clearly, several of the papers in this collection address issues that were highly relevant to the Italian business situation several decades ago but resonate much less strongly today. For example, "The Relationship between the Firm and Its Workforce: Prospects for Change" addresses the adversarial nature of employer–employee relations in a society characterized by socio-economic divisions and class solidarity. The article anticipates the transition from an antagonistic to a cooperative view of the firm though a shift in emphasis from the distribution to the production of wealth, to building social relationships within companies, and to refocusing corporate goals on growth rather than profitability. This conflict between management and organized labor was a feature of Europe's former industrial landscape, but it is less evident today. The reason is not the solution proposed by Coda but more that increasing international competition has caused the interests of workers, managers, and owners to converge around the basic goal of survival.

Similarly, Coda's comments on ownership and corporate governance requirements for the necessary restructuring of poorly performing companies apply primarily to the Italian situation, where family ownership, the role of banks, and idiosyncratic governance arrangements present particular problems for initiating turnaround strategies.

In other respects, several of the papers which specifically address aspects of the Italian business situation contain messages that are as valid today as when the papers were written. In the case of "Ethical Codes and Market Culture," the sources of ethical problems have changed – in fact, multiplied – but Coda's articulation of the role of codes of ethics and the conditions that cover their effectiveness is insightful and pragmatic.

These observation apply even more strongly to the final paper in this volume, "In Support of a Free and Responsible Entrepreneurial Economy." It too speaks to both a time and a place. Written in the mid-1990s, the article looks forward to an Italian economy that has broken free from the corrupt and backward-looking political system that had shackled innovation and economic growth for decades. Coda's inspiring vision of a liberal economy in which entrepreneurship provides the link between individual initiative and the economic well-being of society offered a manifesto for the economic system of the "new Italy" that the "clean hands" scandals of the early 1990s heralded. The inability of the reform movement to sustain itself against the deeply rooted dysfunctions of the Italian political system is the great tragedy of modern Italy. Nevertheless, Coda's call for a liberal market economy in which entrepreneurial initiative unifies the development of both individuals and society as a whole remains an enduring vision.

This raises the broader issue of the extent to which Coda's contributions to management theory are general or have particular relevance to the Italian national context. Such contextual influences are not something specific to the Italian "Economia Aziendale" tradition. The influences of time and place can be identified in most theoretical developments in the field of management: socio-technical systems theory was stimulated by the technological changes of the period after the Second World War (Trist and Bamforth, 1951), the theory of the multinational enterprise was a response to the wave of international corporate expansion during the 1950s and 1960s (Hymer, 1960; Stopford and Wells, 1972), and the knowledge-based view of the firm was stimulated by the emergence of the postindustrial, knowledge-based economy (Nonaka, 1994; Grant, 1996).

However, the fact that circumstances stimulate the development of certain theories does not mean that the circumstances define the domains of these theories. The management thought of Vittorio Coda has clearly been strongly influenced by the continental European context, where there is much less ideological consensus supporting the private ownership of capital and the pursuit of profit as the foundation of the economic system. In articulating a model of the entrepreneurial, capitalist firm embedded in a social system and a values system based on notions of fairness and social responsibility, Coda has developed a view of the business system that is the economic equivalent of the European notion of social democracy within the political system. Indeed, as the Anglo-Saxon model of shareholder value maximization loses its appeal in a decade that has featured the collapse of Enron, obscene levels of executive compensation, and the financial crash of 2008–9, Coda's view of a socially responsible, entrepreneurial business sector offers an attractive alternative to all of the prevailing models of market capitalism: Anglo-Saxon shareholder capitalism, Chinese state capitalism, and the corporatist economies of Japan and South Korea.

References

Allen, W. T. (1992). "Our Schizophrenic Conception of the Business Corporation," *Cardozo Law Review*, 14: 261–81.

Bourgeois, L. J. (1980). "Strategy and the Environment: A Conceptual Integration," *Academy of Management Review*, 5: 25–39.

Collins, J. C. and Porras, J. I. (1995). *Built to Last: Successful Habits of Visionary Companies*. New York: HarperCollins.

Collis, D. J. and Rukstad, M. G. (2008). "Can You Say What Your Strategy Is?" *Harvard Business Review*, 86: 82–90.

De Geus, A. (1997). "The Living Company," *Harvard Business Review*, 75: 51–9.

Gavetti, G. and Rivkin, J. W. (2007). "On the Origin of Strategy: Action and Cognition Over Time," *Organization Science*, 18: 420–39.

Grant, R. M. (1996). "Toward a Knowledge-Based Theory of the Firm," *Strategic Management Journal*, 17: 109–22. Special issue: "Knowledge and the Firm."

——. (2003). "Strategic Planning in a Turbulent Environment: Evidence from the Oil and Gas Majors," *Strategic Management Journal*, 24: 491–518.

Habib, M. M. and Victor, B. (1991). "Strategy, Structure, and Performance of U.S. Manufacturing and Service MNCs: A Comparative Analysis," *Strategic Management Journal*, 12: 589–606.

Handy, C. (2002). "What's a Business For?" *Harvard Business Review*, 80: 49–55, 132.

Hymer, S. H. (1960). "The International Operations of National Firms: A Study of Direct Foreign Investment." PhD Dissertation. Published Cambridge, MA: MIT Press, 1976.

Kim, W. C. and Mauborgne, R. (2009). "How Strategy Shapes Structure," *Harvard Business Review*, 87: 72–80.

Kogut, B. and Zander, U. (1996). "What Firms Do? Coordination, Identity, and Learning," *Organization Science*, 7: 502–18.

Lovas, B. and Ghoshal, S. (2000). "Strategy as Guided Evolution," *Strategic Management Journal*, 21: 875–96.

Markides, C. (2000). *All the Right Moves: A Guide to Crafting Breakthrough Strategy*. Boston, MA: Harvard Business School Press.

Nonaka, I. (1994). "A Dynamic Theory of Organizational Knowledge Creation," *Organization Science*, 5: 14–37.

Porter, M. E. and Kramer, M. R. (2006). "Strategy and Society: The Link between Competitive Advantage and Corporate Social Responsibility," *Harvard Business Review*, 84: 76–92.

Preston, L. E and Sapienza, H. J. (1990). "Stakeholder Management and Corporate Performance," *Journal of Behavioral Economics*, 19: 361–75.

Schultz, M., Hatch, M. J., and Larsen, M. H. (2000). *The Expressive Organization: Linking Identity, Reputation, and the Corporate Brand*. Oxford: Oxford University Press.

Schwenk, C. R. (1984). "Cognitive Simplification Processes in Strategic Decision-Making," *Strategic Management Journal*, 5: 111–28.

Spender, J.-C. (1989). *Industry Recipes*. Oxford: Blackwell.

Stopford, J. M. and Wells, L. T., Jr. (1972). *Managing the Multinational Enterprise*. New York: Basic Books.

Teece, D. J., Rumelt, R. P., Dosi, G., and Winter, S. G. (1994). "Understanding Corporate Coherence: Theory and Evidence," *Journal of Economic Behavior and Organization*, 23: 1–30.

Trist, E. and Bamforth, K. (1951). "Some Social and Psychological Consequences of the Longwall Method of Coal Getting," *Human Relations*, 4: 3–38.

Part I
The Italian Tradition of Management Theory

1
Management Theory:
Its Content, Specificities, and Role

The key questions that lead directly to the heart of the problem are "What is Management Theory?" and "How can the identity of the Management Theory scholar be defined?"

The answers that we attempt to provide in this chapter are the following:

- Management Theory scholars are concerned with issues of economic life, but they should not be confused with economists.
- In Management Theory research, a radical transformation is underway, mainly as a result of advances in fields of study relating to organizational functions.
- Management Theory has significant growth potential, but realizing this potential requires the development of both generalist and specialist research competencies.
- Management Theory scholars constantly grapple with value judgments about what is good or bad management, and they must be well equipped to make these judgments.

Translator's note: "Management Theory" is the suggested rendition of the original Italian term "Economia Aziendale," which refers to the unique approach to the study of firms and other productive institutions (mainly central and local government and non-profit organizations) adopted by most scholars belonging to the traditional Italian framework established by Gino Zappa in the 1920s. Italian Management Theory focuses on those organizations which are responsible for their own future in a free economic system by complying with the rules of market competition and/or institutional rules. In this book, the term "organization" is used with this meaning.

1. Organizations as the focus of study for Management Theory

According to the traditional Italian framework established by Gino Zappa, Management Theory addresses "the conditions of existence and the manifestations of life" of organizations (Zappa, 1927).

As business studies has evolved over time, a variety of definitions for the concept of "the organization" have been offered, each emphasizing different aspects: finance-related issues, organizational structure, operations coordination, or the institutional character which makes an organization an entity that is not contingent on something else but "made to last."

In any case, two recurrent ideas emerge from all of these definitions of the organization: a systemic, teleological order and a scientific interest essentially focused on economic phenomena.

The idea of a systemic order is so prevalent as to result in defining as "non-firms" those organizational entities in which there is insufficient capacity for feedback and the drive toward income is lacking (Saraceno, 1970, p. 76). As to the second idea, the continual emphasis on the economic nature of the organization and on the focus of business-related disciplines means that the topics explored in these fields exclude non-economic phenomena.

This gives rise to a conception of the organization as "the economic order of a (social) institution" (Masini, 1979, p. 18), which might be a family, a firm, a local public body, a business association, a trade union, and so on. Furthermore, Management Theory investigates production and consumption, savings and investments and their ordered occurrence within organizations.

2. The cultural identity of the Management Theory scholar

Management Theory scholars investigate the same phenomena as pure economists (production and consumption, savings and investments, in the context of micro- and macroeconomies, with either a descriptive or a prescriptive focus). Yet the scientific vocation of the Management Theory scholar is distinctly different from that of the economist. There is no room for role confusion, and there is nothing to warrant the former having an identity crisis or inferiority complex in relation to the latter.

The aim of business scholars is to study not so much economic phenomena per se, taken separately from the organized activities in which they occur, but these very activities as they take place in organizations. These activities are essentially management, organization, and accounting. Taken as an interconnected whole, this is what constitutes the object of study for Management Theory, or, put another way, the science of business administration (Zappa, 1927).

A Management Theory scholar would be prone to an identity crisis only if he or she forgot that the "value-added" of Management Theory typically derives from synergetically combining knowledge of management, organization, and accounting. Adequate cultural background in all of these areas is a prerequisite to being a Management Theory scholar. Someone without this background would simply be an expert in a specific field of business knowledge. For example, financial accounting and organizational behavior are two areas in which specialized professionals perform their duties even without training in all of the economic/management disciplines. Management Theory studies might also spill over into other disciplines (for instance, monetary economics). In such cases, if economic culture is lacking, the assumption that the business scholar is a "minor-league economist" finds substantiation.

To sum up, one could conceive of "the science of business administration or Management Theory advocated by Zappa" as a "pure and formal combination of the doctrines of accounting, managerial practices, and organization which had materialized or might develop within the prevailing research stream at the time when Zappa began his work…. But this would mean not having the slightest understanding of Zappa's reasoning," by which a "binding scientific need" impels us to integrate research and doctrines of accounting, managerial practices, and organization (Onida, 1951, p. 99).

3. Recent developments and current trends in Management Theory

In the 1960s and 1970s, major advances were made in economic and management disciplines whose effects were felt in Italy.

The reasons for this progress were the following:

1. developments in function-based business disciplines (which can be clustered into broad categories such as administration and governance, finance, organization, marketing, production, strategy, and information systems)
2. a new and more correct way for business scholars to relate to what occurs in organizations
3. a rich and productive interdisciplinarity among business research streams

Function-based disciplines have a role to play in business studies that must not be underestimated. These disciplines delineate research areas that cross disparate production sectors, though each one taken singly may be relatively homogeneous, and as such well suited to the development of specialized knowledge. Therefore, there are constant calls to compare different contexts, to understand similarities and differences, to verify how prior knowledge might apply to new challenges, and to generate new knowledge to deal with existing problems.

Moreover, function-based disciplines, and the knowledge that these fields gradually generate, lay the essential groundwork for Management Theory to be the science that Gino Zappa hoped it would become: a science that is the result of synergetic integration of the doctrines of accounting, management, and organization, and not simply a formal combination of the three. This sort of integration requires that accounting, managerial practices, and organization individually develop a robust body of internal doctrines. This has proven possible beyond all expectations, as we can see from the proliferation of function-based disciplines in the past few decades.

In Italy, studies centered on functional areas have long been developed within the context of sector-based research (with the sole exception of accounting disciplines). In other words, such research aims to identify profiles for management, organization, and accounting activities in specific production sectors or broad economic sectors.

The scientific precondition for this research stream may lie in a concern not to lose sight of the unitary nature of the organization in the structure of business-related subjects set down in the statutes of schools of management and business. At the very least this tendency seems to have delayed the development of important disciplines in functional areas such as production, marketing, strategy, and organization.

This observation is not intended to suggest a negative view of sector studies. On the contrary, there is a need for research both on sectors and on functions, with each feeding into and drawing from the other. More simply put, the development of function-based subject areas can provide an enormous stimulus for studies such as the economics of industrial concerns, the economics of lending institutions, and the economics of public administration. The contents of function-based disciplines can be interpreted and integrated with an eye to the specificities of these different sectors. By the same token, experts in function-based disciplines are indebted to sector-related studies for a thorough understanding of these specificities.

A second key consideration in understanding recent developments and the advances being made in business studies is the new way that scholars relate to the facts. In Italy's cultural tradition, business scholars have always concerned themselves with measuring their theories against what goes on in organizations. The ability to perceive economic phenomena in material form, and their ordered occurrence in organizations, has always been a point of pride for these academics, a characteristic which differentiates them and their role as scholars from the economists. Nonetheless, what has been missing is the methodical, patient, even menial work of directly observing and documenting what goes on in the world of business, with the aim of compiling case studies for teaching and research.

In the USA, in contrast, reams of empirical material have been produced (case studies in particular) for use in the classrooms of business schools to expose managers (or future managers) to a great number and variety of experiences. However, these data were often compiled exclusively or primarily for didactic purposes and for this reason were of little use for research.

The situation has gradually changed of late. In Italy, case studies are being used more often in management schools and for some university courses. A growing number of scholars have come to realize the importance of compiling cases based on Italian businesses in order to grasp the problems specific to this country. In addition, researchers are beginning to understand that by explicating the empirical data underpinning theoretical statements they can greatly facilitate scientific communication while guaranteeing the historical ground-ing of business research. As for the USA, publishing research findings and gathering empirical data are currently given equal importance as activities, reflecting a close interaction between theory and experi-ence, even when the outcome is not a case study.

All in all, the impression is that today as never before the exhorta-tions of the experts as to "the duties of theories toward the facts" are being taken seriously. This can be seen in the way studies are con-ducted. Researchers approach reality armed with theories that are anchored in what happens in the business world. However, they are also open to whatever they can learn from anything new or unex-pected in what they observe and from the data they gather and pre-sent on occasion as autonomous research findings in the form of business case studies.

Finally, recent advances in business studies are linked to the sub-ject's growing interdisciplinarity, fostered by business scholars and centered on business issues and production problems in general in the economy of both public and private production institutions of every kind.

Real economic phenomena in firms and other production institu-tions are vitally important, as is the "real-life" perspective and know-ledge interests of managers, which business scholars tend to adopt as their own. This is what prompts these experts to tap research which may prove useful to solving management problems they tackle and to take on the role of a catalyst in interdisciplinary dialogue. Some of the non-business fields which provide commonly used input are psycho-sociology, economics, law, and mathematics/statistics.

What should be stressed is that the study of firms alone (and of production institutions in general) prompts the business scholar to act as a promoter of interdisciplinary dialogue. For consumption units, where economic phenomenology has much less impact, schol-ars from other fields would be better suited to filling this role, but in production institutions problems pertaining to information, man-agement, and organization reach such high levels of complexity as to elicit particular interest among business scholars.

To sum up, then, economic/management disciplines are making rapid progress. In these fields, new knowledge is related to (1) the intersectorial nature of function-based disciplines such as organiza-tion and marketing, (2) the interfunctional nature of sector-based disciplines such as the economics of industrial concerns and the economics of credit institutions, and (3) the fact that business studies offers a natural point of intersection and integration for multidisciplinary knowledge centered on production institutions.

Management Theory, which as a discipline includes all management-related topics, is necessarily multisectorial and multifunctional. Furthermore, the discipline responds to the need to promote the synergetic unification of business knowledge in the hands of "generalist" scholars. This role becomes more imperative as sector-based and function-based knowledge becomes more specialized. This underscores the difference in the cultural backgrounds of specialists in the two areas and the consequent challenges they face in communicating with one another.

4. Prospects for developments in Management Theory

Management Theory is heading down a development path of enormous potential, driven to rapid progress by the urgency and complexity of the problems facing organizations. "Today as never before the interest and attention of practitioners and scholars are trained on Management Theory in concrete terms" (Zappa, 1956–7, vol. I, p. 2). These words, written by Gino Zappa around 30 years ago in the introduction to his monumental three-volume work on production in the economy of firms, seem more relevant than ever.

Today, a number of factors make the business scholar the focal point of challenging expectations: critical problems of effectiveness and efficiency that arise daily in complex production organizations, the acknowledged importance "in the field" of knowledge generated by business-related disciplines, and recent developments in these fields, in particular in schools of management.

However, major obstacles lie in the way of completely realizing the potential of business-related topics, at least as regards the situation in Italy. Negligible research resources and the resulting need to optimize existing ones are two such obstacles. For this reason, we need to ask how we can acquire the business competencies that are needed. Here are some ideas in this regard.

First, we must realize the need for both specialized and general competencies. If all business scholars specialized in certain branches of business knowledge, the synergetic integration and development of business disciplines would suffer. If, on the other hand, everyone had only general knowledge, the diversity and variety of competencies which constitute the essential precondition for innovative learning would be missing.

Second, our hope is that generalists and specialists alike can see themselves as business scholars and can communicate with one another fairly easily. They should have a solid foundation of basic knowledge spanning various functions (finance, governance, organization, and so on) and be capable of taking a holistic view of business-related issues, at least to some extent.

Third, it should be clear that the only way for scholars to become good generalists is by having a thorough grounding in at least one functional area and adequate experience in all of the other more important ones. This means that becoming a management generalist is not something that can be improvised; it comes about through a long training period. If it were any other way, the result would be superficial knowledge and not generalized competencies.

Finally, and this problem is acutely felt in Italy (and perhaps elsewhere too), specialized competencies in any area will never be developed if operational issues are neglected. This applies to accounting areas (financial accounting, cost accounting, budgeting, and so on) as well as management issues. Specifically, people cannot specialize in production or marketing if they avoid problems pertaining to operations and focus solely or primarily on strategic management questions. We should remember that in the reality of production organizations these are closely interrelated. What is more, both are vitally important, as are issues of effectiveness (relating more directly to strategic management) and efficiency (more closely linked to operations).

In conclusion, to realize the huge potential for furthering business studies in Italy, we must recognize that functional disciplines are critical to fostering both specialized and general competencies. However, this must not diminish our drive to comprehend the unitary nature of the organization, which is specific to the Italian tradition of Management Theory and has been fostered by sector-based research streams. As we immerse ourselves in the problems of business functions, we come to a deeper holistic view of the firm and various production institutions only if we sustain the momentum of this drive.

If we take these two points as given – the criticality of function-based disciplines and the drive toward a deeper holistic understanding of business phenomena – we no longer have certain conflicting, or even somewhat factitious, juxtapositions between Management Theory in the Italian tradition and management studies developed in the rest of the world.

It is true that when we consider some leading US or British authorities on finance or organization, the impression is that these experts have little in common with our idea of who Management Theory scholars are and the roles they play. This is due to the fact that management studies in the USA is not conducted within a holistic framework, as is the case with Management Theory in Italy. Not only must we constantly keep this framework in mind, but we should also re-energize it by applying the most suitable methods in the most appropriate institutional contexts. (This should be done above all in schools of management, in undergraduate degree programs in business administration, in business schools, and in the Italian Academy of Management Theory, which has already done a great deal to promote business-related disciplines and continues to do so.)

Some may assert that no well-rounded business scholars (as the Italian tradition would define them) can be found among management experts. On the other hand, there seem to be many such scholars among authorities on business policy, for example. Others might affirm that Management Theory must not be confused with management studies because of the inherent difference in focus between the two schools of thought. In other words, the former is essentially a descriptive discipline, focusing exclusively on analyzing and interpreting "the conditions of existence and the manifestations of life" of organizations, whereas the latter addresses entrepreneurs and managers and serves a more prescriptive purpose.

This view, however, does not seem to reflect the reality of the situation. First, it is impossible to draw a clear distinction between prescriptive and descriptive/interpretive management studies. In addition, if they are valid, explanatory theories in this field are invaluable in terms of planning and prescribing what management should be. Furthermore, Management Theory moves steadily forward by means of value judgments which make it possible to differentiate physiological manifestations of life from pathological ones. This is why we continuously move between "what is" (description) and "what ought to be" (prescription) until the two blend together and become one and the same.

The definitions of organization above clearly illustrate the dual significance of economic/management studies, based on both prescription and interpretation. These definitions refer to a "systemic order" which in reality is often not present. Such an order does not materialize spontaneously as a natural state of affairs; rather, it is the result of resolve and determination.

The fact is that for business scholars, "what ought to be" corresponds to "what a physiological situation entails," which is what interests them most. For this reason, when Management Theory scholars ask themselves, "What is an organization?" or "What is a firm?" they are (at times almost inadvertently) posing questions that often tend to overlap and coincide with others, such as "What is an organization asked to do?" or "What is a successful firm, one which completely fulfils its *raison d'être*?" (see, for example, the same definitions for "organization" and "firm" in Italian Management Theory, or the concept of the business idea in Normann, 1977, ch. 3).

5. Values underpinning Management Theory

The considerations above, referring to the interpretive rather than prescriptive contents of Management Theory, lead us back to the key questions about who business scholars are, what conception they have of the organization and related socio-economic institutions, to whom they address business studies and research, and what basic values they hold to be true. Specifically, the previous observations underscore the evaluation side of business-related disciplines, an aspect which we will address more fully now.

Management Theory scholars study "the conditions of existence and the manifestations of life" of the organization, but not in an acritical way or purely to satisfy scientific curiosity. Instead, these scholars make a critical assessment of these conditions and manifestations to decide whether they are expressions of physiological behaviors (that is, a response to the need for long-term functionality of the other socio-economic institutions to which the organizations refer) or pathological ones. In making such judgments, scholars contribute to the improvement of the firm and other production institutions.

For this reason, business scholars investigate what happens in organizations and which mechanisms make them function. At the same time, these scholars apply benchmark models that enable them to evaluate how all of this serves the *raison d'être* of the institutions to which organizations refer. So, for example, scholars examine the logic and methods used for drawing up financial statements for a given type of firm, or the financial structure of firms in a given sector, or strategic paths for firms that operate in a given competitive arena, and they do all of this with an eye to refining their critical assessments. To accomplish this, however, business scholars must use benchmarks that show what good financial statements look like, what a balanced financial structure consists of, what a winning strategy is, and, to sum it all up, what constitutes a well-run firm.

Clearly, underpinning these models are specific value judgments which must be made explicit if the objective is to shed light on the ideological contents and the political significance of Management Theory. Furthermore, we must be fully aware of the basic values embraced by business scholars in performing their cultural role. Only by doing so can we delve into these values, question them, and recognize what to keep and what to throw away or what new contents should replace age-old values. In short, this will point us in the direction that progress in business knowledge should take (Zappa, 1956–7, ss. 19, 21, 31, 39, and elsewhere).

When we scan the profusion of business literature with an institutional bent, a clear impression emerges. In the final analysis, the values in question tie into the selfsame concepts of the organization and of the firm and their unchanging characteristics: continual unity, profitability, relative autonomy, and the quality of endurance.

Specifically, business scholars always refer to the organization or the firm as an entity that transcends the specific interests of the people who are temporarily in control of it or those who are in a position to condition it in some way. Indeed, evidence emerges continuously of the conviction that in every historically established situation, there exists a higher-level interest – the interest of the organization. This has clearly defined contents which management is obliged to reveal and pursue. If the opposite were true, the long-term functionality of organizational institutions would be compromised, with well-known negative consequences on the economic and social levels.

If these are the basic values avowed by business scholars, can we say that they constitute a naturally conservative cultural force, and as such strive to serve the existing power structure? Clearly, the answer is no. Indeed, in recent years the use of production institutions to serve any purpose other than their own institutional one has led to spectacular business failures and is certainly among the ultimate causes for the crisis in public finance. In such circumstances, the values which are inherent in business studies and research take on an almost revolutionary flavor, not to mention the contributions of those business scholars who are working to bring about more or less radical innovations in the rules of the game pertaining to the institutional structure of the firm (Masini, 1964).

In the past 20 years, Management Theory has moved in the direction of corporate and entrepreneurial values, and toward research conducted to identify a better firm and more functional production institutions. The drivers in this movement include studies on corporate ethics, social strategy, innovative corporate processes, and more recently entrepreneurial excellence. These research streams, developed outside of Italy, have been little more than ripples in this country until now. (They are summarized in Coda, 1985.)

These studies deserve to be analyzed, investigated further, and combined with the Italian tradition of business studies. The aim should be to evolve the benchmark models which are so essential to a discipline like Management Theory, which moves forward by means of continual value judgments.

Above all, there is still much to be done to constitute a unitary and dynamic view of the firm which incorporates values such as profitability, sociality, competitiveness, and innovation. Each of these is not in and of itself a "corporate value," but taken together they can and must become one within a clearly defined entrepreneurial mission.

References

Coda, V. (1985). "Valori imprenditoriali e successo dell'impresa" [Entrepreneurial Values and Success in the Firm], *Finanza, marketing e produzione*, 2: 23–56.

Masini, C. (1964). *La struttura dell'impresa* [The Structure of the Firm]. Milan: Giuffrè.

——. (1979). *Lavoro e risparmio* [Work and Savings]. Turin: UTET.

Normann, R. (1977). *Management for Growth*. New York: Wiley.

Onida, P. (1951). *Le discipline economico-aziendali: Oggetto e metodo* [Economic/ Managerial Disciplines: Object and Method]. Milan: Giuffrè.

Saraceno, P. (1970). *La produzione industriale* [Industrial Production], 6th edn. Venice: Libreria universitaria editrice.

Zappa, G. (1927). *Tendenze nuove negli studi di ragioneria* [New Tendencies in Accounting Studies]. Milan: Istituto editoriale scientifico.

——. (1956–7). *Le produzioni nell'economia delle imprese* [Production in the Economy of Firms], 3 vols. Milan: Giuffré.

2
Management Theory in the Late 1950s: Revisiting Gino Zappa's *Productive Activities* and His Posthumous Work

1. The reason for this chapter

Having reached the end of his career and having lost his sight as well, Gino Zappa endeavored to compile a monumental series of books addressing numerous issues. In the context of Management Theory, his intention was first to examine the real economy, followed by the financial economy. Then he would investigate quantitative measures of organizations (consistent with his guiding principle that management must be studied first, and then accounting issues). After dealing with the institutional structure of organizations and their aggregations (coalitions and concentrations), Zappa would conclude with a book entitled *Management Theory*.[1]

The question is, What motivated Zappa to take on such a task?

One likely answer is that with these works, Zappa sought to record the state of the art and potential directions for development in Management Theory, encouraging and contributing to progress in this field. But what was his assessment of the situation? What direction did he believe this discipline should take?

As I sought to answer these questions, memories and reflections came to mind which prompted me to peruse *Productive Activities* and

---

Translator's note: Gino Zappa wrote exclusively in Italian. The titles of his works are given in English here for ease of comprehension. The original titles can be found among the references listed at the end of this chapter.

Zappa's posthumous work (on government institutions and non-profit organizations) again, 40 years on. My aim was to look for the knowledge gaps that Zappa perceived and to discover the research streams to which he was personally committed, to which he strove to contribute, and which he encouraged scholars to follow.

1.1. The skyscraper metaphor

"Management Theory is like a towering skyscraper, but until now we have laid only the foundations." This was Zappa's depiction of the vast expanse of work that lay ahead for new generations of scholars, as described to three young visitors to Venice, accompanied by Carlo Masini, on a brilliant Sunday in June 1958. (Sunday was the only day on which Zappa received visitors, as he spent the rest of the week studying.)

These words give us a clear picture of Zappa's assessment of the state of the art of Management Theory: the groundwork had been laid for a discipline with enormous potential. Yet this gives rise to several questions: What motivated this evaluation? Of Management Theory's fundamental principles and knowledge, what would remain firm, providing the foundations for this discipline? Which research streams should be pursued to further knowledge in this field of study?

How gratifying it would have been to have asked Zappa these questions and listened to his answers firsthand. Unfortunately, I did not ask then (perhaps because I was too shy; perhaps because the conversation moved on to other topics too quickly) and cannot now. We can attempt to satisfy this curiosity only by studying his voluminous work *Productive Activities in the Economy of Firms* and his posthumous work on government institutions and non-profit organizations. When the meeting mentioned above took place, *Productive Activities* had only recently been published (volume I in 1956, volumes II and III in 1957), and Zappa was mostly likely working on the book *Income and Savings, Investments and Consumption in the Economy of Non-Profit Organizations.*

1.2. Life choices

Before we delve into these weighty tomes, they should be framed within the context of the scientific production of Zappa and of his school. Moreover, we must remember that these works came out years after *Income of the Firm*, which was published in 1937. According to a note by the author, this was the second amended and expanded edition of the book *Determining Income in Commercial Enterprises: Using Accounting Values in Compiling Financial Statements*, which was published in two parts in 1920 and 1929. Few other works by Zappa[2] appeared after the publication of the first of these two parts (which would eventually be compiled in *Income*) until *Productive Activities*. What was the reason for this sporadic scientific production?

The answer may be found in Zappa's own life choices, which reveal a highly human, moral, and civic character. Zappa was completely dedicated to the university and made teaching his highest priority. Only after retiring from his university post in 1950 did he decide that the best way to spend his remaining years was to compose a new, challenging series of works. This choice was consistent with his vocation as founder and framer of the doctrine of Management Theory.

"Don't squander your energy in professional careers; be very, very selective instead." This was Zappa's adamant advice to his three young visitors during the meeting in Venice. Not abiding by this advice would have meant betraying his mission to be a teacher and a scholar. But Zappa's life choices entailed another decision: to build a school and dedicate himself entirely to training his pupils.

"Our School" was the title of a short poem about Zappa and his pupils written by a Bocconi University student in the 1920s. This satirical verse describes the zealous activity of the group of scholars who gravitated toward Gino Zappa on the old Bocconi campus in Largo Treves, attesting to the students' clear perception that a Zappian School was coming into being. Since then a profusion of scientific publications by economics and business scholars have been forged under the guiding hand of Zappa that bear the unmistakable mark of the maestro. It is true that in the 30 years before the publication of *Productive Activities*, Zappa wrote little other than *Income of the Firm*, the definitive reference book for generations of economics and business scholars; however, the abundant scientific production of scholars trained in Zappa's School and these scholars' affectionate devotion to their maestro are proof of his steadfast and fruitful commitment to research.

The bond between a student and his or her maestro (in the case of a true maestro, naturally) is known to be one of the strongest and most enduring of all human relationships. Its power and persistence can be discerned in the testimonials of the pupils who studied directly under Zappa. For example, Ugo Caprara was the "first among [Zappa's] devoted disciples to work with him in building the School of Management Theory and in founding the library directed by him." He spoke for all of Zappa's pupils in his message to the participants at a commemoration in Ca' Foscari on 4 April 1981 to mark the centenary of the birth of Gino Zappa: "Nearly sixty years have gone by, but when I happen across his letters telling me how satisfied he was by the research I was doing, I am moved by affection from the bottom of my heart, the affection I always felt for him" (AA.VV., 1982).

Even after the end of his teaching career at Ca' Foscari and Bocconi universities, Zappa took an interest in the scientific production of his pupils, reading their work and offering encouragement and suggestions. But by then his students were either approaching or had already reached the height of their scientific maturity, and Zappa has less contact with new pupils because he was no longer teaching, and so he found himself free to spend precious time on personal study and on the ambitious project of producing a new series of books. This would be his contribution to filling the gaps in economic/management knowledge mentioned above. Perhaps even more, this would provide a stimulus to students (and students of students) to pursue prolific scientific production.

2. Reasons for the knowledge gap perceived by Zappa

Why did Zappa see an enormous gap that needed to be filled? To understand his viewpoint, we must consider his awareness of the largely unexplored systemic and dynamic complexity of economic reality, on one hand, and his conception of Management Theory as a unitary science with immense potential, on the other. According to Zappa, this discipline "tends to collocate the myriad and complex manifestations of the study of economics and management in a single whole, generally ordered by principles" (*Productive Activities*, vol. I, p. 3).

Zappa insistently reiterates the complexity and dynamism of organizational systems and the negligible knowledge we have of them. Unity is the key characteristic and the dominant principle of the economic life of organizations. Systemic unity results from the "complementarity of every production phase in a firm," by the force of which "the technical efficiency and economic productivity of a single factor, operation, or production process can never be separated from the efficiency and productivity of other factors, operations, and processes, which are coordinated to achieve a single end" (*Productive Activities*, vol. II, p. 808; cf. pp. 826, 888, 904, 907).

The variety and dynamism of production phenomena are major causes of complexity: "The variety of productive activities within firms is extreme. Production volumes are constantly being modified; diverse production processes are coordinated and combined in very different ways; product features obtained by single processes vary constantly, under pressure from changing demand and innovative production techniques" (*Productive Activities*, vol. III, p. 62; cf. vol. II, §102).

Little is yet known about these characteristics of production phenomena. "Although affirming in the abstract the need for a dynamic view of organizational phenomena, until today our doctrine has developed this view only in a limited and fragmented way, without ever integrating these developments by rearranging them into an aggregation of interdependent theories" (*Productive Activities*, vol. I, p. 153). The knowledge gap widens: "The contrast between what we know and what we have to learn is becoming more and more stark. Theory must adapt itself to the complexity of the phenomena at hand, in other words, to the reality for which the theory was advanced. It is time to realign our doctrines, within a renewed and concurrent framework, with the unity that is increasingly drawing economic life into a single whole" (vol. I, p. 5).

Management Theory must not fail in its mission to fill this gap. In other words, it should not limit itself to simplifying economic reality in order to build theories which may be logical in a formal sense but have nothing to do with experience. Various factors gave rise to this discipline: "the need to study the economic behavior of people in the complex organizational institutions in which they actually interact with other people, with an affinity of intentions, efforts, and means" (*Productive Activities*, vol. I, p. 62); the refusal to position economic life "on the fictitious foundations of highly abstract hypotheses" (vol. I, p. 62); the drive to lead the way to "a new and unique understanding of economic phenomena" (vol. I, p. 3). Underlying all of this is the awareness that even though these economic phenomena cannot be revealed by Management Theory alone, "many of their most common and conspicuous manifestations can be seen in organizations" (vol. I, p. 172).[3]

Zappa's concrete conception of Management Theory clearly emerges from the following passage:

> It would be detrimental for Economic and Management Theory to disregard the widespread awareness of the growing complexity of production activities in organizations. The intention of the all-too-rudimentary models prized by a doctrine that is far from scientific may be to facilitate the understanding of theories but not to identify simpler ways to solve concrete management problems, with their tight web of technical, monetary, and economic coordination mechanisms intertwining organizational production.

A sharp criticism follows of the conception, "in highly abstract hypotheses, of firms which deal with a single product," "an expedient applied perhaps more than others to simplify organizational production to an extreme" (*Productive Activities*, vol. II, p. 781).[4]

To sum up, Zappa was convinced that the still-unexplored complexity and dynamism of economic life had increasingly significant manifestations in organizations. These factors, together with the intrinsically related realism of the organization-based approach to studying economic problems, resulted in an enormous gap in economic/management knowledge.

3. Research streams deriving from *Productive Activities*

The three volumes of Gino Zappa's *Productive Activities* are extraordinary works of Management Theory, especially if we consider when they were published. Zappa addresses a number of institutional issues in commendable depth and goes on to penetrate previously unexplored territory. The first volume outlines a general theory of organizations and firms; the second provides a structural analysis of the firm in terms of its two factors of production (labor and capital) and the configuration of its functions; the third volume and the final sections of the second investigate the dynamics of production activities within firms.

Now we will focus on some of the fields of study which Zappa explored (or intended to explore) to advance the frontiers of economic/management knowledge:

- the structure of functions within the firm
- the connections between financial and monetary factors, non-monetary quantitative factors, and qualitative factors of dynamic phenomena
- the coordination of economic activities along the production/distribution chain and the adaptation of these activities to output consumption
- the dynamics of production activities within the firm

For each of these research streams, we describe the path of investigation which Zappa tested and evaluate his results, including in light of later advances in economic/management doctrine.

3.1. The structure of productive activities within the firm

Enormous complexity and dynamism are typical of the functions that firms put in place "to compete in different markets subject to various events, to allocate relative risks in an appropriate manner, to achieve a fairly stable volume of business" (*Productive Activities*, vol. II, pp. 792ff.), and, therefore, to shore up the "economic system of corporate production" (vol. II, p. 795).

How can we delve into the dynamic complexity of functions within the firm and grasp how they contribute to economic results and production goals? We find an insightful observation on this subject in *Productive Activities* §§102–9, in a discussion of production processes and how they are combined.[5]

According to the system of thought postulated in *Productive Activities*, the concepts of the production process and the combination of production processes are critical to identifying significant configurations of costs and initial results, and consequently assessing economic advantage (which centers on production processes and how they are combined) and the best approach to management, which "can be appropriately directed only by processes... [which are] diverse and often manifold, and, in turn, consist of specific or general production combinations" (*Productive Activities*, vol. II, pp. 788, 792).

The following observations are relevant in this regard. First, for the more essential aims of production, basic costs and revenues are typically concentrated in processes and specific and general combinations of processes. Second, costs and revenues which do not slot into the consistent succession of processes and combinations of production processes (which give rise to these costs/revenues and which converge to generate profits) are isolated in abstract terms from the uninterrupted management of operations and, as such, have negligible economic effectiveness (*Productive Activities*, vol. II, p. 819). Therefore, we need to know what the production processes are and how they are combined. This knowledge, along with a non-arbitrary determination of costs, revenues, and economic results generated by these processes, opens the way for an intimate understanding of the economics of the firm. This comprehension cannot come from a generic view of functions as a whole or financial statements summaries, nor can it be attained by superficially ascertaining costs, revenues, and results which are not consistent with the reality of the various production processes and their combination.[6]

The innovation in the evolution of Zappa's system of thought is not the centrality of functions; in fact, management and the coordinated operations inherent to it were always the focal point of Zappa's conception of the organization and of the firm. Only an understanding of management can make financial statements clear and meaningful, and make it possible to read these documents and see what is behind the figures. Only by comprehending the specificities of management can we fully grasp the unmistakable individuality of firms. Only in light of relevant management activities can we analyze the structures of resources and assets, assess their suitability, and design them judiciously (see *Productive Activities*, vol. II, p. 805). The innovation lies in Zappa's attempt to govern the complexity and dynamism of corporate functions by applying the concepts of the production process and the combination of production processes. With these conceptual tools we can at least acquire some notion – in the continual flow of operations – of the systemic structure and dynamic profile of production activities within firms, the latter marked by the timing, duration, and cycles and rhythms of production phenomena.[7] This knowledge will reveal the path to significant economic determinations and facilitate judicious decision-making.

This focus on the systemic structure of production activities calls for further explanation. Zappa harshly criticized certain approaches to analytical accounting based on an artificial breakdown of overhead costs and joint costs. This criticism was interpreted by some as a denial of the real information needs of business managers in the name of continual unity in the economic coordination processes of the organization. In my opinion, Zappa was not negating these needs. He simply could not accept the divergence between theory and practice. He was convinced of the practical utility of a solid theory and of the consequent need to advance theory to respond fully to the organization's good governance requirements, which would allow management systems to evolve in complete compliance with the tenets of Management Theory. *Productive Activities* provides confirmation that Zappa had no preconceived aversion toward the measurements of analytical accounting; instead, he was searching for an approach that would fully satisfy both practitioners and scholars. Zappa believed that the way to overcome the divergence mentioned above was through a line of reasoning based on production processes and the specific and general ways they are combined rather than through overhead/joint cost accounting techniques. This search had probably begun long before – at least by the time Teodoro D'Ippolito, under Zappa's guidance, began to study cost accounting. D'Ippolito's later research led in directions that left unsolved the problem of making theory and practice converge, a problem which Zappa must have considered fundamental.

Later developments in economic/management studies left no doubt as to the significance and the potential of research into the structure of corporate functions. These studies, with various aims, leveraged the concepts of the production process and combinations of production processes. In this regard, here I mention only research in the following streams:

- the multibusiness firm, which must be managed with attention to individual strategic business units. These are nothing more than specific sets of coordinated production processes or product/market/technology combinations which lend themselves to a standard strategy and are configured as self-contained organizational units generating distinct streams of income. Strategic business units enable the firm to operate in various competitive arenas, contending with dissimilar needs, customers, and competitors, and therefore with diverse critical success factors and different rules of competitive engagement

- strategic analysis of the determinants of entrepreneurial success or failure, associated with the attractiveness of the sector and the strategic positioning of the firm. This last factor, in turn, relates to how activities in the value chain are configured and performed. More specifically, these can be categorized as "primary" or "support" activities. Primary activities are processes that involve moving materials and products (incoming and outgoing logistics), technological transformation, marketing and sales, and post-sales assistance. Support activities (auxiliary to primary activities) include processes of provisioning, technology development, human resource development, and administrative processes pertaining to the firm as a whole. The basis of sustainable competitive advantage – and consequently higher profits – is that a firm performs these activities with greater efficiency and/or lower costs than the competition and when they are so individualized as to be difficult to imitate

- management accounting and governance systems designed in keeping with the need for effective and efficient management of production processes and combinations of production processes

- re-engineering basic business processes such as filling orders, developing and launching new products, handling customer assistance, and provisioning production input. The aim is to speed up these processes, reduce the costs of production inputs, and enhance the value of output for the customer, and consequently to increase overall productivity

3.2. The connections between financial and monetary profiles and quantitative and qualitative profiles of dynamic phenomena within the firm

This immense field of inquiry is briefly mentioned in *Productive Activities* in reference to management. A more thorough discussion is deferred to later volumes.[8] More than likely, Zappa realized that there was a sizeable gap to fill. Indeed, he must have been well aware that the chance to combine management, organization, and accounting knowledge was at stake, and thus the advancement of Management Theory as a unitary discipline through the systematic integration of accounting with management practices and organization. Consider that progress in the field at the time consisted mainly of perceptive descriptions of these relationships, an awareness that accounting and non-accounting data had to be used in a complementary way, and the search for these relationships in time-series tables and graphs.

In the decades that followed, notable progress was made in this area. Here are a few of the most important advances:

- In Italy, techniques were adopted that had been used for years in the USA for analyzing net working capital flows and cash flows. In addition, the concepts of net working capital and cash flow were integrated in the theory of financial accounting. These transitions were indispensable in enabling scholars to grasp the connections between financial and monetary trends in management in a tangible way, and not merely in qualitative/descriptive terms.

- A compact system for analyzing financial statements consisting of multiple ratios was gradually adopted. This system served both for ex post analysis and for budgeting. It facilitated the transition to an integrated interpretation of the information potential of financial statements in terms of profitability, financial solidity, liquidity, and the dynamics of firm dimensions (on operational and structural levels).

- Cause–effect relationships were meticulously analyzed in terms of profit performance (which can be deduced from annual accounts) and its determinants, represented by economic data typically derived from non-accounting surveys or statistics (price/cost, price/revenue, production/sales volumes, production/sales mix, level of saturation of production capacity, market share, physical output, etc.). This transition was crucial for a deeper reflection on the complementary use of accounting and non-accounting data, and it made it possible to move one step further to link these findings to the decision to activate certain managerial and organizational levers in the face of specific environmental conditions.

- Developments took place in management accounting, from direct costing to activity costing to cost management, which served to increase our knowledge of the connections between the economic and qualitative aspects of managerial phenomena.

- Advances were made in sensitivity analysis with the advent of computerized financial simulations that could immediately respond to a wide range of "what if?"s.
- A set of tools for strategic analysis was perfected. These instruments served to answer questions such as: Why do firms succeed (or fail)? What are the determinants of business success (or failure), in terms of statistical analysis and from a dynamic perspective? The first question hinges on the concepts of the attractiveness of the sector, strategic positioning/competitive advantage, and the value chain. The second perspective is contingent on the concepts of the potential for transformation in sectors and markets (as this gives rise to business opportunities) and the firm's capacity for initiative and innovation (which clearly determines its chances of exploiting these opportunities).
- Progress was made on the topic of strategic governance. This provided a major thrust in the direction of organically reconnecting all aspects of dynamic phenomena described by Zappa, for the purpose of effective and efficient management through monitoring the realization of business strategies (Kaplan and Norton, 1996) or even with an eye to governing the strategic dynamics of the firm (Simons, 1994).
- Developments were made in system dynamics, as applied to management problems. System dynamics is based on analyzing the dynamic cause–effect relationships between relevant variables inherent to a given problem. Among other things, this methodology makes it possible to deal with qualitative variables and consequently to incorporate them into models.

3.3. The coordination of economic activities along the production/distribution chain and the adaptation of these activities to consumer dynamics

This topic is addressed in §110, entitled "Mutual dependence of production and consumption in the economy of organizations connected through trade." A more general discussion is provided in the sixth chapter and part of the seventh chapter of *Productive Activities*.

In these pages, Zappa considers how firms operate through trade "in a long and varied chain of different production activities, from the initial creation of factors of production to the final positioning of output" (*Productive Activities*, vol. III, p. 84). Clearly he saw this as one of the main sources of complexity and dynamism in business management. What emerges is a picture of how at that time (in the 1950s) management opted to deal with the challenge of calibrating production to consumption. The complications included forecasting the dynamics of consumption and identifying production trends and their consequences for firms positioned upstream and downstream in the production/distribution chain.

Another point that clearly arises is the inadequacy of the market as a mechanism for coordinating economic activities along this chain. In Zappa's words,

> Often it is said that as market prices vary, changes in supply and demand take place. But it is not simply a question of higher prices, or greater volumes of negotiated goods, or the myriad conditions which affect negotiations. Consider the many links in the chain of production activities carried out in numerous firms belonging to various production sectors. Remember that this chain is often a very complex one, with intricately interlinking production activities which are combined and complementary. Do not forget the production lags which are so common in lengthy production processes and which require firms to stockpile an enormous variety and quantity of inventory or to make rapid changes in the intensity and volume of production. (*Productive Activities*, vol. III, p. 43)

Furthermore, "market supply and demand cannot be understood by tracking market share alone or even trade alone on a given market" (vol. III, p. 44).

Here, too, we find a field of study which has turned out to be exceptionally fruitful. Suffice it to mention two research streams: industrial dynamics (later, "system dynamics") and networking. The first, beginning with seminal work of Forrester (1961), proved to have tremendous potential for explaining the dynamic phenomena that sparked such intense interest for Zappa. Subsequently, however, concrete applications of system dynamics by business management were quite rare, and initiatives in innovative management and entrepreneurialism moved in different directions. Networks (or coalitions) of firms have taken on greater importance, in particular since the 1970s. Networks are a way of organizing economic activity to achieve two objectives. The first is to control the turbulence and general instability that arise from the inadequacy of the market as a coordination mechanism for firms operating along the production/distribution chain. The second objective is to expand the firm's operations while limiting investments (and associated financial requirements) and the risk of hierarchical bureaucratization. The second of the two research streams mentioned above delves into this important phenomenon (Lorenzoni, 1987, 1992).

3.4. The dynamics of productive activities within the firm

Zappa appears to have dedicated most of his effort and enthusiasm to this research stream in *Productive Activities*. In *Non-Profit Organizations* he takes up this topic with reference to every type of organization. In this posthumous work, a precise description is given of the gap which, more than any other "absence of knowledge," was the focus of the author's attention and energy in writing *Productive Activities*:

> Until today in Management Theory, a model or a theoretical framework has yet to be designed which represents trends in the economic movements of individual phenomena in business management, whether these trends be consistent or contradictory, interconnected or only temporarily independent, and does so without excessive modifications. If such a model were constructed, it would call for a generally valid explanation for dynamism, albeit within the limits of the hypotheses put forth. Dynamism, in all of its various progressions and diverse tendencies, is the distinctive characteristic of management of every kind of organization. (*Non-Profit Organizations*, p. 106)

Productive Activities repeatedly reminds us of the unsound conditions of the firm, the instability of management, and the increasingly distant objective of equilibrium.[9] The conclusion Zappa draws is a drastic one:

> The abused model of the state of equilibrium, which any firm would tend toward in the face of an imbalance, is not made for Economic and Management Theory. In fact, not even in hypotheses which are realistic to some degree can this discipline identify conditions of equilibrium, a concept which is too often referred to as a complex phenomenon [but] which actually lends itself to an exact definition. (*Productive Activities*, vol. III, p. 195)

In no less adamant terms is this opinion echoed in Zappa's posthumous work: "Any theory of the firm built on the abstract hypothesis of a state of equilibrium in a given moment which is not subject to constant disruption, every theory of this kind that is not integrated with the dynamic study of the phenomena in question is one that must utterly alter reality" (*Non-Profit Organizations*, p. 62).

Zappa's criticism seems to target, on one hand, economists' abstract models, whose solution to defining the equilibrium of an economic system is to solve a system of *n* equations with *n* unknowns.[10] On the other hand, Zappa disparages a certain artificial understanding of an organization's management and functionality. According to this perspective, the former involve defining and achieving positions of static equilibrium (typically expressed by statements of assets and liabilities) at fixed periods (*Non-Profit Organizations*, pp. 61ff.);[11] the latter can be revealed simply by analyzing the asset structure.[12]

Zappa's criticism is apparently not directed toward the work of economics and management scholars on the conditions of economic equilibrium of firms. Zappa appears to have recognized and even encouraged these studies – as is the case with Tancredi Bianchi's study of the conditions of equilibrium of banks – given their unquestionable usefulness. Furthermore, previous excerpts from his work leave little room for doubt that Zappa did not believe it worthwhile to continue investing in building a economic/business theory on equilibrium within firms unless such a theory was "integrated by a dynamic study of the phenomena in question."

Now we will try to gain a clearer understanding of the turbulence that marks the life of firms and its manifestations, causes, and solutions. Typical signs of the "turbulent situations" referred to by Zappa are insufficient or excess availability of certain factors of production (in respective provisioning markets), untapped production capacity, excess depletion or accumulation of stock of semi-finished or finished goods, and the unexpected closure of markets in which the firm has traditionally operated as a result of the emergence of new areas of entrepreneurial initiative (undertaken by the firm itself or others).[13]

As for the causes of imbalances, some may result from "incessant changes in the status of markets for production factors and products in which the organization conducts its trade." Others are the consequence of mistaken decisions by management ("unwise management policy") and/or the inability of management to realize policy ("inopportune implementation") (*Productive Activities*, vol. III, p. 64).

In any case, solutions can be found in "incessant modifications in operations, in production processes, and in the combination of these processes," which, in turn, "lead to transformations, often radical ones, in the structure of the firm" (*Productive Activities*, vol. III, p. 64).

This last observation is invaluable, because it implicitly indicates where economics and management scholars should focus their efforts to build a theory of the dynamics of production activities within firms – in other words, a theory that explains how firms can survive in conditions of continuously disrupted equilibrium. The consequent research stream becomes even more apparent in this masterful profile of the dynamic firm that strives to turn a profit in a turbulent environment:

> A firm, which could be taken as a symbol of today's production conditions, is an institution that prospers only with progress. This entity is incessantly transforming, constantly testing out new processes, implementing new production combinations, and demanding increased efficiency from its production units along with expanded financial structures and richer, larger markets. Complex, long-term production coordination is accompanied by frequent technical and economical innovations, a search for new markets, and a heightened sensitivity to new demands. Production activities, as a result, can never stop moving forward and can never achieve sought-after stability, the desired long-term equilibrium, the guaranteed employment and investment. ... By changing production processes and by the myriad ways they are combined, the aim is to manage the production of the firm in the most advantageous and least unstable way. (*Productive Activities*, vol. III, p. 237)

What later advances were made in economic/management knowledge? Has research moved in the direction indicated by Zappa or followed other streams?

The most important research in the decades after Zappa's death followed a course that Zappa would have appreciated. To be specific, study focused on building an Economic and Management Theory of the equilibrium of the firm that explained the fundamental elements of sustainable entrepreneurial success which could withstand various kinds of environmental changes. Scientific publications analyzed leaders in given market sectors or segments who had secured their success and maintained both position and profitability in the face of various contingencies and attacks by hostile competitors. These studies also took into account firms which achieved transient success on fragile foundations. Below are examples of this research:

- successful entrepreneurial formulae (Normann, 1979 [1977])
- mechanisms typifying quasi-monopolistic situations despite competitive market contexts (Rumelt and Lippman, 1982)
- strong strategic positions resulting in a defendable competitive advantage in structurally attractive sectors, which is possible when certain rules of the game are established that promote high profits even in the face of cyclical events (Porter, 1980, 1985)
- business networks clustered around leading firms which have moved beyond the traditional business logic; these firms have succeeded in steadily expanding the boundaries of the activities they control and govern no small amount of turbulence and imbalance between production and consumption, as described in *Productive Activities*

All in all, these studies sought to respond to a recurrent question in *Productive Activities* and *Non-Profit Organizations*: "How can we build a management structure that is relatively sound and not excessively unstable in an economic and social environment rife with continual contrasts and profound transformations?" (*Non-Profit Organizations*, p. 667). Likewise, these studies have provided substance to an idea that pervades Zappa's work: "[t]he winning economic unit that is often a source of prosperous and enduring life, rich with fruitful results" (p. 667).[14] This is the basis for my assertion that Zappa may have had some inkling of the developments that would come from the research streams mentioned above.

Moreover, these are not the only paths of progress for economic/management knowledge pertinent to our objectives. Some research also focused on building a theory of the dynamics of production activities within firms. Specifically, certain studies were prompted by observing firms that followed extraordinary trajectories of diversified growth; others explored crisis situations and the reorganizations which no small number of firms were forced to undertake. More generally, a number of studies strove to contribute to a theory of the growth of the firm, beginning with the pioneering work of Edith Penrose (1973). Further research focused on strategic governance processes in conditions of environmental turbulence. The impetus for these studies, which burgeoned in the 1970s with Igor Ansoff's work, was the energy crisis in the fall of 1973.

Only in the 1980s did further research gradually take the direction indicated by Zappa. This occurred after numerous legendary Western firms (which had been resting on their laurels) collapsed as a result of the rising intensity of a new kind of competition, in particular from Japan. In addition, new myths propagated by literature on entrepreneurial excellence (beginning with the famous book by Tom Peters and Robert Waterman, *In Search of Excellence*, 1982) began to crumble inexorably under the devastating pressure of competitive dynamics.

Currently, competitive contexts are most commonly marked by hyper-competition and discontinuity, the consequences of incredible technological advances (in particular in connectivity technologies) and unprecedented liberalization processes. Today it is impossible for a firm to survive for decades, or even for a few years, on the success of some past innovation translated into a consolidated business idea. For this reason, there is little interest at present in scientific research framed within a theory of constant equilibrium within the firm or in competitive dynamics manifested within the confines of a given sector following specific, constant rules. These studies are useful for analysis and decision-making in terms of strategic positioning; however, researchers are now focused on contributing to a dynamic theory of strategy and production activities within firms. Their aim is to explain not the preconditions for success underpinning superior competitive and profit performance but the managerial and learning processes which generate and continually reproduce this foundation, as well as the behavioral contexts in which these processes occur.

Clearly, today we have moved beyond the archetype of the successful firm as one that applies an innovative entrepreneurial formula created with acumen and conserved over time; indeed, such a firm can be found in far fewer entrepreneurial and sectorial contexts. Instead, the benchmark model – the focus of countless studies – is the dynamic and innovative firm, one that progresses steadily along the path of growing profits and turnover through its capacity for innovation on three fronts: operational innovation, which enables the firm to make ground-breaking advances in productivity; strategic innovation, which allows the firm to contend with threats and seize opportunities generated by environmental discontinuity; and managerial and organizational innovation, which unites rigor and discipline with freedom to experiment and take the initiative. This third type of innovation requires aligning governance and management systems with the complexity of relative responsibilities and effectively dealing with generational turnover.

What scholars and practitioners consider the ideal model of the firm today, a model they are working to create and elaborate, is not far removed from the one described above which Zappa delineated nearly half a century ago. In light of the enormous differences in environmental context, this may appear to be a paradox. Yet the pages of *Productive Activities* that explore this perspective are still relevant today. The reason is that after much dedication and effort – for the most part successful – to stabilize the operations of the firm on more solid foundations, the world of production is experiencing monumental transformations. These changes re-introduce the vital issues of entrepreneurial innovation and refocus the attention of scholars and practitioners on the research of economists such as Schumpeter and Hayek (Eisenhardt, 2002) and on the final works of Gino Zappa. Consequently, his words deserve careful reflection.

4. The contribution of the posthumous work

As mentioned above, *L'economia delle aziende di consumo* (The Economy of Non-Profit Organizations),[15] published posthumously in 1962, is only the first part of a more extensive work that Zappa intended to write and publish, to be entitled *Redditi e risparmi, investimenti e consumi nell'economia delle aziende di erogazione* (Income and Savings, Investments and Consumption in the Economy of Non-Profit Organizations).

Non-profit organizations are one of the key research streams for the Zappian School. The maestro realized that there had not been sufficient investigation or careful analysis of the various classes of non-profit organizations. This issue had been neglected by researchers, who for the most part were intent on studying production organizations.[16] General economists, meanwhile, had dedicated much more attention to consumption phenomena, but without producing significant results for economics/business scholars.[17] This prompted Zappa's desire to compile a comprehensive work that assessed the situation and advanced the frontier of knowledge on this topic.

Sadly, the death of Gino Zappa left an unfinished work which gives us a glimpse of the basic principles and some logical assertions that the author was elaborating but conveys only the intention of how the more imperative issues and problems would be developed as they were identified.

Summarized below are some of the issues that captured the attention and the efforts of Zappa in his study of non-profit organizations, categorized into three groups:

- applying the concept of organization to the study of consumption phenomena
- the "ends" of consumption organizations and how they relate to "means"; the role of goals in management
- a new consumption theory of well-being; analyzing needs

4.1. Applying the concept of organization to the study of consumption phenomena

In his personal analysis and attentive investigation, Gino Zappa perceived the organization as the conceptual category best suited to comprehending and representing consumption phenomena. Using this category has an immediate consequence: consumption is no longer seen as an exclusively individual phenomenon or as a generically collective one. Instead, consumption becomes a phenomenon that involves myriad people within an organization.[18]

As regards consumption organizations, Gino Zappa provides the framework that circumscribes the context and the object of study: "In non-profit organizations, consumption – individual and collective, private and public – takes place to directly satisfy human needs" (*Non-Profit Organizations*, p. 646). This definition encompasses both "local government organizations" (p. 649) and "family units" (p. 651). In addition, Zappa stakes out the boundaries that separate this field from the study of business organizations (p. 557).

Applying the concept of organization to the consumption phenomenon enables the author to use general principles of Management

Theory (such as unitary economics, economic sustainability, dynamism, and autonomy) to study consumption. Zappa pays particular attention to the unitary notion (*Non-Profit Organizations*, p. 597), seeing as critical the interconnections between income and consumption, savings and investments, which he commits to address in later volumes.[19]

The economics and management approach to the study of public administrations is widely recognized as a fruitful one, as evinced by the increasingly abundant studies published during the decades after Zappa's death, in particular since the 1970s.

4.2. The "ends" of the non-profit organization and how they relate to "means"

This particularly relevant issue, addressed by Zappa in his work on non-profit organizations, also involves the concept of the organization in general, and consequently business organizations as well.

First, Zappa illustrates the set of goals of the organization, which are distinct from those of individuals and from the objectives of the core stakeholders: "The ends of organizations…beyond the specific purposes of any individual activity…must not be confused with the ends of its core stakeholder" (*Non-Profit Organizations*, p. 721). From this, we can infer that the organization has a life of its own; it exists for reasons above and beyond the personal interests of individuals or of a category of social bodies. In other words, the organization "is a tool created to pursue its own ends, not only those of its core stakeholder, but also of all those who provide the organization with their labor and capital" (p. 721).

With these assertions, Gino Zappa joins the debate on the *raison d'être* of the organization, clearly implying that the good of the organization cannot be equated with the interest of one category of stakeholder; it is, instead, the "common good." This can be identified in the historical context in which an organization exists, which dominates and encompasses all.

In later decades, a number of researchers explored this question more fully and advanced the frontier of knowledge (for example, Giannessi, 1969; Masini, 1970). In the international literature the issue was the focal point of a heated debate which over time gave rise to two main perspectives: the shareholder view and the stakeholder view, the latter undoubtedly being closer to the approach of Zappa and various other exponents of Italian Management Theory.

A second object of study is also linked to the finalism of consumption organizations – and, more generally speaking, of every organization. This is the relationship between ends and means, and, indirectly, the role of goals in managerial activity.

From Zappa's perspective, choices regarding goals cannot be separated from decisions as to resources: "A conscious determination of ends can be made only in relation to the means that are or will be available" to the organization (*Non-Profit Organizations*, p. 717). Consequently, "both needs and means in non-profit organizations should be determined, at least in consideration of the numerous correlations that link income production and consumption simultaneously in the short term" (p. 718).

As his recurrent references to the topic confirm, the ends–means relationship held particular significance for Zappa (see *Non-Profit Organizations*, pp. 683, 717, 723). It was also a major theme in the development of economic/business knowledge in later decades. Over time, experts on strategy have generated and consolidated two contrasting basic views with specific, if not exclusive, reference to firms. The first does not include the definition of goals; rather, the aim of organizational management is to pursue pre-established goals, and, as a result, the focus is on improving how resources are organized to achieve these goals. (The leading proponent of this view is Ansoff in his 1965 book *Corporate Strategy*). The second view incorporates the definition of goals into the concept of strategy, expanding strategic management of the organization to include setting goals as well as identifying resources (see Chandler, 1962; Andrews, 1971).

4.3. A new consumption theory: the welfare theory

In *Non-Profit Organizations*, Zappa pays special attention to defining and structuring a new consumption theory: the theory of well-being. Zappa's position, which supports a theory of well-being, comes from his dissatisfaction with the consolidated theory of personal gain, which he believed did not fully explain the complex phenomenon of consumption.

The transition from the traditional economy based on personal gain to a new one centering on well-being implies a radical transformation in basic assumptions in two main respects. The first is a rejection of utilitarianism and individualism and an affirmation of altruism and sociality as essential human traits (*Non-Profit Organizations*, p. 686). Particularly influential for Zappa was

O. F. Boucke's work *A Critique of Economics*, which challenges the ego-istic view of needs in favor of an altruistic one. Second, the interests and needs of individual members of organizations are not reduced to mere material and economic necessities. Rather, they encompass moral, social, political, religious aspects, and so on (p. 595). Zappa emphasized the idea of the common good, a concept which cannot be condensed into a set of specific interests (p. 714).

On the basis of these assumptions, Zappa posits a theory of con-sumption that takes the pursuit of the general and overall well-being of the individual as the objective function, and not the maximiza-tion of consumption of material goods, as is the case with the theory of personal gain.

How does one pursue well-being? Only by consuming more mater-ial goods? Or by conscientiously curbing one's needs? Zappa's opin-ion on the matter leaves no room for doubt: "For each individual it is beneficial to realize that often well-being is attained not by increas-ing one's wealth but by judiciously limiting one's needs" (*Non-Profit Organizations*, p. 566).

Obviously, limiting strictly material needs can serve as a mechan-ism for attaining personal well-being only because the model encom-passes individuals' spiritual, ethical, and moral dimensions. From this perspective alone can the individual comprehend and appreci-ate curbing material needs to fulfill those of a higher order, which have to do with the spiritual and altruistic facets of a person. None of this was admissible in the traditional theory of personal gain, which held that more material goods always meant greater benefit for the individual.

In the end, on one hand, the theory of consumption and of non-profit organizations must be extended to the pursuit of individual well-being, encompassing moral, social, intellectual, and religious aspects. On the other hand, and actually because of more compre-hensive moral, intellectual, and social needs, limiting material needs becomes a way to pursue well-being.

In the model that Zappa attempts to outline, he draws no distinc-tion between non-economic and economic aspects of the individ-ual sphere. Moreover, he does not attempt to isolate the latter in an abstract manner in order to apply traditional categories of max-imum utility and individual gain. Instead, Zappa does the oppos-ite: he preserves the complex interconnection between economic and non-economic needs and ends. This intuition foreshadows the necessity for a new theory of well-being in which the overall well-being of the individual is the central focus of study and economic factors serve to achieve economic and, more importantly, non-economic ends.

Two key issues arise within this broad perspective encompassing ethical, moral, and spiritual aspects of the individual. The first is that we must have a clear understanding of human needs, both material and non-material. This understanding is a vital prerequisite for any study on consumption. Indeed, Zappa explicitly states that quantitative measures of needs must be constructed to make consumption studies concrete and to render the theory useful for understanding real consumption processes. At the same time, Zappa emphasizes the complexity of identifying such measures. He then goes on to propose a scale of individual needs, in order of intensity, extension, and duration, so as to provide an initial classification (*Non-Profit Organizations*, p. 574).

The second issue pertains to the fact that individuals participate in a number of organizations. According to Zappa, in this way – and not only through direct consumption of utility goods – individuals satisfy their need for belonging. The result is a complex web of interrelations among organizations. Zappa believed that this phenomenon had to be taken into account in advancing economic sciences (*Non-Profit Organizations*, p. 700).

The importance of Zappa's comments becomes apparent in the intense drive in later years toward a better understanding of consumption and underlying human needs. First and foremost is Maslow's work, which offers an ordinal classification of needs which is widely used in leadership studies, and more generally in research on organizational behavior, which saw momentous progress during the 1960s and 1970s (Maslow, 1964).

As regards consumer behavior, over time so many advances have been made on this issue that it has grown into a separate field of research, with the founding of the Association for Consumer Research in the USA in 1969 and the publication of the *Journal of Consumer Research* in 1974. Moreover, a great many marketing studies address consumer behavior and choice (Gandolfo and Romani, 1998).

To sum up, what emerges from reading *Non-Profit Organizations* is that Zappa succeeded in identifying and anticipating some of the key issues which still capture the attention of, and stimulate prolific efforts by, numerous scholars today.

5. A rich source of research hypotheses

The wealth of Zappa's contribution with his final works is apparent not only when we consider the research streams he indicated to scholars, which absorbed Zappa himself. More specifically, we can see *Productive Activities* and *Non-Profit Organizations* as sources of myriad research questions and hypotheses. These books provide numerous observations that deserve to be verified, enhanced, and investigated through appropriate study. Here are some examples taken nearly at random from the pages of *Productive Activities* and *Non-Profit Organizations*.

As regards management strategy and goal-setting, Zappa writes,

> [An organization] cannot structure an appropriate management policy if it does not pursue specific aims. Defining goals in an ambiguous fashion blurs the clear view of what paths to follow and how to organize the means that serve to achieve these ends. An uncertain perception of ends makes a conscientious orientation and conscious implementation of management impossible. ... Objectives that are too distant are always problematic and pointless; they imply unfounded expectations of needs. ... Clearly, a definite purpose of a judicious management policy is not simply the generic goal which private firms often set for themselves, i.e. attaining an acceptable income in the long term while exploiting the resource and asset structure of the organization to the fullest. (*Productive Activities*, vol. II, p. 784)

Reading this passage gives rise to myriad questions: What are the actual goals of management policies in any given area or the general management policy of a firm? How should we define and identify management policies? How can we measure and evaluate whether ends are defined or undefined? What determines a clear (or unclear) perception of goals by those called on to manage an organization judiciously and conscientiously? As Zappa affirms, "Objectives that are too distant are always problematic and pointless." How should we interpret this in light of research revealing the critical role that an ambitious "strategic intention projected into the long term" can have in strategic governance processes within firms? How can we hypothetically reformulate the "general goal" that private firms tend to strive toward? Shouldn't we specify this goal for each class of private firm (for example, differentiating listed firms and private equity ventures from other enterprises)? How can we test these hypotheses empirically? How does a general goal shape concrete managerial orientation? How can we express such a goal effectively? What tools should we use to do so?

In terms of the different ways we can view managerial phenomena along space/time dimensions, Zappa observes, "When phenomena are analyzed in groups of operations that are too small, or in short timeframes, management seems to elude all rules, any preset convenience, any form of risk mitigation" (*Productive Activities*, vol. II, p. 118). This simple sentence gives rise to a number of questions: How does management aggregate or disaggregate functions? What time horizon(s) does management apply in dealing with these functions? What processes does management use to come up with specific management maps? What mental models form the basis of these aggregation or disaggregation processes? How do they develop? What impact do they have? What is the relationship between these maps and firm performance? What levels of aggregation or disaggregation are appropriate? What time horizons are appropriate?

With clear reference to familiar cases of bad management familiar, Zappa observes,

> In firms of a certain size, management cannot be carried out through the inert repetition of habitual operations for the sake of convenience. Management cannot productively persist in performing operations dictated by blind empiricism, by uneducated intuition, or by simple feelings. Management cannot even gain any advantage by following the paths of firms run by managers known for their astuteness. (*Productive Activities*, vol. III, p. 188)

Each of the issues mentioned in this passage (inertia, empiricism, guesstimation, and imitation in managing medium-sized firms) deserves further investigation in an appropriately selected sample of firms that are thriving or failing, located in districts or otherwise, competing in sectors with different degrees of competitive pressure, and so on.

This brings us to an example from *Non-Profit Organizations*. In these organizations, here is how Zappa interprets the principle of "continual unity of management, which is an inalienable trait of any effective administration." Different phases in consumption management (that is, procuring income or financial results; accumulating savings or financial surplus; constituting, transforming, and as far as possible augmenting investments; realizing consumption) are always, without exception, reciprocally bound by a continual series of mobile relationships and connections. When trends in these relationships and connections in their various manifestations are carefully followed, together they create a valid source of the frequently cited unity of management in any given organization.

Let us now ask ourselves whether the principle and the concepts described above can still constitute the basis for interesting research in economics and management in public administrations. Wouldn't operationalizing these concepts be a challenge for researchers even today? Let us say, for example, that we wanted to study certain local bodies to understand whether and how they could enhance productivity by linking this goal to objectives for investing the resources which efficiency gains would free up. How could such a study be structured?

Now consider this next excerpt:

> Too often non-profit organizations seem to neglect the constant search for economic advantage, both in various forms of profit and income procurement and in channeling investments or utilizing the capital raised. But before drawing hasty conclusions on the economic sustainability of the management processes in question, one must consider the continual mingling of processes focused on economic ends and those directed toward moral, social, and political ends. The latter can never be subordinate to the continual application of the principle of personal gain without numerous limitations. (*Non-Profit Organizations*, p. 587)

The question arises as to whether the "mingling of processes focused on economic ends and those directed toward other ends" would call for further study even today. This should entail not purely theoretical deliberations but empirical research to identify different types of "mingling" and to discern which types evidence good or bad administration.

The examples above suffice to enable us to recognize that *Productive Activities* and *Non-Profit Organizations* can be tapped as rich sources of ideas and stimuli for future research. This should not be surprising, considering the acumen of the author and his particular conception of scientific research, which he saw as an activity that served to develop generalizations and uniformity based on empirical observations in individual organizations (or organizations in a single sector). These organizations were studied in depth – naturally with the tools available at that time (with which we are familiar from the numerous studies by Zappa's students) – without even making the empirical correlations very explicit. The resulting knowledge typically takes the form of descriptive or explanatory hypotheses of given phenomena, which are precisely identified and open to further study. "The more stimulating and worthy of further study, the greater the genius and more penetrating the vision of the scholar who posited these hypotheses." Zappa would also add, "after necessary reflection and indispensable concrete observations, always with eyes and mind focused on the high mountain. It is only from here that the light comes which illuminates the way for men of good will" (Zappa, in Amaduzzi, 1991).

6. Some questions for debate

A number of relevant questions arise from this revisitation of *Productive Activities* and *Non-Profit Organizations* by Gino Zappa. Here are a just a few of the many that come to mind:

- How far have we come in building the "skyscraper" of Management Theory? How can we measure the progress made so far? Does this progress fulfill Zappa's expectations? To what extent? What lies ahead?
- Are the foundations Zappa referred to still valid today? Or, as some assert, should Management Theory be refounded? In the years since Zappa died, have these foundations been solidified and/or restructured to some degree?
- What is the impact on the economic/management knowledge gap of the revolutionary changes taking place? Are there many more floors in the skyscraper still to be built than Zappa believed in 1958?

- Are the fields of research delineated in *Productive Activities* and *Non-Profit Organizations* still bearing fruit? Which research streams have the most potential today?
- Today's young researchers may be interested in current issues in economics and management in organizations and aggregates of organizations. Is it worthwhile for them to spend energy reading, consulting, and commenting on Zappa's *Productive Activities* and *Non-Profit Organizations*?
- What progress has been made in the field of research methodologies? What dangers should we be wary of? What, if anything, is obsolete and what is still valid in the method underpinning Zappa's last works?
- Given that research methodology depends on the object and knowledge objectives of the study, we should ask ourselves what constitutes a scientific contribution today. Has this evolved since Zappa's time? What parameters are appropriate today, and were so then, for assessing the contribution of a scientific publication?

My hope is that an exhaustive debate will address these and other questions relevant to the scientific community of Italian economics and business scholars. This would serve to define more clearly our shared scientific identity, allow us to relate more effectively to one another and to our international colleagues, and enable us to find a more cognizant and incisive way to contribute to progress in Management Theory and the various disciplines it encompasses.

This is and must be the deeper significance of revisiting the writings and teachings of the maestro: advancing the frontier of knowledge. Gino Zappa's words in this regard, written to Aldo Amaduzzi from Venice in 1955, are eloquent: "I do not have, nor have I ever had, certified followers. The only people who belong to my school are those who have taken the first steps with me, and are capable of going beyond the limits I've achieved" (Amaduzzi, 1991).

Notes

1. Here are Zappa's words, taken from the Preface to *Productive Activities*: "This new series of writings is dedicated to exploring 'production and consumption phenomena in the economy of firms and non-profit organizations.' The three books we present here to the reader regard *Productive Activities in the Economy of Firms*. A second volume will immediately follow, *Income and Savings, Investments and Consumption in the Economy of*

Non-Profit Organizations. Other books are forthcoming: *Costs, Prices, and Results in the Production and Consumption of Organizations*; *Money, Credit, Bank, and Stock Markets in the Economy of Firms and Non-Profit Organizations*; *Accounting and Non-Accounting Data in Firms and Non-Profit Organizations*. These last books, ideally published in progression, illustrate concepts and problems that were not considered or not fully elucidated in previous volumes, but always connected by logical coherence. Some less important writings on joint-stock companies, coalitions and concentrations of firms, and economic/management inquiry are separate from the major books for simplicity's sake. All of these works, the fruit of in-depth investigation and prolonged meditation, are already compiled in the form of outlines and initial detailed drafts; they will be published shortly" (*Productive Activities*, vol. I, p. 1).

As we know, in addition to the 2,200 pages of *Productive Activities*, Zappa managed to write 800 pages of his work entitled *The Economy of Non-Profit Organizations*, which was published posthumously in 1962. This constitutes the incomplete work that Zappa intended to publish with the title *Income and Savings, Investments and Consumption in the Economy of Non-Profit Organizations*. The fact that *Non-Profit Organizations* is an unfinished work is clear because, of the three chapters it contains, only one addresses these organizations. The first, "Introductory Notions," takes up some of the issues touched on in *Productive Activities* and develops them further, and the second is dedicated to human societies and their surrounding environment. The third chapter is only an introduction to non-profit organizations and explicitly defers a discussion of management problems in such organizations to later chapters (p. 615).

2. These include the following: the acclaimed introductory essay *Tendenze nuove negli studi di ragioneria* (New Tendencies in Accounting Studies, 1927); the famous commemoration *Fabio Besta, il Maestro* (1935); the exacting study of *La Nazionalizzazione delle imprese* (Nationalizing Firms, 1946); accounting textbooks for technical schools (written with Azzini and Cudini, and on applied accounting in public entities with Marcantonio). Among these textbooks, *Ragioneria Generale* (1949), the book on general accounting, contains chapters framing the concepts of organization, assets, and management. These topics are explored deeply and developed fully in *Productive Activities*. Finally, Zappa published various articles on topics addressed in *Productive Activities* in the final decade of his life, for the most part in the journal *Il Risparmio* (Savings).

3. On economics and management and its relationships with political economics in Zappa's thought system, the following excerpt from *Non-Profit Organizations* is also enlightening: "Economics and management, which has recently emerged yet has been rapidly and continually growing, is not the last among economic sciences. It offers political economics a large collection of facts practically ignored until now and presents economists with a view of a system arising from numerous coordinations of myriad facts, which converge in the unity of the organization as the economic institution most befitting man's economic behavior" (p. 648).

Note that within the economic sciences, economic and business inquiry had a problem of legitimacy which would persist throughout the 1960s. This is substantiated by certain economic and business scholars, some of whom later moved in directions different from studies strictly in economics and business inquiry (for example, industrial economics or monetary/credit economics). Others sought to distinguish themselves as economists, losing sight of the issues of management, organization, and accounting in business and how the three interrelate. This problem was gradually overcome as a result of developments with a functional bent in economic and business fields (organization, finance and financial analysis, auditing, marketing, production, logistics, research and development). Additional progress included management research applied to the sphere of financial brokerage and public administration, as well as studies on institutional structure and governance problems in organizations and different types of organizational associations. Today, far from there being a problem of legitimacy for economics and business scholars, economists are increasingly engrossed in problems that are the central focus of scientific interest for economic and management inquiry.

4. The simplified hypothesis of the single-product firm must be rejected because it leads us to ignore "all of the more fascinating correlations which make the changing system of production within firms a continual whole" – in other words, "the technical and economic conjunctions of production activities," "the numerous factors common to some, to many, to the general set of production activities implemented jointly, which perhaps intersect by phase, simultaneously and over time," "price connections and their infinite repercussions on every phase and in every sector of production, even if prices are linked only to generating revenue," the "conception of overall product cost and product cost per unit," and "the economic complementarity which, as an essential trait, draws the entire economy of every single firm into a dynamic industrious combination."

5. By a "production process" Zappa means a coordination of operations or facts or events within the sphere of management which are normally expressed in terms of costs, revenues, or other accounting values, or in some cases in terms of physical/technical quantities (*Productive Activities*, vol. II, p. 790, n. 1).

6. As further confirmation of what is asserted in the text, consider the following passage, which clarifies the link between process costs and data on operations: "on the basis of process costs, we can make a calculation either directly or by a progressive succession of specific combinations of production activities. The result of this calculation gives us operating costs or components of cost and revenue in general, and other values pertaining to the general production combination of the firm. In other words, we can compute overall operations for a given reporting period" (*Productive Activities*, vol. II, p. 822). Later, Zappa observes that "to compile more comprehensive cost configurations, we do not need to know basic ordinary and extraordinary costs, grouped into appropriate categories." He adds, "If we choose to ignore the more important and less important

functions and their interconnected and continual economic occurrence, we neglect no small number of essential characteristics of the overall production of a firm, and we hinder the conscious constitution and judicious interpretation of the numerous components of general operating results" (vol. II, p. 824).

7. See the famous §109 in *Productive Activities* entitled "The characteristics and the circumstances of dynamic business functions: the timing and duration of production phenomena, cycles and rhythms of production activities within firms."

8. "In economic and management inquiry, as we know, dynamic phenomena must normally be observed from numerous perspectives. Economic, financial, and monetary aspects, non-monetary quantitative aspects, qualitative aspects, all mutually related, were already briefly illustrated in our discussion on management. The connections mentioned here will be thoroughly investigated in later volumes in this series of books" (*Productive Activities*, vol. III, p. 117).

9. Here is a compelling comment in this regard: "The dynamics of production activities within the firm never flows at a constant rate, accelerating or decelerating for established reasons. Scholars would prefer to ignore the urgent appeals of continual changes in market and corporate circumstances. Because of these changes, management appears perpetually unstable, and on occasion is completely overwhelmed. Administration constantly attempts different ways to achieve a supposed state of 'systematic advantage.' Almost as if it were an unfixed aim, it moves further and further away the moment we believe we have attained it. Even normal 'advantage' is a supposition based on groundless hypothesis, as a tangible demarcation would involve knowledge of long-term trends which are entirely unreliable" (*Productive Activities*, vol. III, p. 194).

10. "To our knowledge, until today analytical expressions of organizational phenomena have not opened new paths to renewed economic and management research. The hypotheses advanced by analytical economics are so simplistically illusory as to render devoid of any meaning the representations so laboriously constructed with absolutely no bearing on real economic life in the organization. The initial positions... used to structure analytical equations are normally so rudimentary and abstract as to make it impossible, even following the long trail of subsequent approximations, to arrive at effective results in terms of practical management of an organization" (*Non-Profit Organizations*, p. 106).

11. It is precisely the reference to these financial positions, understood as expressions of situations of static equilibrium, which prompts Zappa to add, "The theory of annual corporate accounts itself is developed irrespective of knowledge of organizational production processes and movements, persistent disturbances in the circumstances of the organization and the market. [This theory] neglects the concrete facts and comes down to a set of unrelated, abstract arguments which predict and perhaps disguise any positive experience, and which are unable to disclose the various options and potential results" (*Non-Profit Organizations*, pp. 62 ff.).

12. "Do not expect to find signs, not entirely unstable and unsound, of the so-called functionality of an organization from a single analysis, even a comprehensive one, of the so-called asset structure or, worse still, from a few ratios derived from relationships among a large or small number of items on a balance sheet, or from a final statement of accounts, or even from the so-called liquidity report consisting of items from the same statement of accounts. An induction drawn by a few ratios, however correlated, gleaned from the usual corporate documents and statistics, is in fact unsuited to illustrate a necessarily complex situation, or to shape judgments on past management, or to make substantiated projections regarding future management possible, or to structure comprehensive plans and specific programs that extend beyond the immediate future" (*Non-Profit Organizations*, p. 592).

13. Here are Zappa's words: "In individual firms, the turbulent situations we mention are fairly often accompanied by a surplus or lack of factors of production; non-functioning factors of production; a shortage or excess of stock, semi-finished or finished products on hand; or else some benefit or advantage, gained by following age-old management paths, unexpectedly ceases to exist, and new fields come into being which are advantageous to producers' initiatives" (*Productive Activities*, vol. III, p. 64).

14. Consider the books on successful business ideas capable of generating superior profit performance and the similarities among the constituent elements (Normann, 1979 [1977]). Also relevant are works on strategy which address the systemic consistency of the numerous activities along the value chain and the value system which serves as the foundation for sustainable competitive advantage (Porter, 1996).

15. In this chapter, "Non-Profit Organization" is the suggested rendition of the original Italian *Aziende di consumo/Aziende di erogazione*, terms which in traditional Italian Management Theory include families, not-for-profit organizations, and central and local government.

16. "The study of non-profit organizations is very much neglected, even though this topic is so closely linked to business organizations that the different structures are often evoked" (*Non-Profit Organizations*, p. 584). In addition, "Until now, Economic and Management Theory has not attributed the great importance to consumption that it deserves, nor does this theory consider divisions into classes useful in practical terms for managing an organization" (*Non-Profit Organizations*, p. 647).

17. "In general economic theory, many noteworthy papers have addressed consumption phenomena; most, however, have little practical meaning in business. In studies on economic situations during various periods, consumption has been the focus of a number of significant observations and arguments. However, it is difficult to find a relationship between these often-unconnected observations and the consumption theory. In fact, consumption must be investigated by class, in light of the very dissimilar trends and the very diverse tendencies of each type of consumption, if theory is to be effective with respect to resource and asset

structures and the management of the organization" (*Non-Profit Organizations*, p. 648).

18. "In short, to conduct the investigations called for by our studies correctly, we need to distance ourselves from a hypothesis which is customary in other sciences, which posits the existence of unitary elementary economies pertinent to single individuals. We must do likewise with another hypothesis, also not uncommon but no less illusory than the previous one, which posits a unitary social economy made up of humanity in its entirety, or at least the whole of civilized peoples. It is correct to affirm that today's economic unit of measure can no longer be men, but organizations" (*Non-Profit Organizations*, pp. 552 ff.). Reference is made to studies in macroeconomics and microeconomics (*Non-Profit Organizations*, p. 704).

19. "Earmarking income for savings (that is, investments) or consumption is extremely relevant in non-profit organizations, as we will state in a later volume" (*Non-Profit Organizations*, p. 746).

References

AA.VV. (1982). *Le determinaziori del reddito nelle imprese del nostro tempo alla luce del pensiero di Gino Zappa* [The Determination of Income in Modern Firms, in Light of Gino Zappa's Works]. Padua: Cedam.

Amaduzzi, A. (1991). "Ricordo di Aldo Amaduzzi" [Aldo Amaduzzi Remembered], *Finanza Marketing e Produzione*, 4.

Andrews, K. (1971). *The Concept of Corporate Strategy.* Homewood, IL: Irwin.

Ansoff, H. I. (1965). *Corporate Strategy.* New York: McGraw-Hill.

Chandler, A. (1962). *Strategy and Structures.* Cambridge, MA: MIT Press.

Eisenhardt, K. M. (2002). "Has Strategy Changed?" *Sloan Management Review*, 43: 88–91.

Forrester, J. W. (1961). *Industrial Dynamics.* Cambridge, MA: Productivity Press.

Gandolfo, A. and Romani, S. (1998). "Il comportamento dei consumatore nella prospettiva di marketing: contenuti e categorie concettuali" [Consumer Behavior according to Marketing Perspective: Contents and Conceptual Categories], *Finanza, Marketing e Produzione*, 3.

Giannessi, E. (1969). "Considerazioni critiche intorno al concetto di azienda" [Critical Thoughts on the Concept of Firm], in *Scritti in onore di Giordano Dell'Amore. Saggi di discipline aziendali e sociali.* Milan: Giuffrè.

Kaplan, R. S. and Norton, D. P. (1996). *The Balanced Scorecard: Translating Strategy into Action.* Cambridge, MA: Harvard Business School Press.

Lorenzoni, G. (1987). "Costellazioni di imprese e processi di sviluppo" [Constellations of Firms and Development Processes], *Sviluppo & Organizzazione*, 102.

——. (ed.) (1992). *Accordi, reti e vantaggio competitivo. Le innovazioni nell'economia d'impresa e negli assetti organizzativi* [Alliances, Networks and

Competitive Advantage. Innovation in management Theory and Organizational Settings]. Milan: Etas Libri.

Masini, C. (1970). *Lavoro e risparmio* [Work and Savings]. Turin: Utet.

Maslow, A. (1964). *Motivation and Personality.* New York: Harper & Row.

Normann, R. (1979 [1977]). *Le condizioni di sviluppo dell'impresa* [The Conditions for Firms' Development]. Milan: Etas Libri.

Penrose, E. T. (1973). *The Theory of the Growth of the Firm.* Oxford: Blackwell.

Peters, T. J. and Waterman, R. H. (1982). *In Search of Excellence: Lessons from America's Best Run Companies.* New York: Harper & Row.

Porter, M. E. (1980). *Competitive Strategy.* New York: Free Press.

Porter, M. E. (1985). *Competitive Advantage.* New York: Free Press.

Porter, M. E. (1996). "What Is Strategy?" *Harvard Business Review,* 74: 61–78.

Rumelt, R. P. and Lippman, S. A. (1982). "Uncertain Imitability: An Analysis of Interfirm Differences in Efficiency under Competition," *Bell Journal of Economics,* 13(2): 418–38.

Simons, R. (1994). *Levers of Control: How Managers Use Innovative Control Systems to Drive Strategic Renewal.* Boston, MA: Harvard Business School Press.

Zappa, G. (1927). *Tendenze nuove negli studi di ragioneria* [New Tendencies in Accounting Studies]. Milan: Soc. an. Istituto editoriale scientifico.

——. (1935). *Fabio Besta, il maestro* [Fabio Besta: The Maestro]. Milan: Giuffrè.

——. (1946). *La nazionalizzazione delle imprese* [The Nationalization of Firms]. Milan: Giuffrè.

——. (1957). *Le produzioni nell'economia delle imprese* [Production in the Economy of Firms]. Milan: Giuffrè.

——. (1962). *L'economia delle aziende di consumo* [The Economics of Consumption Firms], Milan. Giuffrè.

Part II
The Framework of Strategic Management

3
The Evaluation of the Entrepreneurial Formula

How can we discover whether a firm has a valid entrepreneurial formula? And how can we recognize when the entrepreneurial formula calls for renewal?

To answer these questions, we need to conduct an analysis at both a strategic business unit (SBU) level and a corporate level.

To identify the management traits of a firm for each of its SBUs, two critical dimensions must be considered: competitive success and economic success. Only if both are strong is the entrepreneurial formula internally coherent or stable at an SBU level, assuming that the entrepreneurial formula is not invalidated by threats which can be dealt with only through a radical renovation. If competitive and economic success is not strong, the ensuing instability can lead, even immediately, to corporate economic crisis. To complete our diagnosis of the entrepreneurial formula at a firm level, we then need to correlate economic success with social accomplishments. This pertains to the firm's ability to satisfy the expectations of different members of the organization. Striking a balance between the performance/contributions of different stakeholders and the remuneration that the firm can and will provide is essential to its enduring economic success.

1. Introduction

In the strategic governance of firms, evaluating the entrepreneurial formula is key. Strategic management differs from operations: instead of taking the business approach as a given and making it work as efficiently as possible, strategic management challenges this approach and changes it when required. The problem in initiating any strategic action is understanding what the business approach is, assessing its validity, and determining whether at least its baseline aspects should be renewed.

After clarifying what we mean by entrepreneurial formula and what constitutes a successful one, in this chapter we address the assessment problem, differentiating between the two basic levels of analysis: the SBU and the firm.

The approach proposed here uses only a small subset of the wealth of analytical tools offered in the literature on strategy analysis, evaluation, and formulation. The distinguishing feature of our approach is that we explicitly base it on a fairly simple conceptual network, one which nonetheless elicits a theory (albeit a germinal one) of corporate success or failure. In addition, we posit a small number of guiding hypotheses which serve to focus analysis on the key issues that management must address.

2. What is an entrepreneurial formula?

A firm's entrepreneurial formula is the outcome of basic choices regarding

1. the markets to target, and more generally the competitive system (or systems) in which the firm operates[1]
2. the products and/or services offered, with all of the constituent elements of the offering or product system of the firm – in other words, the product's features, both material (quality, range, technological level, reliability, etc.) and intangible (prestige, elegance, health, safety); related services (rapid and on-time delivery, pre- and post-sales assistance, application engineering, etc.); and strictly economic terms of trade (price, terms and methods of payment, transportation conditions, guarantees, insurance, etc.)
3. the project that is to be proposed (more or less explicitly) to the economic and social forces with which the firm can (potentially) get involved or partner for its realization (workers, managers, shareholders, lenders, union representatives, financial/credit institutions, members of the local community, etc.), offering specific prospects and asking for specific contributions or consensus
4. the system of stakeholders[2] – the target of the proposal – with their expectations of the firm and their power to influence it

5. the structure that enables the firm to launch its offering on the market and to propose the project in question to its stakeholders. The word "structure" is used here in a broad sense, encompassing the organizational structure and operating mechanisms (such as planning and control systems, human resources management systems) and all of the resources (human and non-human) which make up the technological, commercial, managerial, and financial assets of the firm

These five aggregate variables (competitive system, product system, prospects offered to and contributions requested from stakeholders, system of stakeholders, and structure) can be found in every firm. Their interconnections bind them into a single entrepreneurial formula which can be divided into two subsets. One subset consists of how the firm operates in a given competitive arena (its approach to a specific sector of economic activity); the other corresponds to how the firm operates within the system of economic, political, and social forces where it seeks the resources and consensus it needs (Figure 3.1). Put another way, the first subset reflects the positioning and competitive strategy of the firm, and the second reveals its positioning and "social" strategy.[3] From an analytical/evaluative viewpoint, we can assert that structure determines the product system, which, in turn, enables the firm to carve out its place in the market; at the same time, structure contributes to shaping the competitive system. Finally, the competitive system provides the structure with the continual flow of information which provokes short- and long-term adaptations, and the flow of resources which represent compensation for the exchanges made with this system. Similar considerations apply to the second subset: the structure expresses the project proposal, which attracts certain social forces that guarantee it the essential collaboration it needs.

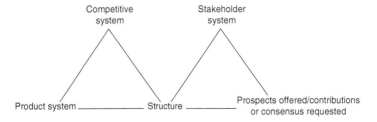

Figure 3.1   Components of the entrepreneurial formula

In essence, the entrepreneurial formula takes on the configuration of two circular subsets, both revolving around the structure, which is a synthesis of the firm's history in all its various dimensions (entrepreneurial learning, commercial launch, financial aspects, etc.). At the same time, the structure represents the firm's proactive ability with regard to the competitive system and other social forces, contributing to them and receiving stimuli, resources, and collaboration in return.

Note that Figure 3.1 is a schematic of the entrepreneurial formula of a single-business firm. For firms which compete in several business areas, we need a model for each SBU, each with its own components, all clustered around a central structure. It would be constructed in a similar way, and the entire entrepreneurial formula would still revolve around the structure.

3. What distinguishes a successful entrepreneurial formula?

A successful entrepreneurial formula has unmistakable attributes that are worth examining for each of the two subsets – that is, business unit and firm level – mentioned above.

First, for simplicity's sake, we'll take the example of a single-business firm. With respect to the product systems of rival companies, the entrepreneurial formula adopted by a firm has clear competitive advantages which serve to fulfill specific market needs or attain critical success factors. The firm is able to achieve these advantages owing to a structure that has clearly identifiable distinctive competencies compared with the structure of competitors.

In successful firms, the product system and the structure are internally coherent. Moreover, the product system adapts well to the characteristics of the structure (fully exploiting its strengths) and the competitive system (capturing certain opportunities). Finally, the structure is well fitted to the market (or, more often, the market segment or niche) and is sufficiently flexible or rigid to compete in this arena effectively.

In short, all components of the entrepreneurial formulas of successful firms are highly coherent. In a sense they represent logical developments of a central idea about how to be competitive in a given branch of industry. This idea is the outcome of an often-intuitive initiative which unites perceived needs and the prospect of satisfying them economically. It is a simple idea conceptually, the fruit of linear reasoning rather than convoluted considerations. As such, the idea captures our attention because of its intrinsic validity. It is coherent with the basic evolutionary paths of the environment and the sector, even though on occasion a highly innovative idea can appear to be non-conformist or in sync with social values shared only by a minority of people.[4]

This coherence among components in the entrepreneurial formula which are centered on an intrinsically valid central idea serves as the basis for competitive and economic success. Competitive success is achieved because coherence generates an enduring (not transient) competitive advantage on one or more critical success factors (and not on less important competitive variables), which leads the firm to a leadership position in the market segment or niche. In addition, economic success is achieved because profitability is the consequence of the ability of the product system to satisfy market needs and contend with structural constraints, and to some extent exploit those constraints. This, in turn, reflects the coherence between structure and the business niche carved out by the firm in the context of the relevant competitive system.

This describes the subset of the entrepreneurial formula which constitutes the firm's competitive strategy. The other subset in some senses represents a higher-level entrepreneurial formula than the entrepreneurial formula of a specific business unit. This subset has clearly identifiable features in firms which are moving forward on the path to success. Specifically, the offering proposed to the stakeholders who are asked for their resources and their consensus is distinguished by certain differential advantages. That is, the proposal is perceived by those who accept it as something that can satisfy their basic expectations better than any alternative. Nevertheless, clearly the path ahead may call for sacrifices, and the future holds unexpected events and risks. For example, stockholders may be requested to relinquish their share of profits to ensure the survival and autonomy of the firm, or workers may be asked to make a special effort to maintain competitive advantage. Finally, in its constituent elements that more directly affect the higher-level entrepreneurial formula, structure is generally marked by a strong corporate culture made up of shared values.

Most notably, these values include continuity, autonomy, profitability, and sociality. Continuity leads us to regard the firm as an institution that transcends the life and individual interests of the parties temporarily responsible for it. This institution must be preserved and handed down intact to future generations. Autonomy causes us to see in the firm a typical, fundamental expression of economic systems with largely decentralized decision-making. A corollary to these first two values is profitability, because survival without profitability inevitably results in a loss of autonomy. Profitability, in turn, in "excellent" firms is indivisible from sociality; the two tend to be linked by reciprocal functionality.

A culture anchored in these values represents a powerful motivational force that encourages dedication to corporate interests. Such a culture forms the basis for long-term success, which results in the ability to attract the requisite resources and collaboration. Consequently, we can see how the "superordinate" entrepreneurial formula is a coherent set of elements which generates consensus, trust, and satisfaction, centering on corporate strategy. All of these conditions are vital for the firm to carry out its social role as a producer of wealth in the best possible way.

Figure 3.2 illustrates the distinctive traits of an entrepreneurial formula in successful firms.

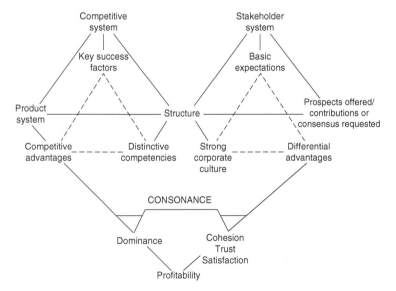

Figure 3.2   Components of the entrepreneurial formula and their distinctive traits in successful firms

4. How to evaluate an entrepreneurial formula: introductory comments

An entrepreneurial formula should be evaluated both at an SBU level and at a corporate level. The former calls for analysis and assessment of the competitive strategy behind the firm's entrance into key SBUs; the latter involves evaluation of the aspects of the entrepreneurial formula which are dominant and shared by the different SBUs.

There are several possible approaches to evaluating the validity of an entrepreneurial formula at these two levels. The one that perhaps most directly serves our assessment purposes entails answering the following questions:

- What is the positioning of the SBU in question or of the firm as a whole, as compared with the typical aspects of business success (that is, success at an SBU level in terms of competition and profits, and social and overall economic success at a corporate level)?
- What is the reason for the positioning of the SBU or the firm? What path was followed to get there?
- Assuming that the positioning is optimal and can be explained by a process of learning a successful entrepreneurial formula, are there impending threats which might undermine the basis for success – threats which the firm must contend with by revolutionizing its entrepreneurial approach?
- Assuming, instead, that a firm's positioning is not advantageous, at least in terms of one of the dimensions mentioned above, owing to the inadequacy of some aspect of the entrepreneurial formula, what are the resultant needs for entrepreneurial innovation?

Generally speaking, an entrepreneurial formula is valid if the SBU or the firm enjoys an advantageous position with respect to both dimensions of success and no impending threats necessitate a drastic transformation. A valid entrepreneurial formula must be protected and consolidated. In every other case, the entrepreneurial formula requires more or less radical renewal.

Now we'll examine how to evaluate the entrepreneurial formula more closely, beginning with the business strategy.

5. Evaluating the entrepreneurial formula at an SBU level

At an SBU level, business success relates to competition and profits. This gives rise to an initial key question: Is the firm successful (as far as the SBU in question is concerned) at the level of competition and/ or profit?

This question can be answered by identifying and evaluating the signs of success, even if they are only circumstantial or symptomatic, and carefully determining whether they are proof of past or present success.

As regards the competitive aspect, relevant proof of success may come from various types of information pertaining to absolute and relative market share, extent of market coverage, the qualitative level of the target clientele, and the degree of penetration among different customer segments.

Clearly, this information shows us the score in the competitive game and not the causes behind it. These causes can be revealed by shifting the focus of our investigation to competitive differentials and the distinctive competencies of each competitor. But these should be examined later, when we want to understand the reason for our success or failure. Contemplating causes at the initial stages of our analysis would serve only to complicate matters; worse still, the distinction between the concepts of competitive success and economic success might become blurred. If, for example, at this point we compare our corporate cost structure with those of our competitors, we run the risk of blending our evaluation of competitive and corporate economic success into a single whole. The simple reason is that competitiveness in terms of cost structure is a causal factor of the ability both to compete and to generate profit. To sum up, then, this initial analysis is the formation of an indicative opinion as to the level of competitive success based exclusively on evidence garnered from results without taking into account competitors' behaviors or structures.

As regards the profit component of success, we must focus our evaluation on operating profit from investments (earnings before interest and tax divided by total assets net of risk and contingency funds) and not net return on equity – that is, ROI not ROE. (The latter is an indicator of profitability, used to evaluate the entrepreneurial formula at a corporate level.)

It is not always possible to obtain information on ROI. This is the case with multi-SBU firms, in which substantial fixed costs and sizeable earning assets may be shared by SBUs, in which case it may be technically impossible to measure ROI for each. Moreover, a reliable set of financial statements may simply not be available. In such cases, we can still form an opinion as to level of economic success by using other earnings indicators linked to operating profit, such as contribution margin ratios, current asset rotation ratios, turnover (or value-added) per employee, markup on base cost (to calculate sales price), and discount policies.

Once we've positioned the firm (or the individual SBU) in the matrix of the indicators of business success at an SBU level, it's crucial that we find an explanation for this positioning by answering questions such as: What is the basis for simultaneous success in terms of competition and profits? How can a firm make a profit, achieving some degree of economic success, even if it has not achieved a high degree of market penetration? or, How can a firm fail to make a profit despite established market success and an excellent reputation? or, Why isn't the firm successful, either competitively or economically?

Normally we look for the answer to these questions using the guiding hypotheses given in the matrix in Figure 3.3.[5] To be specific, if

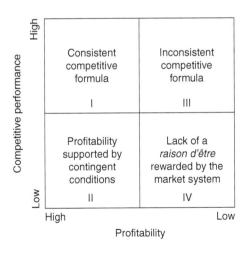

Figure 3.3 Tool for the initial diagnosis of the strategic formula at the strategic business unit level

the firm is successful in a given SBU both competitively and economically, the reason is quite probably that the business strategy works efficiently, there is coherence among its constituent elements, and these revolve around a central idea that is intrinsically valid. We may also assert that the attainment of competitive and economic success at the same time validates the hypothesis that the former causes the latter, which, in turn, enhances the former. But this virtuous circle is no coincidence; it is proof that a successful, well-thought-out business strategy is working. The cornerstones of this strategy are most likely certain distinctive competencies which enable the firm to enter the market with a certain competitive advantage, which, in turn, empowers the firm at least as regards a certain market segment (or niche) for which the structure is well fitted.

With firms which enjoy significant economic success without a substantial market presence, the situation is different. The explanation here might be found in the impact of favorable external conditions that facilitate the task of generating profits. Examples are demand that exhibits continual and consistent expansion; entrance barriers for newcomers such as customs duties, import quotas, economies of scale, and other cost advantages (linked to low pay rates, to qualifying and using particular skills, or to the low cost of money); advantages relating to quality, distribution channel, or other factors which are not accessible or are too costly for potential newcomers; effective agreements among producers for limiting competition; a chronic lack of bargaining power among suppliers, who have excess production capacity and are unable to agree on price-stabilizing measures. The entrepreneurial formula of these firms is probably a straightforward one, sparse on entrepreneurial content, based simply on the idea of exploiting favorable external conditions and the implicit or explicit assumption that they are destined to last indefinitely.

In contrast, with firms that are successful competitively but not economically, we usually find a complex entrepreneurial formula made up of various interlinking factors which explain market success. However, this firm is unable to achieve the same level of success on an economic level because of internal inconsistencies in the entrepreneurial formula, such as a positive quality differential without a corresponding price differential; a structural imbalance between the size of the target niche and production capacity, which is systematically underutilized; a structure weighed down by a "culture of waste" which becomes intolerable in the face of intense competitive pressure; a high proficiency in product innovation which is not accompanied by equal aptitude in exploiting these products economically. All of this is caused either by some obstacle that prevents the business culture from evolving toward an advanced industrial level or by a production organization which is structurally inconsistent with the demands made on it in terms of flexibility, cost, quality, service level, and so on.

Finally, firms that are not successful either competitively or economically owe their situation to the absence of a *raison d'être* rewarded by the market system.

To gain a clearer understanding of the hypotheses that explain the positioning of SBUs in the matrix presented above, it's useful to consider the most common success or crisis paths that lead to a certain position in the matrix.

Box I in Figure 3.4 represents the finish line in a process of entrepreneurial learning, which typically tracks the following sequence of stages, some of which partially overlap: conceiving an entrepreneurial vision (the so-called sensing stage), and then developing, realizing, and consolidating this vision (Normann, 1977, §4.3 "A typical growth cycle"). This learning process (which normally progresses through a series of more or less serious trials and errors) can be set in

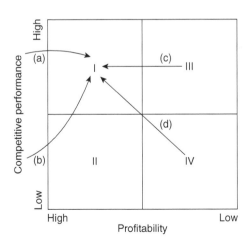

Figure 3.4   Success paths of a business area

motion from the moment the decision is made to enter a certain field of business, or it may begin in an SBU that has been active for some time. It may be continuous or suspended for long periods.

Only when the process starts from the moment the entrepreneurial initiative is conceived and continues on track without interruptions does the SBU go directly to Box I without crossing through any of the other boxes (Figure 3.4, path a).

What has often happened in Italy's recent industrial history, instead, is that initiatives are undertaken by people who pass themselves off as entrepreneurs. They are equipped with some degree of technical competency and a minimum of financial resources; they are highly motivated and want to take advantage of a favorable market situation. In such cases, the SBU initially slots into Box II in our matrix. Only later, as the successful entrepreneurial formula – one made up of several elements with profound shared coherence – gradually takes shape does the SBU shift into Box I (Figure 3.4, path b).

This success path is typical of entrepreneurial initiatives during the rapid-growth stage of an industry. In such circumstances, the desire to waste no time in exploiting a favorable situation overcomes the need to refine an elaborate entrepreneurial formula. Building the durable foundations for success is put off to a later stage.

It is inconceivable for an entrepreneurial initiative to follow a similar path in mature sectors where total consumption is stagnant. Here firms have to contend with selective and shrewd demand and cut-throat competition which has already been put to the test.

For successful entry into these sectors, the prerequisite for an entrepreneurial intuition is originality, to be developed and verified through a series of activities: gathering technical and commercial information, testing, running feasibility studies (in technical, commercial, and financial terms), and evaluating economic aspects. All of these actions are typical of the sensing stage and the development stage of an entrepreneurial formula.

Beyond these two hypotheses for actualizing a successful entrepreneurial formula (one typical of the rapid-growth phase of industrial sectors; the other commonly found in the maturity phase), an SBU experiencing some level of crisis (positioned in box III or IV) can move into Box I of our matrix only through a reorganization. The action that an SBU must take to move from Box III to Box I (Figure 3.4, path c) depends on the type of dissonance or incoherence that has to be resolved within the entrepreneurial formula. It might require rationalizing or completely transforming the entrepreneurial formula. Usually, rationalization must come first, with the aim of surfacing potential for improving the current profit level. Putting this into action may be quite simple (for example, increasing sales price) or relatively complex (such as initiatives for efficiently administering working capital); it may be effortless or extremely painful (for instance, cutting back on personnel); sizeable investments may or may not be required.

However, rationalization does not always solve the problem, in which case the entrepreneurial formula may not be valid and may require a radical re-orientation. Rationalization is open to criticism if it necessitates the use of scarce available resources which would be more gainfully channeled in other directions.

Transitioning from Box IV to Box I (Figure 3.4, path d) entails a relatively problematic reorganization process because it means following all of the steps in the development process of an entrepreneurial formula, starting from a situation that is extremely compromised in every way. Fortunately, positive potential can be found even in the most catastrophic situations, although it may be obstructed by any number of conservative forces which block the implementation of the reorganization. This proves to be a difficult path from the outset, and it appears to follow certain obligatory stages, each calling for certain specific conditions (Guatri, 1983; Coda, 1983). In any case, reorganization often remains an open option even in the face of a very severe crisis.

The description above pertains to typical success paths which explain how an SBU can end up in Box I in our matrix. Figure 3.5 examines the crisis paths which most often lead to Boxes III and IV.

Dynamics which risk forcing an SBU from Box I to Box III (Figure 3.5, path a) are typically the following:

- The entrepreneurial formula gradually deteriorates. This may be due to higher competitive pressure (typical of sectors in the maturity phase) or a lack of impetus toward profitability in a firm afflicted by corporate complacency.
- A seriously flawed growth strategy is implemented which disrupts the internal coherence among various elements of the entrepreneurial formula without causing a drop in short-term

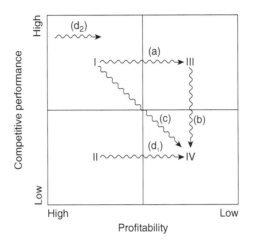

Figure 3.5   Crisis paths of a business area

competitiveness. For example, expanding production capacity on the basis of erroneous market forecasts upsets structural equilibrium in relation to the size of the niche controlled by the SBU.

- Demand shrinks for non-transitory reasons (for example, permanent shifts in consumption). This results in underexploiting the structure, which consequently becomes oversized.

Once an SBU is positioned in Box III, it will inevitably and fatally lose its competitive force and slide into Box IV (Figure 3.5, path b) unless effective action is taken to recover solid economic success. Defending the competitive position calls for continual use of resources which are not easily mobilized unless there are concrete prospects for economic success.

A successful SBU can also fall directly from Box I to Box IV (Figure 3.5, path c) This is the case when the foundation for success of an entrepreneurial formula is destabilized by revolutionary new technology or the introduction of substitute products.

Finally, we can find other typical crisis paths where favorable external conditions which once facilitated the task of generating profits cease to exist. In such circumstances, an SBU positioned in Box II inevitably slumps into Box IV (Figure 3.5, path d_1). Clearly, even SBUs in Box I shift toward the right, at least initially (Figure 3.5, path d_2). However, whereas SBUs in the latter situation continue to be economically viable, in the former situation this is no longer the case.

In addition to the success and crisis factors described above, movement by SBUs in our matrix can be caused by failed attempts to follow success paths. An emblematic case is the firm which has disastrous economic results even though it achieves ambitious goals in terms of market share and levels of productivity. Another example is the firm in crisis which sells the family jewels to survive, pruning the organization and trimming left and right, without implementing or advancing a serious reorganization process with continuity.

Positioning an SBU in the matrix of indicators of business success and understanding the reasons behind this positioning, even in approximate terms, give rise to a series of crucial questions. By answering them, we can discern the directions in which the firm must focus renewal efforts and develop an informed opinion on the validity or invalidity of the entrepreneurial formula. The need for renewal, in turn, elicits key questions which serve to evaluate the competence of management: Is management aware of the strategic problem of the SBU? Are appropriate steps being taken to deal with the problem? Is there the will to change? Is management capable of contending with problems?

Table 3.1 indicates the questions and the directions of strategic management which emerge from analyzing the position of an SBU within our matrix. In brief, if the SBU is located in Box I, we are interested in finding out (1) whether the firm can stay there, (2) what type of strategy it should use (consolidation or change, minor or major), and (3) what type of management is required (maintaining the present management or not). For SBUs in Box II, the problem is evaluating (1) the chances that the favorable external conditions which form the basis for economic success will last and (2) the willingness of management to move beyond the "speculator" mindset to adopt an authentic entrepreneurial attitude and culture. Finally, if the SBU is positioned in Box III or IV, we have to focus our assessment on (1) the potential for boosting economic performance without modifying the entrepreneurial formula in any significant way, (2) the strategic threats and opportunities which call for a radical renovation of the entrepreneurial formula, and (3) the available managerial and financial resources to implement a reorganization.

Table 3.1 Questions for the appraisal of an entrepreneurial formula (EF) at the strategic business unit (SBU) level

SBU positioning in Figure 3.3	Questions on the consonance of the EF	Need to innovate the EF	Questions on management quality
I: High competitive performance/high profitability	– Is success threatened by changes underway/in the foreseeable future? Where are these threats on the time horizon? How serious are they? How likely? Can we deal with them without radically renewing the EF? – Is success consolidated? If not, can it be consolidated?	Depending on the circumstances, the EF might need to be – radically reoriented – redefined – consolidated	Is management aware of the strategy issue? Is action being taken accordingly? Or is management investing in the wrong direction, aiming for consolidation instead of diversification or vice versa?
II: Low competitive performance/high profitability	– How much longer will favorable conditions last? What will the impact be on profitability when they end? – How much longer before the industry reaches maturity? If this stage is close, is the firm far behind competitors in molding a valid EF? If maturity is far off, what role can the firm play in the industry?	Depending on the circumstances, firms must – accelerate the process of learning a successful EF – gradually shape the EF as strategic uncertainty associated with the industry's initial life cycle stages decreases; the aim is to play a major role in the future structure of the industry	Does management have a clear understanding of the current development stage of the industry and the relevant macroeconomic scenarios? What is management doing to gain control over strategic uncertainties inherent in the environment, to discover and accomplish the corporate mission, and to anchor profitability in more sound and stable foundations?

III: High competitive performance/low profitability	– Can the internal inconsistency of the EF be easily corrected? Are highly competent managers needed to do so? How much time will it take? Are investments necessary? – What is the potential for improving profitability? What obstacles lie in the way? What are the strategic opportunities?	Depending on the circumstances, the EF has to be – rationalized and/or – radically reoriented	Is management aware of the anomaly of competitive success not being confirmed by profitability? How is this explained? What is being done to put the situation right?
IV: Low competitive performance/low profitability		Without neglecting the chance for short-term financial improvement, a new and valid entrepreneurial vision must be developed and implemented	Is there a new entrepreneurial vision that deserves support? If not, what is being done to come up with one? How is management contending with the problem of short-term survival?

6. Firm-level assessment of the entrepreneurial formula

Our assessment of the entrepreneurial formula at a corporate level can also stem from the matrix of business success indicators. In this context, the dimensions of success are social and economic. The former is evidenced by the degree of satisfaction of parties who have a stake in the fate of the firm (notably workers and shareholders). Social success is also apparent in the firm's ability to attract the necessary resources, collaboration, and consensus; to compete effectively with other firms; and, more generally speaking, to find alternative uses for scarce resources. The economic aspect is expressed by ROE, calculated with the following variables: ROI, cost of borrowed capital, level of indebtedness (the measure of all of these variables determines the effect of leverage), and tax burden.

Here, too, when we have positioned the firm within our matrix, we need to understand the reasons behind this positioning, which we can do by conducting our investigation using the guiding hypotheses in Figure 3.6. If, for example, the firm is positioned in Box I, success most likely stems from the "critical circles" functioning in a virtuous way, where profitability is vitally linked to the degree of satisfaction of certain stakeholders.

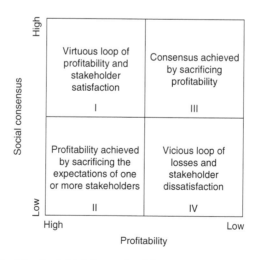

Figure 3.6   Tool for the initial diagnosis of the entrepreneurial formula at the corporate level

Examples are a chemical company with factories operating 24/7 year-round where the attention and concern of management are focused squarely on production personnel, and a bank which actively pursues profitability to satisfy the expectations of its stakeholders, who are often called on for capital increases, on the basis of the well-founded notion that a solid level of capitalization is a prerequisite for profitability (especially in times of high inflation). A final example is an airline that stresses a customer service orientation, shored up by an equally steadfast commitment to employee well-being; this is based on the tried and true conviction that the well-being of personnel and the satisfaction of passengers are interconnected variables critical to economic success, which, in turn, enhances competitive success (keeping the quality/price ratio for service high compared with competitors) and success with employees (by satisfying their expectations about wages etc.).

In Box I, as we see from these examples, economic success is pursued with an eye to satisfying the expectations of stakeholders (in particular core stakeholders). The well-being and satisfaction of stakeholders, in turn, are achieved on the basis of the proven assumption that workers, shareholders, lenders, and so on who are satisfied with their relationship with the firm allow it to attain high levels of productivity, efficiency, and profitability. This, in all likelihood, lies at the heart of the higher-level entrepreneurial formula of firms positioned in Box I. Often, management is not fully aware of the scope of this idea, and as a result it is only partially, almost spontaneously, applied (in far fewer contexts than it could be). Nonetheless, to some extent this idea functions.[6]

In Box II we find firms that have systematically underestimated their social responsibility toward one or more categories of stakeholders (workers, majority shareholders, local residents where factories are located, etc.). These firms enjoy the support of legislation and, even more importantly, a social climate (political, economic, socio-cultural) which permits or tolerates negligible satisfaction of these parties' interests. Naturally, as this climate becomes more demanding (owing to initiatives by workers or unions, non-manager partners, the judicial system, etc.), conflicts arise which have devastating consequences in terms of the firm's profitability. The years since 1968 are replete with examples (not only in Italy).

Firms positioned in Box III, unlike those we have just described, carry the unmistakable mark of socially enlightened leaders who are sensitive to promoting the social and economic interests of workers; open to the problems of the community, in which they are frequently involved; exacting toward ownership; and willing to accept meager remuneration. Despite all of this, such organizations are incapable of giving impetus to objectives of profitability, which is necessary given that external conditions facilitating the production of wealth are lacking. Sooner or later social success will turn out to be short-lived unless it is shored up by and channeled into achieving solid economic success.

The firms in Box III pursue the well-being of workers (and other stakeholders) with determination but do not bring the same determination to achieving high profitability. A strong corporate culture develops around solid entrepreneurial values, yet the profit motive is lacking, almost as if it had negative connotations regardless of how this objective is pursued or used. The consequence is solidarity and identification with the firm, but there will come a time when the firm is undercapitalized and lacks the capacity for self-financing. As a result, it will be incapable of maintaining the levels of social success it has achieved.

Finally, in Box IV we find firms dragged down into a spiral of crisis. In these firms, a vicious circle eventually emerges that consists of falling profitability and rising dissatisfaction among stakeholders, which drives social tensions and/or devitalizes the willingness to collaborate. If this spiral is not dramatically interrupted in these firms by reversing course and moving toward reorganization, either insolvency will ensue or the crisis will stabilize in some way. In the latter case, firms leverage funding mechanisms typical of welfare economies, where social tensions are exploited to obtain the resources to survive without profitability. Consequently, in Box IV we regularly find firms operating with a higher-level entrepreneurial formula which is diametrically opposed to that of companies in Box I. Whereas Box I firms are based on self-sustaining cycles of success, where high profitability is conjoined with high levels of stakeholder satisfaction, Box IV firms stay afloat without profitability owing to the combination of losses and social tensions which justify the request for and granting of subsidies. These funds, which are allocated according to a welfare rationale (and as such are too little, too late to support serious reorganization projects) only serve to perpetuate the crisis.

For a better understanding of the matrix in Figure 3.7, it is useful to explore possible behaviors of firms contending with two situations: an overall increase in the expectations and social demands made of them or a sharp rise in environmental pressures on profitability, regardless of variations in the expectations of stakeholders. If social demands intensify, firms in Box I are likely best suited to respond appropriately. Unlike firms in Box III, Box I companies enjoy a level of profit which allows them to satisfy these demands without compromising the economic equilibrium of the business. Moreover, unlike companies in Box II, Box I firms have all of the prerequisites for interacting with stakeholders on the basis of open and constructive relationships. In addition, where they have developed a managerial culture of positive synergies between corporate profitability and the satisfaction of stakeholders, these organizations probably know how to seize growth opportunities from changing environmental conditions, at both the social and the profit levels.

Among companies which have achieved a fairly stable position in Boxes II and III, the differences in inherent entrepreneurial values

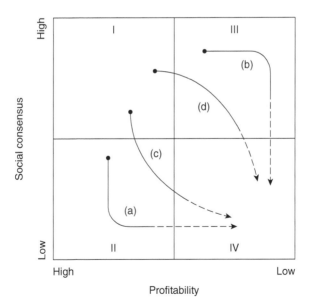

Figure 3.7 Crisis paths at the corporate level

mean that the former are likely to resist increased social pressure and resort to dangerous breaks in established employee relations. The latter will probably comply with these demands within the limits of the profitability and liquidity margins still available, heightening the risk of disrupting economic equilibrium.

As regards firms in a state of chronic crisis with established positioning in Box IV, probable reactions would focus on containment, keeping the level of losses within a politically acceptable limit. This would entail incomplete actions aimed at recovery and efforts to restrain social pressures.

We can make the same basic observations about possible behaviors of firms in Boxes II, III, and IV in the face of a sharp increase in environmental pressure on profitability. Here, too (excluding the hypothesis of a complete turnaround, which would call for changes in corporate culture and values that are not easily implemented), it is likely that firms in Box II will attempt to defend their profitability, asking certain stakeholders to make additional sacrifices. Firms in Box III will seek to defend levels of sociality they have attained without disrupting the financial equilibrium. Finally, Box IV companies will work to contain losses within politically acceptable limits.

In relation to firms in Box I, it is helpful to differentiate between those whose profitability is based on internally coherent entrepreneurial formulas and those whose economic success is influenced significantly by favorable external conditions which may cease to exist. The first group of firms are in a better position not only to withstand higher pressure on profitability but even to take advantage of such a situation. The second group, in contrast, embark on a crisis path which may lead either to Box III, if the corporate culture is permeated by sociality and is not greatly affected by economic considerations, or to Box II, if the opposite is true.

These descriptions allow us to draw some typical crisis paths in our matrix (Figure 3.7). Paths a and b show firms with initial positioning in Boxes II and III. These organizations have defended their profitability or sociality to the breaking point and have then fallen into Box IV. Paths c and d represent firms previously positioned in Box I which start down a crisis path subsequent to high pressure on profitability. At first they move vertically and horizontally, respectively, and then they too make a diagonal descent into Box IV. This reflects an initial holding pattern for profitability or levels of stakeholder satisfaction (because some of these parties, in particular owners, readjust their expectations). Subsequently, however, a vicious circle of dissatisfaction and losses spirals these firms down into Box IV.

Above we have described crisis paths. As far as success paths go, for firms positioned in Boxes II, III, and IV, these routes always involve radical cultural change. For firms in Box II this means opening up to sociality. Organizations in Box III have to introduce the value of profitability – clearly defined and diffused throughout the firm – into their managerial and corporate culture. This is the basis for a solid capacity for raising capital, which, in turn, is a prerequisite for recovering broad freedom of choice and flexibility in management. As for Box IV, to reactivate healthy funding mechanisms based on trust, these firms must break free from the chains of welfare economy values and logic. Unfortunately, this kind of turnaround is rare unless it is spurred by traumatic events which cause the crisis to intensify rapidly and/or a change in the group that controls the firm.

As for firms which are already positioned in Box I, there are conceivable growth paths which make improvement possible, both on a social and an economic level, which may continue indefinitely. This involves moving forward with continual entrepreneurial learning, centered not only on economic and social variables in a broad sense but also on competitive variables pertaining to the firm's SBUs.

So far, we have intentionally omitted the connections between social and competitive success to focus on the relationships between economic and social success that are established in excellent firms. However, the examples used above to illustrate the virtuous circles connecting corporate profitability and levels of stakeholder satisfaction show how these circles, far from being disassociated from concrete competitive systems, are key factors in winning competitive strategies.

Consequently, we can assert that a valid entrepreneurial formula is oriented toward simultaneously pursuing success on the competitive, social, and economic levels. In addition, such an entrepreneurial formula tends to set in motion self-perpetuating success circles which intersect these different levels, as illustrated in Figure 3.8.

The connections between social and competitive success are particularly evident and immediate when the stakeholders in question

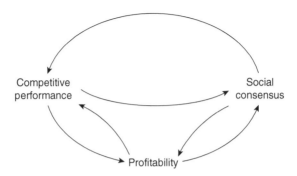

Figure 3.8   Causal loops of a consistent entrepreneurial formula

are the workers. These connections are less obvious and direct when it comes to other stakeholders, such as shareholders or banks. This is especially true for multibusiness firms.

As we can clearly see, however, in these cases, too, and for other types of stakeholders, significant connections are established between social and competitive success, which converge in a shared corporate mission. The contents of this mission, even when they are not verbalized, materialize in the concrete work of the firm in specific competitive areas and according to certain criteria or conditions of success.

7. Concluding comments

To sum up, the entrepreneurial formula assessment approach proposed here is based on determining and evaluating the results achieved by a firm in terms of competition, profits, and satisfaction of stakeholders' expectations.

Thus, after identifying the categories of the SBUs and of the firm (using the matrix above), we investigate the causes of success or failure by means of an analysis that follows certain guiding hypotheses which, though generic, suggest a likely explanation.

Clearly, this analysis can be taken to different levels depending on the specific knowledge needs of interested parties. In any case, on the basis of these hypotheses, we generally get a exact explanation which reveals whether the entrepreneurial formula should be renewed.

In searching for this explanation, we must not neglect a review of the history of the firm in terms of relevant factors which have contributed to shaping its current profile. Only with a historical perspective encompassing the firm and the sector in question can we reconstruct the success or crisis paths of the firm and in doing so understand how and why it has attained a given position.

The paths in question, as we have seen, tend to take on typical configurations which can also be represented on well-known matrices. However, beyond these possible representations, it is important to plot the timing of a firm's course and the individual transitions that mark the major turning points.

Notes

1. The term "competitive system" is used here in a broad sense, in keeping with Porter's (1980) definition. Hence, in addition to competing companies, the competitive system includes firms which are customers, suppliers, potential entrants, and those offering substitute products.
2. By "system of stakeholders," we refer only to those parties who play a part in running the firm but have no involvement in the competitive system. In this chapter, for brevity's sake, we use the terms "participants," "interested parties," and "stakeholders" interchangeably. The reader should be aware, however, that in the literature these terms often include some actors in the competitive system, such as customers, suppliers, and competitors (Freeman and Reed, 1983).
3. The components of the entrepreneurial formula we describe here coincide more or less with those outlined by Normann (1977): niche or market segment, product system, structure. We say "more or less" because our concept of the competitive system is more vast than that of a market niche or segment. Also, our conception of "structure" encompasses every kind of resource available to the firm (including financial resources), with their qualitative and quantitative, structural and functional characteristics. To get a better understanding of Normann's conceptual network, it is useful to recall that he uses "business idea" to denote the success formula of a firm in a given niche or market segment.
4. This means that coherence among the components of a successful entrepreneurial formula is not incidental, nor is it the result of meticulous planning of the idea itself. This coherence, instead, is the outcome of an entrepreneurial internalization process which, at least from a certain point, focuses entirely on developing and realizing a credible entrepreneurial intuition. This intuition is an "anticipatory vision" or "embryo" of the successful entrepreneurial formula.
5. An initial version of this matrix was presented in an article published in *Sviluppo e Organizzazione* (Development and Organization), the journal of the Bocconi School of Management in Milan (Coda, 1981).

6. It should be emphasized that this is not a misleading or manipulative idea used to engineer the consensus of certain stakeholders; rather, it is the expression of corporate values which serve to ensure long-term success for the firm. This idea serves as the foundation for a strong corporate culture. The socially responsible firm which is able to respond to political and social challenges is the focus of a specific stream of literature which developed mainly in the 1970s, as the social demands on firms intensified and problems relating to legitimacy deepened (e.g., Anshen, 1974; Ackerman, 1975). The firm in Box I, instead, calls to mind the case studies in the research on "excellent" firms which developed following growing competitive pressures and changes in competitive scenarios in numerous sectors (e.g., Deal and Kennedy, 1982; Peters and Waterman, 1982).

References

Ackerman, R. W. (1975). *The Social Challenge to Business*. Cambridge, MA: Harvard University Press.

Anshen, M. (ed.) (1974). *Managing the Socially Responsible Corporation*. New York: Macmillan.

Coda, V. (1981). "Impatti ambientali e potenzialità di crescita imprenditoriale" [Environmental Impact and Potential for Business Growth], *Sviluppo e Organizzazione*, November–December.

——. (1983). "Crisi e risanamenti aziendali" [Corporate Crises and Reorganizations], *Sviluppo e Organizzazione*, January–February.

Deal, T. E. and Kennedy, A. A. (1982). *Corporate Cultures: The Rites and Rituals of Corporate Life*. New York: Addison-Wesley.

Freeman, E. E. and Reed, D. L. (1983). "Stockholders and Stakeholders: A New Perspective on Corporate Governance," *California Management Review*, Spring.

Guatri, L. (1983). "I piani di risanamento delle imprese: obiettivi e condizioni" [Corporate Reorganization Plans: Objectives and Conditions], *Finanza, Marketing e Produzione*, December.

Normann, R. (1977). *Management for Growth*. Chichester, UK: John Wiley.

Peters, T. J. and Waterman, R. H., Jr. (1982). *In Search of Excellence: Lessons for America's Best-Run Companies*. New York: Harper & Row.

Porter, M. E. (1980). *Competitive Strategy. Techniques for Analyzing Industries and Competitors*. New York: Free Press.

4
The Purpose of the Firm: Physiology and Pathology

Corporate success or crisis often originates in the conception of the firm underlying the behavior of management and ownership. This conception consists of guiding ideas or basic principles which underpin the concrete choices which lead the firm to operate in particular competitive arenas, apply specific managerial and organizational practices, and give priority to certain objectives.

Particularly important are ideas that define the firm's goals, although the logical or chronological prioritization of these goals is not necessarily in line with the specific corporate mission and managerial/organizational philosophy.

Goals are, by definition, guiding principles; the conception of these goals which determines the action of the firm constitutes the focal point of the firm's basic strategic orientation. In other words, this conception is what enables the firm to get to the heart of the existential dilemma and respond to key questions such as: What does the firm represent for its core stakeholders? What does profit mean to them? What role do they want to establish for the firm in the competitive arena? How do they shape the firm's relationships with other stakeholders?

The "why" of the firm's actions, in other words, has a crucial impact on "what" it does and "how," even if the firm's goals are defined not in abstract terms but within the framework of choices pertaining to what and how to produce. Likewise, consonant views of the purpose of the firm (described in Section 3 of this chapter) are inconceivable if the products or services the firm offers offend or upset the conscience of its workers or the community at large.

For these reasons, it is useful to focus on the purpose of the firm. In doing so our hope is to elucidate and evaluate the different views of this purpose.

1. Aspects of the purpose of the firm

The purpose of the firm is a complex concept with a number of aspects: producing goods or services for specific markets, satisfying the expectations of certain stakeholders, and generating wealth, that is income or profit (here we use the two terms interchangeably). In addition to these institutional aspects of the purpose of any firm, there is a fourth fundamental dimension pertaining to the goals and individual motivation of the firm's core stakeholders.

Within the framework of these institutional aspects, goals and objectives are constructed and connected to one another. In this way, they take on a specific motivational meaning for core stakeholders (and others, too, in well-run firms). This is what defines the purpose of a given firm.

Thus, we find ourselves dealing with an issue that can no longer be reduced to a few elementary statements such as "The firm must strive to maximize profits." Such an assertion would erroneously assume that there is one unequivocal way to view, pursue, and use profits. Instead, we can summarize some typical views found in the economic world and evaluate them in an attempt to pinpoint which serve to ensure the survival and enduring prosperity of the firm and which do not.

Of course, all of the institutional aspects of the purpose of the firm are relevant. However, the economic dimension is undoubtedly central to shaping the goals of the firm, on one hand, and the motivations and basic objectives of the core stakeholders, on the other. To understand why, consider the fact that the firm is an institution created to generate wealth. Furthermore, the type of relationship that people (and specifically core stakeholders) establish with wealth is what has the greatest impact on determining both corporate goals and individual motivations and objectives. (Here wealth consists of current and future corporate assets.) In addition, the centrality of the economic dimension emerges clearly in all scientific debate on the profit/income objective and the admissibility of alternative goals. For this reason, we believe it is fitting to open our discussion by looking at profit and attempting to clarify its meaning and role in the various conceptions of the purpose of the firm, beginning with pathological ones. Subsequently, we distinguish the common traits among conceptions which serve to ensure the vitality and long-term survival of the firm.

2. The pathology of profit

Because firms are institutions established to create wealth and not to consume or destroy it, these organizations cannot avoid incorporating income or profit into their basic strategic orientation. But what part should profit play? Should profit be the primary purpose of the firm, with every other aim subordinate to it? Or should profit be a secondary goal which comes after other, more important ones?

We can argue from various standpoints that these two antithetical ways of understanding the role of income in a firm are both seriously detrimental to the firm's long-term well-being, as available evidence confirms.

2.1. Absolutizing the role of profit

Let us consider a profit ideology which absolutizes the economic role of the firm and renders profit an end in and of itself. This rationale inevitably leads to the exploitation, to some degree, of all of the vital relationships that make up the life of the firm, beginning with customer and employee relations. A profit ideology is unavoidably reflected in both interaction with customers (which is the negation of a genuine customer service orientation) and interaction with employees (which, at the very least, hinders employee identification with the firm and its goals). If profit is considered by corporate management as the highest good, superior to every other value, attitudes and behaviors will inevitably result which seek out any and every opportunity to make a profit that the system and circumstances will allow. As a result, management underestimates the negative repercussions that such a single-minded search for profit may eventually have on the firm's competitiveness and the social consensus it enjoys, and hence on profitability itself.

Of course, a customer service orientation is not a corporate requirement, nor is making an effort to encourage employees to identify with the firm and take an active part in it. But this is true only while firms do not have to contend with experienced competitors who strive to perceive customer needs and attempt to respond to them economically, leveraging highly motivated and well-trained human resources who are committed to the success of their organization in the competitive arena.

The evolution of the competitive game obliges firms to improve product and service quality without affecting costs, or to boost productivity and flexibility at the same time, in response to a market that demands higher quality and faster delivery, wider assortment, and more frequent product innovations. In such circumstances, the human factor is vital. The reason is that employees are called on to learn new ways of producing and competing in the market and to be willing to take on the firm's problems and everything such a move entails in terms of dedication and personal sacrifice.

One could argue that in this type of competitive context, the need for economic rationality based on income targets is actually what forces firms to rethink how they interact with customers and how they treat employees. So the bottom line is the pursuit of profit. This is true provided we are aware of the following considerations: (1) The profit we refer to is not the same as before; instead, profit is long term, and it is systematically linked to objectives of competitiveness and sociality. (2) This calls for a radical renovation of values and attitudes, the philosophy of management, and corporate culture. (3) Such a change is not and cannot be the automatic outcome of the same economic rationale that once drove the firm in the opposite direction. Such reasoning is the cause of managerial myopia which makes a profound transformation unlikely unless the corporate situation is so critical as to make this kind of a reversal unavoidable.

Absolutizing profit is inherent in the research model of entrepreneurial success based on exploiting simple opportunities to make profits. Essential requirements for such opportunities are advantageous environmental conditions, such as strong growth in demand, an abundant supply of low-cost labor, the chance to take advantage of special terms of credit and sizeable tax breaks, most-favored access to provisioning for materials in short supply, a chronic lack of bargaining power among suppliers, a cartel which effectively maintains sales prices and regulates supply, protectionist trade barriers, and so on.

Although the profit-based model is still in use, it is less common today than in the past, when competitive and social pressures were less intense. In reality, the dissemination this approach once enjoyed was not impervious to the explosion of anger from trade unions in what was called the "Hot Autumn" of 1969 in Italy, which affected all but a few companies. At that time, firms were inspired by a very different conception of profit. Moreover, this model lay at the root of a widespread crisis which followed an increase in competitive pressure (owing to the entrance of new players onto the market and a drop in demand) and an outbreak of social unrest.

Absolutizing profit and subordinating all other business aims (competitive and social) are phenomena which can occur even in firms with solid business ideas. A wide variety of phenomena, not always readily or fully understood, may explain the transition from a long-term profit orientation, one focused on competitiveness and social cohesion, to a search for short-term profits by sacrificing the foundations of enduring success to varying degrees. These complex issues involving loss of entrepreneurial vitality may be linked to myriad factors (economic, cultural, biological, etc.) which can engender attitudes and feelings of estrangement, mistrust, and fear of taking on new investments among owners and managers. Or else a new corporate leadership may take the helm, bent on quick success and orienting all business activity toward short-term results.

The second case is typical of firms taken over by an ambitious leadership that has a financial background but is culturally and physically detached from the competitive, technological, productive, and commercial problems of the strategic business units. We find such situations in the US experience, which is characterized by an economic downturn and rapid de-industrialization.[1]

The first case is often linked to the life cycle of the entrepreneur and the question of succession being left partially or completely unsolved. Typically these situations emerge in times of economic crisis, when there is widespread pessimism about the potential of the sector and the chance of economic recovery.

2.2. Downgrading the role of profit

No less detrimental to the future of the firm are views that hold profit as a secondary goal, to be sacrificed to varying degrees to other objectives, which might relate to technical excellence, social concerns, prestige and power, or growth. Clearly we are not referring here to situations in which these objectives are fittingly pursued for the sake of long-term profitability, as in such a case profit would not be downgraded to a secondary or negligible goal. Rather, our discussion pertains to cases in which the fundamental purpose of the firm becomes the pursuit of one of the objectives listed above. We will examine each item in turn.

(2.2.1) It is not uncommon for technical excellence to become an end in itself when a firm is headed by dynamic technicians or inventors who lack a grounding in economics and business. These people are motivated essentially by the desire to see their inventions work. Their mentality does not embrace a thorough understanding of the competitive system or the development of a strategy that would enable the firm to win a solid market position and keep it by leveraging technological superiority. All of this would require certain cultural instruments of which these technicians/inventors are not even aware. As these people have no business background, the economic rationale of the firm and efficient operating mechanisms are beyond their comprehension. Consequently, despite the validity of their product, these would-be entrepreneurs cannot create the conditions for enduring financial equilibrium.

What is basically missing in these situations is an authentic entrepreneurial spirit, driven by a strong impetus toward economic sustainability and capable of turning technical creativity into a winning business idea. If this were the spirit of the firm, the necessary business and management skills would gradually be developed. Moreover, profit would not play a marginal role in basic strategic orientation but would be a value effectively applied by the firm.

(2.2.2) Circumstances are different for firms in which a misconceived sociality dictates the order of priority for the goals to be pursued, neglecting the social value of the economic role of the firm. Here the motivation at play is the prioritization of social objectives over economic ones. Even if the intention is good, in practice this opens the way to a distortion of the nature of the firm.

Inherently, the social goals in question are commendable: protecting jobs for employees, creating new job opportunities, industrializing economically depressed areas, and so forth. But the firm is not the appropriate instrument for pursuing these goals, except to the extent that they are conducive to economic sustainability within the context of valid entrepreneurial initiatives (in other words, self-sustaining ventures with competitive potential). By the same token, public entrepreneurialism plays a part in achieving social objectives only insofar as it takes on wide-ranging entrepreneurial projects that private players avoid even though these projects are valid in economic terms. Otherwise, the firm loses its inherent quality as a wealth-generating institution and turns into a dispenser of resources, in continual need of subsidies.

Here we should point out that when applied to the business world, the theory that social objectives are superior to economic ones can open the door to base political objectives camouflaged as sociality. An additional risk is the political/social pressure that comes to bear on management, which cannot rely on the firm's capacity for self-financing and so has little decision-making autonomy. Furthermore, we must not forget that wherever the principle of survival without economic sustainability takes hold, it becomes extremely difficult to sustain a drive toward efficiency and profitability targets. A case in point is when firms facing impending bankruptcy are placed under the control of the Agency for the Management of Industrial Shareholdings, or GEPI (the Italian acronym).

The inappropriate use of the firm for social ends is likely even when the conceptions adopted of the purpose of the firm tend to establish a link between profit goals and social objectives but do so outside any framework of entrepreneurial logic. Here we refer to views that firms (public institutions in particular) ought to pursue social objectives, allowing for the constraints of economic sustainability, or should focus on profit-related goals, allowing for the obligation of a few social objectives.

The problem with combining economic and social concerns in the real business world can be solved not by obliging firms to set social objectives but by creatively integrating social needs and market demands in a winning entrepreneurial vision with intrinsic economic validity. This is the only route to a solution compatible with the nature of the firm and its *raison d'être*. This path involves developing entrepreneurialism that is particularly sensitive to certain social issues but despite this is no less authentic and no less focused on producing income. Otherwise, firms would be suffocated, paralyzed in the face of competition, weighed down by obligations which unfortunately affect the underlying spirit of initiative and, as a result, entrepreneurial vitality. However we appraise it, this situation cannot be rectified. Indeed, any such expedient would do nothing more than cause the damage to continue and compound.

There is a view of the firm which holds that economic objectives are necessarily the antithesis of social ones, and thus the latter must be sacrificed. Clearly, this conception underpins, on one hand, an idea of economic sustainability identified with an opportunistic search for short-lived profit and, on the other, an idea of sociality completely detached from the social significance of the wealth-generating function of the firm. There is no doubt that this understanding of economic sustainability and sociality is mistaken, and its consequences in terms of the purpose of the firm are misguided. Equally clear is the distorted view of the firm that results. This view was widely held in Italy throughout the 1960s and 1970s in the context of state-owned firms. The result was catastrophic effects of enormous proportions, to the extent that recovery initiatives implemented in the early 1980s have yet to remedy the situation completely.

In the 1970s this warped conception of the firm had a major impact on medium-sized private enterprises. This was not because the Italian Manufacturers' Association embraced this view, which at one time found the same consensus at the Ministry of State Investments. Instead, the reason for the effect of this conception was that it resonated with the leading political and union forces of the time. Private business owners would not or could not adequately counter this view; instead, at some level they succumbed to it. In practice, this meant that objectives tied to profits and competitiveness were often upstaged by a misconceived sociality.

Irrespective of these phenomena, in the sphere of private enterprise a misconception about the sociality of the firm can still be seen. This notion is connoted with socially inspired management, sensitive to the needs and well-being of workers, who, in turn, come to identify intensely with the organization. Yet there is no impetus toward economic sustainability, and as a result no way to make all organizational levels and functions aware of the economic aspect of the firm's operations. Behind this type of business model we usually find an idealistic entrepreneur, who may be inventive and innovative, bent on bonding with his or her collaborators and employees. But this person might not be equally determined to pursue solid, long-term profitability, with everything that this involves in terms of renewing the business strategy and, more importantly, continually increasing productivity and operational efficiency.

As long as pressure from the competition is relatively restrained, such models usually hold up well. However, their limits become apparent when the competitive game demands far-reaching revitalization to continue on the uphill path toward profit. When the firm contends with these challenging phases – when the very survival of the firm may be at stake – the quality of employees and their relationship with the firm are crucial strengths.

(2.2.3) Yet another set of circumstances arises in other firms, mostly in the sphere of private enterprise, where objectives related to prestige or power take precedence over profit-related goals.

The search for prestige can manifest in a number of ways: by creating a public relations cult; in subsidizing unwarranted entertainment expenses which encourage a culture of waste in the organization; in maintaining a meticulous corporate image policy which is not combined with a strategy of continuous improvement of the firm, and as such is not used to generate and disseminate an impetus toward improvement; in a high-class leadership handling money with elegant detachment and appearing to consider the drive to produce profits a disagreeable subject, even when profit margins are narrow. In the search for power, the firm can be exploited in much more serious ways for purposes that are not intrinsic to it.

Interesting to note is how the objectives of prestige and power are commonly disguised as corporate interests, given how easily the line blurs between the prestige and power of key players and those of the firm itself. Despite this fact, it is not hard to see the signs of an unmistakable devaluation of profit goals in the context of corporate goals.

(2.2.4) Finally, growth – when it is not geared toward long-term profitability – is a goal which can be associated with objectives of prestige, power, or survival without economic sustainability. In this last case, growth in firm size is connected with financing mechanisms which enable the firm to survive and delay the "moment of truth." In this way, management neglects basic problems in the vain hope of finding a painless solution.

3. Profit in a physiological conception of the purpose of the firm

The profit pathology described above shows the wide variety of circumstances in which profit, within the framework of the purpose of the firm, is not a central value in terms of enduring functionality. But what are the profiles of entrepreneurial excellence in this regard?

We can easily recognize these profiles on the basis of our discussion thus far. Clearly, we cannot avoid the dysfunctions that lead to absolutizing the profit goal or downgrading profits to a secondary goal unless we acknowledge the following points:

1. As good or fair as a certain goal might be, the firm cannot allow itself to pursue it without linking that goal to profitability. If it does not make this link, the risk is a division of objectives leading to the negation of the economic role of the firm and its *raison d'être*.
2. Profitability built on solid, long-lasting foundations cannot exist without intense competitiveness and a strong consensus and social solidarity centering on the firm; consequently, income targets must be combined with competitive and social objectives.
3. The pursuit of income as a goal – which encompasses every other objective and goal of the firm and, in turn, ultimately serves to promote competitiveness and social consensus – must inevitably focus on the long term. Only over an extended time horizon can the firm activate the virtuous circles in which economic results, competitive results, and social results are linked synergistically.
4. Short-term income should be persistently pursued, but without sacrificing the foundations of enduring success. Indeed, short-term income should be seen as a means to obtain the financial resources required for investments which serve as the basis for building the long-term future of the firm.

The first premise is relevant when stakeholders lack a deep understanding of the firm: what it is, its unitary nature, its *raison d'être* – all of which necessarily encompasses the economic dimension. The other three assumptions take on particular significance whenever a detrimental orientation toward short-term profit emerges which destabilizes the foundations for long-term success.

According to a physiological conception of the purpose of the firm, in other words, profit does not factor into the hierarchy or pyramid of goals and objectives, because its inclusion in this hierarchy inevitably leads to absolutizing profit (with the only constraints being legislation and the bargaining power or political weight of various stakeholders) or diminishing the importance of profit (thereby eliminating the impetus toward economic sustainability which is essential to the survival of the firm, today more than ever). Profit, instead, is a key element in the circular movement of other equally important goals and objectives and must combine synergistically with them.

From this viewpoint, profit is qualified by the fact that it originates from a superior ability to serve the needs of the customer and to satisfy the expectations of stakeholders. This engenders trust, dedication, cohesion, motivation – all key factors in superior competitive performance. This virtuous circle is then reinforced by other relationships that "short-circuit" the variables at play (Figure 4.1).

Note that this view of the purpose of the firm sees the firm's prosperity and stakeholders' satisfaction as indivisible; the two blend into a single whole. But for this to take place, we must reject any notion that productivity and economic sustainability are irreconcilable with respect for human beings (those who work for the firm, consume its products, or live near its production hubs), and we must also deny any conception of social goals that might lead to a

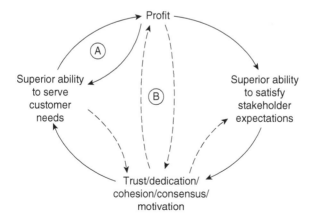

Figure 4.1 Profit in a physiological view of the purpose of the firm

negation of the economic role of the firm. To sum up, it is critical that the human dimension (in the broadest sense) and the economic dimension of the firm merge. When this happens, profit is no longer absolutized, because it serves people's well-being and progress, but neither is profit underestimated or downgraded, as it is essential for attaining these objectives

4. The dominant "circular" views of entrepreneurial goals in the Western world

(4.1) In Western businesses we often find a circular view of the purpose of the firm, but this is limited primarily to setting in motion virtuous cycles which combine profitability and competitiveness (Figure 4.1, Circle A). In contrast, it is quite rare to find firms capable of establishing a close connection between workers' well-being/stakeholders' satisfaction and the long-term prosperity of the organization. This would lead to a superior ability both to satisfy the expectations of workers (and other stakeholders) and to compete on the market (Figure 4.1, Circle B).

To clarify this point, working to activate a Type A circle means developing distinctive competencies (technical-productive, for example) to achieve a competitive advantage (for example, a higher-quality product). This, in turn, generates profits which are earmarked for honing these skills.

Basing competitive ability on a Type B circle involving all workers means linking the prosperity of the firm and the well-being of employees in such a way as to anchor the former in excellence which pervades the organization. This manifests in a competitive advantage (such as differentiation), accompanied by high performance in other competitive variables (leading to low costs, for example). This excellence, in turn, is possible as a result of the commitment and enhancement of the firm's human resources, which would be entirely inconceivable unless every employee completely identified with corporate objectives. Moreover, this identification is contingent on the satisfaction of myriad expectations of workers, including job security and continual enhancement of conditions for worker participation in the life of the firm and its results.

It is beyond the scope of this chapter to detail the specific tools and concrete actions which can lead employees to identify fully with corporate objectives. The crucial point is that a shared circular view of the purpose of the firm should be fully embraced by owners and management. This view will then be creatively expressed in various ways, giving evidence of a sincere interest in workers' well-being, a desire to improve work and wage conditions, and a systematic willingness to share certain corporate information on the results achieved and the goals to be attained, to create a dialog and an open interface, and to implement other forms of participation as required. All of this should take place within a framework of continual improvement and growth of the firm and its economic functionality.

(4.2) In the Western world, it is quite rare to find a circular view of entrepreneurial goals as described above (that is, one which manifests in Type B circles). Antagonistic views which cannot see beyond a conflict-ridden, abstract vision of the interest of owners and labor are still common. Also frequent are paternalistic conceptions, which are rarely able to promote the kind of cohesion and motivational drive that give free rein to all of the individual potential available to the firm.

One consequence of progressive intensification of competitive pressure and labor disputes is to compel firms to incorporate the idea of certain distinctive competencies into their basic strategic orientation. These competencies are necessary to form the basis for a defendable competitive advantage. Another outcome is that firms are prompted to pay closer attention to the social dimension of their operations. Nevertheless, rarely do we find learning paths that lead to a harmonious and synergistic conception of the firm and its myriad objectives.

For many years, larger firms were the setting for social conflict, and the efficiency and competitiveness of the production system were almost entirely the preserve of small companies which were specialized in short phases of the production cycle and very close to the market. A large number of these ventures opened in traditional mainstays of the economy, from the mechanical sector to textiles, clothing, footwear, and so on. Italy's economic development during this period was dangerously derailed in large firms and state-owned companies, but at the same time the country experienced entrepreneurial vitality in the sphere of small businesses. In any case, there was no room for community conceptions of the firm to emerge, only classical Schumpeterian views or worse. This was the case with models based on the misconceived supremacy of social concerns over economic ones, which resulted in the firm's inherent function as producer of wealth being negated and in base political actions being depicted as socially motivated.

When the reorganization phase began in the late 1970s, the economic role of the firm and its fundamental social value were rediscovered. Factories and offices no longer set the stage for social conflict and began once again to win respect as workplaces where the value productivity also played a part; ideological justifications for anti-corporate behaviors were unmasked and rejected.

The early 1980s saw a major reversal in the conception of the firm, its purpose, the role of management, and so on; certain basic truths, forgotten for more than a decade, were rediscovered. However, this was by no means enough to reveal the route toward community views of the firm, even though the reorganizations that occurred were the demonstration of a renewed and hard-won collaboration between management and trade unions. If anything, what was revealed was the path toward re-establishing the conceptions that existed before the years of social struggle.

Subsequently, and as a result of increasingly dynamic international competition, firms have had to take strategic initiatives which require them to be able to mobilize resources in ways they never have before. This has led firms to begin to look at the Japanese managerial paradigm and the loss of competitiveness in the USA from a new perspective. An idea is gaining ground that competition in international markets is also a contest between different views of the firm and its purpose, rooted in different systems of entrepreneurial values which must be clarified and critically assessed.[2]

5. Situations shaped by a physiological view of the purpose of the firm

(5.l) The Japanese managerial paradigm reflects the physiological view of the purpose of the firm presented above. In contrast, in the industrially depressed USA, a pyramid view is espoused which absolutizes economic goals and objectives, placing them at the apex. Consequently, American firms strive for short-term profits.[3]

However, there are cases in the Western world of prestigious companies run by enlightened, competent leaders who have successfully brought together economic and human needs in the way described above. In addition, a growing number of Western firms are attempting to face the radical changes in culture and strategic/organizational structure required to move in the direction of the model illustrated above.[4]

In these circumstances, views of corporate goals are established or emerging which are capable of aligning and integrating the economic and human dimensions of the firm. Behind all of this lies a process of growth and learning which involves corporate leadership, management and all personnel, trade unions, the financial market, and political parties.

(5.2) Individual and collective learning is undertaken by economic and social agents who have a certain stake in the life of the firm. In the Japanese experience, this process centered on the key value of productivity, initially developed during the mid-1950s with the establishment of the Japan Productivity Center. The JPC became the hub of the Japanese movement for productivity in the private sector and is still active today.

The JPC rejected the Taylorist view of productivity, which was based on mechanistic rationality. This framework neglected the human aspects of methods for increasing efficiency and the impact of technological progress on employment. Instead, the JPC associated "respect for the individual to promote personal well-being" with the concept of productivity, embracing the European version of the latter advanced by the movement for productivity which was gaining momentum at that time (Japan Productivity Center, n.d.). In addition, the JPC adopted the guidelines set down at the First Productivity Liaison Conference on 21 May 1955, attended by representatives of the government, workers, entrepreneurs, and managers.

The following basic principles were established:

1. Productivity is instrumental in increasing long-term employment.
2. Government, management, and all people must work together to find the best way to deal with employment problems that may arise in the short term, before economic and occupational growth targets are achieved.

3. Workers and management are committed to collaborating in the most appropriate way for each firm to discuss, study, and debate concrete measures for enhancing productivity.
4. The results of improved productivity must be distributed fairly among firms, workers, and consumers, in a manner consistent with the national economic situation. (Japan Productivity Center, n.d.)

In response to these guiding principles, the Confederation of Japanese Trade Unions (most of whose members are unions representing company workers) listed eight principles clarifying their position on the productivity movement. It is worthwhile to record these statements in their entirety to gain a better understanding of the arrival point in a learning process for the workforce which had an incalculable impact on economic development in Japan.

1. The so-called individualistic rationalization movement and the efficiency movement differ from the productivity movement, which should center all its policies on improving the life of the nation and rendering the Japanese economy self-sufficient.
2. The productivity movement should promote not more intense work but improved working conditions, salaries, and actual income.
3. The productivity movement should increase employment by expanding and developing the economy. Therefore, employers and the government must take steps to stabilize employment and eliminate the risk of unemployment.
4. The productivity movement should not give rise to a higher concentration of capital; rather, it should stabilize small and medium-sized firms and improve the quality of working life in these firms.
5. The profits resulting from enhanced productivity must be earmarked for lowering prices, improving working conditions, and refurbishing factories and production facilities.
6. For the productivity movement to succeed, total industrial democracy is needed, and a rational system of industrial relations must be established.
7. As regards concrete actions for improving productivity, collective agreements should be drawn up to ensure these actions are carried out without acrimony.

8. Centers for improving productivity in Japan will solicit opinions from the unions involved on the basis of a sincere interest in the workforce. (Japan Productivity Center, n.d.)

On the basis of these principles, the Confederation of Japanese Trade Unions joined the productivity movement. In practice, this represented a shared development plan for the country which, at a microeconomic level, was entirely consistent with views of the purpose of the firm described above (see Figure 4.1).

The union statements expressed in the eight points listed above, taken individually, seem to coincide with demands advanced by the unions in several countries. Specifically, these include requests for higher wages, better working conditions, and job security. However, the context in which these demands were raised is completely different. In Japan, the predominant mentality in negotiations is not an economic one. Negotiations do not take place between parties oriented more toward the past than the future, and without undertaking any serious planning (Costa, 1986). Rather, the Japanese context was a wide-ranging strategic plan projected far into the future, even though it became operative immediately, because widespread commitment was secured and appropriate managerial mechanisms were programmed.

Moreover, the understanding reached in 1955 regarding the productivity movement reflected a conception that had already been adopted in some firms, notably Toyota. Since the early 1950s, management and unions at Toyota had shared an idea of the firm's goals in which corporate development and improvement of working conditions were indivisibly and reciprocally connected and were given the same consideration as dependent variables for growth in productivity. The joint resolution of 1982 fully reflects this mindset and the spirit of understanding achieved in the early 1950s (Toyota Motor Corporation, 1984).

Beyond the deep-seated institutional and cultural differences that are rooted in the unique history of each country, it is important to emphasize here that we are dealing with a view of the purpose of the firm with the following traits:

1. This view is essentially a universal one because it simply reflects the natural vocation of the firm to bring together market demands

and social expectations in an economic context. This view can also be found in some Western firms.

2. This conception is the outcome of innovative learning processes which call for management and trade unions to do away with past mental maps and prior ways of thinking and doing.
3. For there to be a constructive change of direction in union relations, this view must be shared.
4. Management and unions, within the framework of their respective roles, must remain faithful to their commitment to collaborate fairly and constructively, sparing no effort in putting this conception into practice.

(5.3) Adopting this view of the purpose of the firm may also affect the behavior of the financial market. For a short-term profit perspective to be abandoned, investments are needed that may give rise to a temporary fluctuation in a firm's economic performance. As a result, the financial community must develop assessment skills which allow lenders to recognize and appreciate management groups who are working along a long time horizon. These abilities are definitely not well regarded by those economic experts and analysts who make indiscriminate use of corporate rankings based on annual financial statements or semi-annual or quarterly results, or who comment on short-term variations without investigating what management is doing to ensure the long-term continuity of the firm.

6. The system of entrepreneurial values underpinning circular views of the purpose of the firm

(6.1) Views of the firm based on hierarchy essentially focus on a single value, a basic goal/objective that tops the pyramid, be it profit, a social goal, corporate growth, technical excellence, or whatever. A circular view, in contrast, must necessarily focus on a system of values. Each of these values is clearly not a corporate value on its own, but only insofar as it combines with others within a dynamic system, as illustrated in Figure 4.2.

This system encompasses values which clearly relate to categories of the institutional dimensions of the purpose of the firm – profit, efficiency, productivity, economic sustainability, and so forth – which are correlated to the competitive dimension. Respecting and

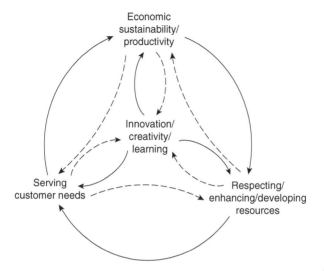

Figure 4.2 Corporate value system underpinning circular views of the purpose of the firm

enhancing human resources, respecting the environment, respecting and augmenting savings, and the like are all values relating to the social dimension. In addition, there are values which slot into categories such as innovation, creativity, and learning, which to some extent represent the creative hub and engine of the entire system.

Each of these views has a positive ethical value. For example, it is right to enhance available resources and not destroy them, to serve customers and not cheat them, to economize on resources and not waste them, to realize creative potential and not restrain it. But what gives these concepts something more than inherently ethical value – what makes them practicable in a firm – is how they come together in a unitary and unifying entrepreneurial vision. Far from allowing for diverging objectives, this vision is what focuses all efforts on achieving that moving target of entrepreneurial excellence.

This holds true for any circular view of the purpose of the firm, even an incomplete one which does not wholly match the model in Figure 4.2. In this case, we should clarify that the principle of respect/ enhancement/development should apply to every resource utilized, according to the nature of each. In this regard Russell L. Ackoff (1986) makes an astute observation, referring to corporate managers who aim to improve the quality of their working conditions and achieve their desired standard of living: "I see no reason for apologizing for this kind of objective. The only thing that's wrong with it is what it covers. It should be extended to cover the quality of working conditions and the standard of living for all employees" (p. 2). Ackoff's assertion can easily be expanded to encompass financial and natural resources in the guiding principle of respect/enhancement/development of resources.

(6.2) It is no coincidence that Ackoff asserts that management should focus attention on human resources and take responsibility for the needs of all of the people who work in the firm. The quality of working conditions and the standard of living of all personnel "cannot improve without making a profit, without paying adequate dividends to attract investors, without enhancing productivity to be competitive and without growing to absorb the employees crowded out by increased productivity" (1986, p. 2). This is like saying that among all of a firm's stakeholders, the people who work there – as the active element – are critical components of the circle around the achievement of competitive/economic/social objectives. The activation and optimal functioning of this cycle depends on employees, specifically on their inventive and creative potential. The highest level of physiology is attained when the firm pursues their interests as far as possible, within the logical framework of the functioning of this cycle (that is, striving for competitiveness and profitability and satisfying the needs of other stakeholders in due measure).

The same cannot be said for the view of the purpose of the firm built on the idea of maximizing share value or seeking to satisfy shareholders' expectations as far as possible. Unlike the view encompassing the needs of all personnel, by its very nature this idea cannot be translated into a circular conception of the purpose of the firm or become its driving force. The reason, quite simply, is that the commitment of management is not enough unless all employees collaborate completely and realize their full potential. This collaboration and realization of potential cannot be attained unless management dedicates the constant and careful attention that befits the most valuable of corporate resources.

In other words, to satisfy the interests of shareholders as fully as possible, executive management in a given firm may place at the top of its list of priorities augmenting share value and boosting the usual economic performance indicators (for example, earnings per share or price/earnings ratios). These goals take priority over concern for the well-being of employees at every level, above and beyond anything else. In such circumstances, management cannot but fail in its intention to attain the level of collaboration which today's competitive and technological context demands, and in doing so jeopardize the interests of shareholders in the long run.

Needless to say, the centrality of the human element described above is fully corroborated in excellent Western and Japanese firms, and the centrality of shareholders' interests is typical of the dominant culture in the USA. In the work cited above, Ackoff's intention is to correct this situation when he concludes, "Giving personnel at every level an interesting and well-paid job, one which offers each employee the opportunity for individual growth, is something to be proud of, not to apologize for or hide. This can give firm's shareholders and the surrounding community something to be proud of too" (1986, p. 3). "In a society which sees and treats firms like social systems, as tools to serve the interests of their stakeholders [and not only their shareholders] firms that are run like machines have no chance for survival or growth" (1986, p. 19).

(6.3) If, within the system of stakeholders, all employees (including management) constitute the most important group, there is no doubt that within the competitive system, the key players are customers. Firms must examine customer needs closely to understand and fulfill those needs as best they can. Relations with suppliers can be critical as well, but only with respect to serving the needs of the end consumer. As far as different types of competitors (direct or indirect, present or future) go, these are players in the competitive system who should be kept under careful surveillance. The purpose of this surveillance is for the firm to serve its target customers better and to fulfill their relevant needs, or possibly to establish partnerships to enhance the offering or to relieve competitive pressure on the customers in question (at least temporarily). To sum up, then, among all of the players in the competitive system, customers, with their needs and the possible alternatives available for satisfying these needs, are positioned directly in the circle of producing competitive/economic/social results in which a harmonious conception of the purpose of the firm is realized.

(6.4) All of this leads to the conclusion that well-run firms have a strong impetus toward economic sustainability, but with a dual focus: on customer needs and on the requirements and potential of company personnel. Entrepreneurial innovation is what takes on the economic role of the firm, favoring the emergence of the potential of human resources channeled toward satisfying customer demand. This, in sum, is the proper interpretation of the system of entrepreneurial values represented in Figure 4.2.

Notes

1. See the seminal article by Hayes and Abernathy (1980), "Managing Our Way to Economic Decline," and the extensive literature that followed. The *Harvard Business Review* opened an interesting and noteworthy debate based on the most relevant articles in an attempt to delve into the micro- and macroeconomic aspects of this complex phenomenon. At the same time, the journal sought to raise awareness of the severity of the situation (cf. *Harvard Business Review*, 1987 issues 3, 4, and 5).
2. Here we refer to the research stream on "excellent firms" which originated in the early 1980s. Among this stream's many products, noteworthy are the works by Ouchi (1981), Deal and Kennedy (1982), Peters and Waterman (1982), and Abegglen and Stalk (1985).
3. See note 1.
4. Two special reports in *Business Week* provide important proof: "Japan, U.S.A." in the 14 July 1986 issue and "The Push for Quality" in the 8 June 1987 issue.

References

Abegglen, J. C. and Stalk, G. S., Jr. (1985). *Kaisha, the Japanese Corporation*. New York: Basic Books.

Ackoff, R. L. (1986). *Management in Small Doses*. New York: Wiley.

Costa, G. (1986). In R. D. C. Nacamulli, G. Costa, and L. Manzolini, *La razionalità contrattata* [Contracted Rationality]. Bologna: Il Mulino.

Deal, T. E. and Kennedy, A. A. (1982). *Corporate Cultures: The Rites and Rituals of Corporate Life*. Harmondsworth, UK: Penguin.

Hayes, E. H. and Abernathy, W. J. (1980). "Managing Our Way to Economic Decline," *Harvard Business Review*, 58: 67–77.

Japan Productivity Center (n.d.). *The Productivity Movement in Japan: The Basic Concept of Productivity and the Development of the Productivity Movement.* Tokyo: Japan Productivity Center.

Ouchi, W. G. (1981). *Theory Z: How American Business Can Meet the Japanese Challenge.* Reading, MA: Addison-Wesley.

Peters, T. J. and Waterman, R. H., Jr. (1982). *In Search of Excellence: Lessons from America's Best-Run Companies.* New York: Harper & Row.

Toyota Motor Corporation (1984). *Toyota Motor Corporation Company Report,* January.

5
Governing Strategy Dynamics

Vittorio Coda,
Bocconi University, Milan

Edoardo Mollona,
University of Bologna

In this chapter we analyze strategic management processes in an organization. Our interest is to understand how top management develops strategic intentions and how those intentions can turn into realized strategy. In our study, we consider both theoretical work and empirical evidence. Our research is greatly influenced by the premise that a systemic approach to strategic governance in organizations is beneficial. Such an approach takes into account the dynamic interaction of numerous processes that affect an organization. In particular, we examine learning processes which give rise to the strategic intentions of top management, managerial processes which top management enacts, and organizational behaviors instigated by top management or developed independently of the executive body. All of these processes unfold in environments which, as a rule, are in a state of constant flux. Our aim, therefore, is to propose a dynamic model of strategy-making (realized strategy) which can be useful to management as a frame of reference for understanding and effectively governing the dynamics of the organizational system and strategy in action. Our model can be applied both in cases where a radical change is needed and in cases when innovation follows an incremental, evolutionary logic.

1. The literature on the strategic management process

The literature on the process of strategic management has posed a number of questions, such as: What does it mean to manage a firm strategically? How should (realized) strategy be evaluated? How should (intended) strategy be defined? What other activities are relevant to the strategic management process? When we attempt to respond to these questions, the theoretical contributions on the strategic management process can be categorized according to the position they take on the following topics:

- the interpretation of strategic management as a purely analytical/ rational process or as complex learning-by-doing
- strategic management as a top-down process or a bottom-up process
- the role of top management in governing this process

The Harvard tradition, for example, established schools of thought that Mintzberg (1990a) re-christened the Design School (Andrews, 1971) and the Planning School (Ansoff, 1965, 1979, 1984, 1991). According to these schools, the process of strategic management is an analytical/rational one in both the formulation and the realization phases (which essentially refer to planning and creating an organizational structure in a broad sense, subsequent to strategic choices). This approach is decidedly top-down and is based on the premise of total rationality in decision-making and logical consequentiality in realizing these decisions.

Previously, Normann (1977) had averred that formulating a business idea in an organization is always a learning-by-doing process. With Mintzberg's work (1978, 1979, 1990a, 1990b, 1991), the divide between thought and action is eliminated. Strategy is the outcome of a learning process that progresses along two lines: a deliberate strategy that embodies the top-down, analytical/rational side of strategy and an emerging strategy, the output of a trial-and-error process, which is decidedly bottom-up (Figure 5.1). In contrast, Bower (1970), Burgelman (1983a, 1983b, 1983c, 1991, 1994), and Noda and Bower (1996) posit that strategy is essentially a bottom-up process in which the CEO plays a dual role. On one hand, the CEO takes charge of designing the strategic/organizational context in which strategy takes shape; on the other, the CEO only fine-tunes corporate strategy ex post, supporting and officializing the results of the strategies that survived the selective pressures of the strategic/organizational context.

Figure 5.1   Mintzberg's model
Source: Mintzberg (1978).

This set of studies holds that strategy is the result of a continual learning process rather than the outcome of an ex ante analytical process. Also included in this group is the work of Quinn (1980, 1981), who sees strategy as a process of logical incrementalism in which corporate leaders channel flows of activities and events into conscious strategies.[1]

Finally, evolutionary economists Nelson and Winter (1982) arrive at an extreme in this direction. They virtually nullify the role of corporate management as the conveyer of global rationality and instead give priority to strategic process, meaning the process resulting from the evolution of organizational routines. Environmental changes force organizations to enact learning processes by which certain inefficient routines are replaced with efficient ones. However, there are tight interconnections and hierarchical links among all routines, from production-related routines to managerial processes. To replace a routine, these changes must be communicated inside the organization. According to this theory, it is management's responsibility to facilitate the learning process, eradicating inefficient routines, removing any obstacles to the transmission of the change inside the organization, and encouraging change in routines through innovation or imitation (Mintzberg et al., 1998). But the true agents of the evolution of corporate strategy are the subsystems in which organizational routines take place.

As a result of their emphasis on learning processes in formulating corporate strategy, the works cited above (from Normann to Mintzberg, Bower, Burgelman, and Noda, and perhaps even Quinn, and finally Nelson and Winter) can be grouped into what Mintzberg et al. (1998) called the Learning School.

2. Open issues

As we have seen, the work of Normann, Mintzberg, Bower, and Burgelman highlights certain key aspects, including the crucial role of learning and the spontaneous and emerging component of strategic activity in the organization. In addition, their work helps us reinterpret the role of the corporate leader. These authors give us perspective on the behavior of the inspired leader who has the situation completely under control, and they call attention to the no less important role of the designer or architect of complex systems (Burgelman, 1983a).

From this starting point, we now attempt to make some headway in clarifying certain issues left open by the studies cited above. First, although Normann, Mintzberg, Bower, and Burgelman clearly reveal the spontaneous and emerging component of strategy, based on learning-by-doing processes, we need to examine more closely the content and key players in these processes.

It is one thing to assert that the CEO learns by observing the result of the strategic action undertaken. It is another thing to say that the CEO monitors, approves, and integrates the results of emerging strategic initiatives into corporate strategy ex post. Such initiatives are generated by front-line managers or other collaborators, including researchers or people in close contact with customers and the market, not necessarily by members of the firm's management team.

In the first assertion, we do not move far from the hypothesis of the existence of a single, global rationality as the driver of strategic change. The key player in the learning process is the CEO, who observes emerging events and information, and who may or may not revise strategic intentions. Whatever the case, the CEO learns to be more effective in realizing these intentions. In this situation, starting with Mintzberg's model in Figure 5.1, we have a process in which information output from the strategy in question reaches the CEO, who processes it and personally promotes the emergence of strategies (loop 1 in Figure 5.2). Subsequently, the new realized strategy, which now also incorporates the results of the emerging strategies, can contribute to the modification of intended strategy (loop 2 in Figure 5.2).[2] The personal involvement of top managers in the entrepreneurial activity of strategic innovation is typical in small and medium-sized firms with limited hierarchy and low complexity.

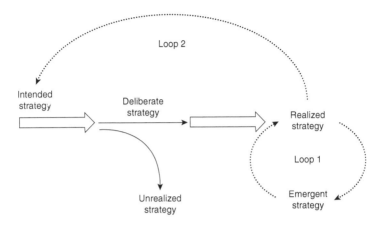

Figure 5.2   Managerial loops in Mintzberg's model
Source: Adapted from Mintzberg (1978).

When we consider large, complex organizations with a multilevel structure, on the other hand, the process is noticeably different. Here the CEO plays a multifaceted role in governing feedback loop 1 in Figure 5.2. First, this top executive manipulates the strategic/organizational context to induce[3] emerging strategic initiatives rather than developing them personally. The contents of these initiatives fall under an "umbrella strategy." Second, the CEO decides how far to endorse or discourage behaviors and strategic initiatives which, as they emerge, do not fall under the organization's umbrella strategy.[4] If the CEO opts to let this kind of strategic initiative take root, he or she will have to shift the umbrella ex post to encompass the contents of these emerging strategic innovations, as in loop 2 of Figure 5.2.

Clearly, in the second interpretation of the strategic learning process, the agents who contribute to learning are located throughout the organizational system, and loop 1 apparently functions as a result of a joint effort. On one side are players who gradually enrich the strategy in action from the bottom up with new content, both within the boundaries set by management and in totally new directions. On the other side is management, which contributes by designing the strategic/organizational context of the firm and by adjusting strategic intentions. This adjustment is made as initiatives emerge which appear valid and promising even though they were not originally included under the umbrella strategy. A form of specialization is established, with top managers creating the strategic/organizational context and designing corporate strategy (for example, structuring the portfolio strategy) and middle and front-line managers handling the development of specific strategic initiatives (such as new product development). In this case, learning takes place on a system level and consequently evolves as the result of the aggregation of input from different areas and hierarchical levels in the organization.

A third interpretation of the strategic learning process, which represents extreme specialization, is described by Burgelman (1991) in the Intel case. After gradually shifting its production from semiconductors to microprocessors, this firm officially declared it had left the business of semiconductors only after 10 years.

The nature of this last type of learning process could be described, in terms of Figure 5.2, by stating that corporate management governs loop 2 while front-line management or other members of the organization handle feedback loop 1. In other words, we can say that the Intel case is Burgelman's description of the strategy-making process taken to the extreme. It leads to the ultimate division of labor in the context of the strategy-making process, with corporate management controlling loop 2 and other members of the organization taking the lead in loop 1.

In the corporate world, it is not unlikely that learning processes in which top management plays differing roles and makes different contributions will coexist and blend. But with an eye to understanding and governing the mechanisms that are the basis of the evolution of corporate strategy, we should differentiate the traits of processes which are inherently different. Mintzberg does not use the concept of the feedback loop; he focuses on identifying a generic learning process, one in which the truly spontaneous and evolutionary component of strategy-making is not easy to pinpoint.

Burgelman, in contrast, is interested in revealing the feedback mechanisms that form the basis of processes for formulating strategic intentions and emerging strategies in a large organization. In this context, we must distinguish among different levels of management and a complex network of players who contribute to creating corporate strategy in various ways and to varying degrees, as Burgelman theorizes.

A second area which calls for further discussion relates to the managerial implications of viewing strategy-making as a circular process, with thought stimulating action and vice versa, merging formulation and realization activities into a single process. One implication of this view is that the CEO needs operational and conceptual tools to govern the strategy dynamics. In this context, it is crucial to distinguish between sub-processes that are components of the process of strategic management and the products, or outcome, of that process. Processes and results connect in a single theory of strategic behavior. Products represent the state of a dynamic system and can be modified only by overcoming inertia. Sub-processes are levers management can use to affect the state of the organizational system.

Referring back to Mintzberg's model (Figure 5.1), we notice that some of the concepts illustrated here refer to processes and others seem more like the observable results of these processes.

Intended strategy, to begin with, appears to be an observable result of processes which generate intentions and strategic objectives. As far as deliberate strategy goes, however, some doubts arise. Should we consider it an observable result of processes that deliberately aim to realize strategic intentions? If this were the case, deliberate strategy would be the intentional component of realized strategy – in other words, something that is already encompassed by the concept of realized strategy. It would be more constructive to interpret deliberate strategy as a continuous flow of realized managerial actions which deliberately aim to implement strategic intentions. But then why call it a "deliberate strategy," which is a term we associate with a variable of state. Why not "realization processes (of strategic intentions)"?

To continue our analysis, realized strategy can no doubt be considered an observable product, for example, in the physical/technical, organizational, and asset structure of a firm. But what does "emergent strategy" mean? The processes that modify realized strategy from the bottom up, or the outcome of the strategic management process, or both?

In this case, too, the distinction between processes and results is an obligatory starting point for an accurate description of strategic management mechanisms in organizations. If we consider emergent strategy a product, it is interesting to understand where and how we can observe that product. We could identify emergent strategies as the various initiatives undertaken without the official blessing of top management, or as ongoing research and development projects, or as trials and testing that top managers encourage to fine-tune the strategy in action. If, on the other hand, we think of emergent strategies as processes, we need to understand the morphology of these processes and to identify the relevant sub-processes.

To describe the dynamic that typically underpins strategy formulation accurately, we need to start with a clear distinction between processes and process products. The former are observable over a period of time; the latter, at a specific moment in time. As regards process products, one significant factor to consider is the behavioral context which they define, either fully or partially. It is vital to realize that in addition to the product of certain processes, variables of state (fully or partially) define the context in which certain other processes originate.

Consider intended strategy, for example. In addition to being the product of certain processes (strategic planning, visioning, etc.), intended strategy defines a desirable situation to strive toward, which directs and channels the managerial action undertaken to realize this situation. As far as realized strategy goes, beyond being the product of implemented top-down and bottom-up processes, this type of strategy defines the context which gives rise to learning processes that occur in the field, resulting in operational innovations and strategic initiatives.

3. Governing the strategy dynamics: a systemic model

In this section, our aim is to propose a model of the strategy dynamics, described in three phases. In the first phase, we highlight level variables. In the symbolic language we use here these variables represent the state of a system at a given moment in time, as the result of one or more processes. The question we ask in this initial phase is: If we imagine the strategy of an organization as a dynamic system in which various processes intersect, what are the observable products of these processes at a given moment in time? In other words, if we could freeze the system of corporate strategy at a specific instant, what level variables would crystallize its state?

In the second phase, we detail processes, or flow variables, which derive from level variables and influence their state.[5] Finally, in the third phase, we underscore the causal texture that links level variables and flow variables. We use a grounded approach (Glaser and Strauss, 1967) to build the model and select the variables, on the basis of case studies of organizations which have undergone significant strategic/organizational change.[6]

3.1. Level variables

In keeping with the orientation provided by our analysis of the literature and the results of empirical studies, we have selected four relevant level variables to describe the state of the system of corporate strategy at a given moment in time: the basic strategic orientation and the intended strategy of the CEO, the realized strategy, and the portfolio of strategic and operational initiatives/innovations.[7]

The CEO's *basic strategic orientation* (Coda, 1989) is the level variable that incorporates this person's mental models – in other words, the values, convictions, and underlying attitudes the CEO has developed over time with experience. Although basic strategic orientation is not a tangible variable, it constitutes one of the cornerstones of the entire system of corporate strategy. All processes involving formulating and realizing strategic intentions, analysis, and interpretation and control of results are permeated by interpretive patterns which have been consolidated over time (Argyris, 1982; Argyris and Schon, 1978).

The second relevant level variable is the CEO's *intended strategy*. This variable includes strategic objectives and ambitions, as well as potential plans to realize them. The concept can also encompass strategic intent, as proposed by Hamel and Prahalad (1989), which is associated with desired market leadership and criteria for monitoring progress toward that position. Strategic intentions can be ascertained from official documents such as shareholders reports and statements by top management during interviews, press conferences, meetings with colleagues, and other communications events. In any case, strategic intentions should be measured against the facts – in other words, with messages conveyed by managerial action undertaken to realize these intentions.

The third level variable we consider is *realized strategy*. This includes variables and relationships that delineate the structure of the corporate system at a given moment in a specific environmental context. (Examples are strategic positioning, organizational structure, and corporate culture and values in action.) Realized strategy also encompasses variables which evidence economic, competitive, and social performance observed over time. In the description of the state of the system, these variables slot in as rates or rhythms, generators of results that accumulate in level variables (for example, monthly rhythms of profits or losses, monthly turnover rates) or relative performance levels (level of customer satisfaction or employee motivation, for instance). Realized strategy is, therefore, an extremely complex aggregate variable. With its systemic and dynamic complexity, realized strategy designates the situation that top management is strategically governing at any given moment.

The final level variable we consider is the *portfolio of strategic and operational initiatives/innovations*. This entails projects and business ideas being tested and developed, as well as innovations, ideas, and proposals not yet integrated into operating procedures. These aim to cut costs, improve quality, speed up processes, and grow productivity. Obviously, this category consists of two different level variables, but for simplicity's sake we combine them in our model.

3.2. Flow variables

We now move to a description of processes, represented by flow variables, which modify the state of level variables over a given period.

We consider five groups of processes which alter the state of the four level variables described above: learning values and mental models, formulating intended strategy, realizing intended strategy, generating innovation, and selecting and realizing innovations.

Learning values and mental models are processes which influence the basic strategic orientation of the CEO and top management, enriching, modifying, and/or reinforcing its contents. Members of the executive body learn and assess the appropriateness of their mental models by observing the results of their decisions, incorporated into realized strategy. For example, these managers recalibrate their ambitions depending on whether they prove unrealizable or unchallenging. Or top managers adapt their basic convictions to the attitudes of members of the organization or other stakeholders, after observing their behavior.

The second group of processes constitute *learning intended strategy* – all of the processes that are responsible for informing the contents of desirable strategic prospects worth realizing. We can assume that the learning process of strategic intentions emerges as the combination of various sub-processes. Likely examples of these are analyzing the (corporate and environmental) situation at hand, using benchmarking to do visioning (the ambition of top management to reach challenging goals materializes here), strategic decision-making and planning from an analytical/rational and organizational perspective, and ex post learning.

We posit that empirical analysis would verify that these sub-processes occur in different weights and proportions. Theoretically, these differences might be explained in light of the degree of organizational formality/informality, top management's ambition level and leadership style (more or less hands-on), the ability to analyze problems in depth, the creation of contextual conditions which serve to stimulate strategic creativity, and the view that the CEO has a specific role and a unique, personalized way of interpreting it.

In the third group of processes, we include those that involve *realizing intentional strategy* – that is, managerial processes that follow from strategic intentions for the purpose of realizing these intentions. These processes can be grouped in the following classes:

- communicating and sharing intended strategy
- building the strategic business unit portfolio, organizational structure, and operating mechanisms
- launching corporate challenges and managing projects developed in response to these challenges
- handling basic managerial processes (decision-making, planning, budgeting, and controlling, evaluating, and managing human resources)

The fourth group consists of processes that involve *generating innovations* – that is, processes which aim to produce operational innovations and internal entrepreneurial processes that engender strategic innovations. Innovation-generating processes are fueled in various ways by environmental opportunities and the cultural and morphological characteristics of the corporate context. By morphology of the organizational context, we mean the formal and informal mechanisms by which internal entrepreneurialism/initiative is encouraged or discouraged. As far as informal mechanisms go, the culture, history, and folklore that imbue corporate life form a layer of accumulated information that reveals common attitudes toward innovation.

These attitudes are often formalized in programs or routines, and in remuneration, promotion, or incentive systems. Take General Electric's "Foundry of Ideas" program, initiated in late 1988. This program involved setting up an employee forum which met regularly to give employees the chance to present ideas and proposals for making the business more effective, and offering them an immediate reaction to the initiatives they presented. At 3M, the drive to

innovate is embodied in the "15 per cent rule," which allows personnel to allocate that proportion of their time to working on ideas they
believe have potential. In addition, the target for every division is
to achieve 30 per cent of its turnover from products released in the
previous four years.

The final group of processes we examine are those that involve
selecting and realizing innovations, which serve to filter the various
emergent initiatives. These filters may be official, and as such a part
of formalized routines. In this case they arise from periodic assessment of the financial, commercial, and strategic potential of each
emergent strategic initiative or from feasibility studies on these initiatives. Selection processes may entail evaluating opportunity costs
and the chance for improving effectiveness and efficiency that operational innovations might allow. These processes are usually linked
to resource allocation mechanisms which enable initiatives to survive, to be strengthened, and to emerge definitively. There are also
informal mechanisms which encourage or discourage emergent strategic and operational initiatives. As Burgelman (1991) explains, for
example, strategic initiatives can survive and be financed outside of
the context of official assessment and selection mechanisms.

3.3. Causal texture

We now link flow and level variables by designing feedback loops. We
focus specifically on four basic loops: strategic control, formulating
strategic intentions, internal entrepreneurialism and initiative, and
learning/revising mental models and the basic strategic orientation.

3.3.1. Loop 1: strategic control

In the first feedback loop management monitors the realization of
intended strategy. Once strategic intentions have been modeled, and
in some cases drawn up into strategic plans, the resulting realization processes aim to minimize the gap between strategic intentions
and realized strategy (Figure 5.3). Periodically, managers check the
distance between objectives and results, and assess implementation
processes to govern the dynamics of the system, without acting on
the intended strategy, which is a given. Loop 1 is a mechanism that
involves strategic control;[8] as such it acts as a thermostat. This mechanism conserves the homeostasis of the system of corporate strategy
if the business idea in use does not need to be regulated. Otherwise,
if management opts to change the current business idea, this loop

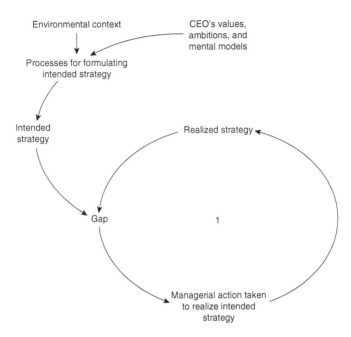

Figure 5.3   Loop 1: strategic control

drives the system on a new evolutionary trajectory. We can compare this to the "first-order learning loop" proposed by Argyris (1982).

The strategic control loop demonstrates a organization's ability to carry out a given strategy promptly and effectively. For example, when Lou Gerstner arrived at IBM in 1993, he complained that the company emphasized defining strategy but showed dangerous gaps in effectively implementing that strategy. As a result, Gerstner saw, strategic plans stayed on the drawing board and were never realized. It is no coincidence, then, that one of Gerstner's first moves was to incorporate the concept of *execution* into the assessment criteria for management performance – in other words, the ability to realize strategic intentions rapidly and effectively.[9]

In loop 1 the key variable is the gap between the desired situation and the actual situation, between objectives and results. This gap should be considered not only in terms of size but also in terms of quality. On one hand, we expect loop 1 to keep this gap under control, to hold it to a minimum; therefore, we are led to believe that a desirable situation is a limited gap. On the other hand, the need to close the gap between objectives and results acts as a driver; therefore, the gap will never be completely eliminated, physiologically speaking.

What follows is the necessity to examine the quality of the existing gap. Quality depends above all on the comprehensiveness of our analysis of the situation calling for strategic management and on what values and ambitions form the basis of strategic intentions. Lofty ambitions and superficial analysis give a negative connotation to the gap, which, in turn, triggers a destructive tendency. This can occur even when in-depth analysis is conducted without the support of an ethical conception of the firm (which is bent on serving the interests of the controlling body). Take the example of a gap that generates creative tension, such as the one perceived by Nicolas Hayek when he took the helm at SMH. The quality of the gap in that case was marked by a meticulous analysis of the competitive challenges and the situation among Swiss watch companies, and by basic values and convictions which proved unquestionably legitimate.

A persistent gap which gives rise to positive pressure is the starting point, the spark that ignites a process of generating efficiency and growth in the company. For example, General Electric completely restructured its strategic business unit portfolio in light of the strategic intention to be number one or two in each of its businesses and an analysis of the existing competitive system. (The company disinvested in 200 businesses and acquired 370.) Given the high degree of bureaucracy at GE, the aim of creating a "streamlined and flexible" company led management to redesign the organizational structure, to pare down the number of staff positions, cut back employees in the strategic planning group by 50 percent, and reduce the number of hierarchical levels from nine to four. The intention of becoming streamlined and flexible later led to drawing up a best practices program and launching the corporate challenge to "outdo yourself."

At IBM, Gerstner's strategic intention was to win a leadership position in Internet-related services, and in connectivity technology in general. As a result, the firm channeled 25 percent of its research and development budget into projects relating to the Internet. This decision was made in 1994, long before any other large group in the sector made such a move. A study group was also set up to visualize the attributes of the emerging sector and the new products that had to be developed. After around a year of work, in September 1995, the study group presented its conclusions, and in October the crucial decision was made to allocate 300 million dollars for the creation of an Internet division.

3.3.2. Loop 2: formulating strategic intentions

Top managers take charge of the process represented by the second loop: they make constructive deductions from their observations on realized strategy which help them review and fine-tune strategic intentions (Figure 5.4). Note that in our model, we distinguish between the two processes of formulating strategic intentions and learning values and mental models. Our hypothesis is that although strategic intentions may be modified on the basis of the observed results of past actions, this does not necessarily imply that the basic convictions and values of top managers must be modified as well. For example, managers in a firm may rethink market-share objectives once they realize they are unable to attain those aims. Revising objectives within the context of strategic intentions can alleviate

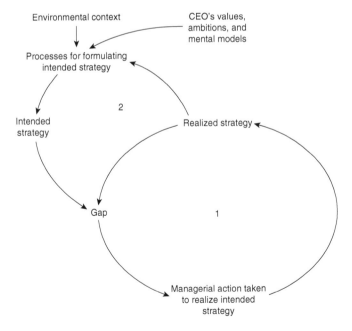

Figure 5.4   Loop 2: formulating strategic intentions

stress on the organization at a given moment and allow time to regroup corporate forces and then attempt to achieve the more challenging goal once again. This can be done without abandoning a deep-seated conviction that the ambitious market-share goal is attainable at some point. For these reasons, we use the word "learning" where there is an adjustment of mental models, and we opt for the expression "formulating strategic intentions" where these intentions are modified not as a consequence of updating mental models but as a result of the progressive expression and increasing awareness of mental models, or the tactical need to control the gap.

A concrete example of how this motor works can be found in an interview with Jack Welch, CEO of General Electric, in the late 1980s, when his company's reorganization had been underway for a few years. "In mid-1988, the hardware sector, the structural part, was more or less locked in. We liked our business. The time had come to work on software." We can see how observing what had been achieved led to the progressive enrichment of the content of strategic intentions, yet without modifying basic objectives.

To sum up, then, in loop 1 (strategic control), examining realized strategy is a way to monitor the degree to which strategic objectives have been met. In loop 2 (formulating strategic intentions), observing realized strategy is preliminary to fine-tuning these same objectives. In the first case, objectives are immobile and serve as benchmarks for control; in the second case, objectives evolve as realized strategy changes.

3.3.3. Loop 3: internal entrepreneurialism and initiative

The third loop illustrates bottom-up innovation which is the expression of internal entrepreneurialism (as with strategic innovations) or simply of engrossing projects which aim to generate operational innovations to boost productivity.

In Figure 5.5, loop 3 comprises a series of factors. The process centers on a stock variable, *strategic and operational initiatives*, which reflects the results of sub-processes upstream or downstream of the stock variable which modify its level. The choice of this particular stock variable is the answer to a specific research question: At a given moment in time, what evidences the energy, tensions, and resources in action which engender innovations in the strategy or in the operations of a firm? The patents a firm holds, for example, are the results of innovative initiatives which were selected, financed, and executed

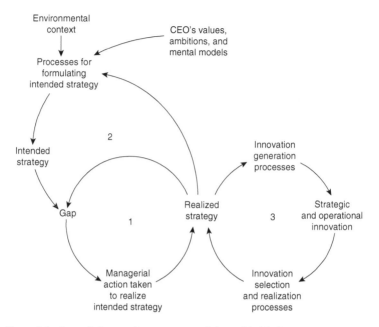

Figure 5.5   Loop 3: internal entrepreneurship and initiative

and which became part of the realized strategy. There are also ideas and projects for which the firm has not yet identified the requisite resources or energy. These denote the wealth and cultural fecundity of a given organizational context; as such they are elements of realized strategy but do not yet constitute "initiatives."

In representing the strategic and operational initiative variable, we are trying to take a snapshot of the moment when stimuli and incentives embedded in the organizational context took shape and came together in initiatives. These initiatives are under development and have not yet modified the strategic/organizational context. This snapshot enables us to observe processes upstream and downstream of the stock of strategic and operational initiatives.

Upstream, initiative-generating processes, which take place in the strategic/organizational context, add to the stock of strategic and operational initiatives. Downstream, processes of selection and realization by which individual initiatives are assessed and financed deplete the stock of initiatives. Once an initiative has been selected and realized, it contributes to modifying the realized strategy, becoming an integral part of it.

In this manner, realized initiatives define the cultural environment in which subsequent initiatives will emerge. This description is consistent with the work of Burgelman (1983a, 1983b, 1983c, 1991), who emphasizes how strategic initiatives generated within a firm, which are key elements in strategic innovation (both incremental and revolutionary), are both the product of certain strategic/organizational contexts and the impetus to modify these contexts.

The challenge is to describe the causal, circular structure that links the generation of innovative initiatives with the strategic/organizational context of the firm, while accentuating the dynamic phenomena that result from this circularity. The behavior of firms – and specifically the ability to generate strategic and operational initiatives from innovative contents – may be forced to continue along trajectories established in the past, which clearly entails problems of self-referentiality. However, this same behavior and ability may, instead, emerge in the form of totally new and unexpected self-organized phenomena which do not originate within a top-down framework and so are not products of top management rationality alone. These phenomena come from the bottom up, as the outcome of interaction reiterated within a context of strategy/organization and individual and local behaviors.

For an example of how the loop 3 mechanism might work, we can look at Honda's conquest of the US motorcycle market in the late 1950s/early 1960s (Pascale, 1982). In 1958, Honda was the leading firm in Japan's domestic market. The company's intended strategy was to activate an internationalization process, beginning with the California coast in the USA. This simple strategic intention led to decisions and actions that established a tiny bridgehead in Los Angeles. This outpost had just a few staff, negligible financial resources, and a small stock of low- and high-horsepower motorcycles. The manager put in charge of this affiliate was a man whom Mr. Honda and his partner, Takeo Fujisawa, trusted to make do with the meager available resources.

The small crew successfully developed radically innovative learning in the field which soon revealed the existence of a market for low-horsepower motorcycles in the USA which they had not even imagined initially. In addition, the team expanded the outlets for medium- and high-horsepower bikes in a new segment differentiated by a use function that had previously been neglected: motorbikes for pure fun. This was much larger than the segments in which European producers and Harley-Davidson were positioned. The new subsidiary also opened new channels and shifted the balance of bargaining power with the trade in Honda's favor.

The Honda case is useful for illustrating and clarifying loop 3. Specifically, we see the critical nature of realized strategy as a set of variables which shape the strategic/organizational context in which learning-by-doing can occur. The strategic innovation that can arise from this learning represents the heart of a successful business idea. Furthermore, the relationship between top management and front-line management is crucial in determining the quality of the behavioral context in which the latter operates and in modeling the processes for the selection and retention of innovation in practical terms.

In some situations, within the framework of realized strategy, the repository of internal entrepreneurship has a key role. This might be due to the fact that strategic intentions are defined only in very general terms, as when the environment is an uncertain one. Or new opportunities may emerge when a strategy is implemented that enrich or modify the contents of the strategic intentions.

In the Honda case, the managers who were sent to the USA successfully exploited the resources they were given within the context of realized strategy. They did so through a learning process consisting of trial and error, and they behaved like true entrepreneurs.

3.3.4. Loop 4: learning/revising mental models and the basic strategic orientation

The process represented in loop 4 in Figure 5.6 shows the impact of observing the results of strategic action and the effect this observation has on learning the mental models of the CEO and top management. Compared with the mechanism illustrated by loop 2, the learning process in loop 4 goes deeper. Taking inspiration from the impact on realized strategy of processes which are positioned upstream and downstream of that strategy, the learning that goes on in loop 4 modifies the mental models of management. In other words, it goes to the very heart of strategic intentions. Therefore, loop 4 describes a mechanism which is very similar to the "second-order learning" described by Argyris (1982).

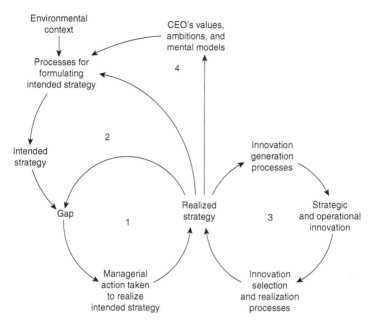

Environmental
context

CEO's values,
ambitions, and
mental models

Processes for
formulating
intended strategy

4

Intended
strategy

2

Innovation
generation
processes

Gap

Realized
strategy

Strategic
and operational
innovation

1

3

Managerial
action taken
to realize
intended strategy

Innovation
selection
and realization
processes

Figure 5.6   Loop 4: learning and revising mental maps and the basic strategic orientation

For example, in the IBM reorganization initiated by Gerstner at the end of 1993, the loop 4 driver allowed the firm continually to refine its basic convictions relating to IBM's field of action, its role in related competitive arena(s), its essential nature and modus operandi, and the significance it assigned to profit as a measure of success.

As regards field of business specifically, an in-depth study was conducted of IBM's distinctive competencies and the arenas in which the company competed. After this study, Gerstner soon realized that the IT sector was undergoing a radical change. Value for the customer could be created not so much in producing as in bundling info-tech services. Gerstner's strategic objective became to make IBM an integrated info-tech service organization that could create value by offering new solutions to old problems and by inventing new competencies. Later Gerstner further refined his definition of the field of business, and in 1995 the concept of IBM as essentially a service company was realized even more fully. The result was the strategy to make IBM not only a big service company in the IT sector but also and above all the biggest service company linked to what Gerstner in 1995 called "network-centric computing." This term referred to the ability to communicate and exchange information in real time, through interconnected computer networks and various kinds of digitized information, such as video, high-definition images, voice, and music.

Gerstner realized that network-centric computing and its main engine, the Internet, would revolutionize the culture and way of life and, consequently, the business strategies of customer organizations. IBM would make it its mission to accompany firms through this technological and cultural transition.

To sum up, then, the model we present suggests that managing strategy calls for a recognition of the existence of the four engines described above. This applies to strategy as a continuous process or as a single radical transformation.

The first engine highlights top management's ability more or less effectively to implement managerial actions with the aim of realizing the contents of intentional strategy. The second engine relates to top management's ability to update strategic intentions if need be, taking into account structural changes in the environmental context and corporate circumstances. This is also a way to control the gap, by striving to maintain high levels of motivation among collaborators without generating stress. The third engine allows firms to realize the innovation potential inherent in the human and cultural fabric of the firm to the extent that energy, knowledge, and creativity are unleashed. These forces move in the direction marked out by a strategy for growing production and creating new spaces for initiative and entrepreneurial responsibility. The possibility to shape strategy from the bottom up increases the adaptability of the corporate system, making it quicker to perceive changes underway in the environment and to come up with the appropriate responses. Finally, the fourth engine reflects top management's capacity for self-reflection and learning, and for challenging personal mental models.

3.4. Coordinating the engines of the strategy dynamics

To manage a firm's strategy successfully, management must learn to run all four engines smoothly and simultaneously, while governing two delicate areas. The first area is coordinating the strategic control engine (loop 1) on one hand, and on the other the engines for formulating strategic intentions and learning mental maps and basic strategic orientation (loops 2 and 4). Making the first engine run requires an ability to reduce the gap between realized strategy and intended strategy. Jack Welch (GE) and Lou Gerstner (IBM) are examples of leaders capable of effectively realizing strategic intentions, moving resources around inside the organization, redesigning operational mechanisms, and eliciting the motivation needed to pursue new objectives with resolve.

However, high-profile strategic management also calls for an executive management team which can govern loops 2 and 4 to reopen the gap between realized and intended strategy, creating a constructive impetus that pushes the organization toward new, challenging goals.

In the government of the strategy dynamics, therefore, the first area of attention can be called "handling the gap." Management must be able to govern the gap. A constant and sizeable divergence between strategic intentions and relative results achieved can be the outcome of superficial analysis or unrealistically high ambitions. This results either in objectives which cannot be realized or inconsistency between plans and actions for realization. In either case, the consequence is the generation of pointless stress and negative tension within the organization. At the other end of the spectrum, if we enjoy a consistently comfortable state of well-being where there is no gap, this could be a sign of a dangerous equilibrium, one lacking positive tension. In such a situation, the firm is inclined toward a state of inertia which threatens its very existence.

The second area of focus pertains to coordinating loops 1, 2, and 4 on one hand, and loop 3 on the other. The first set of engines is directly driven by the CEO, who takes on a key role in directing this movement. Through loop 1, CEOs govern the realization of strategic intentions; with loop 2, they adjust strategic intentions, and, by means of loop 4, they review and update their mental models and consequently the firm's intended strategy. Loop 3 is only indirectly governed by top management. Potential protagonists of loop 3 can be found throughout the organization, and they are all capable of developing new ideas and initiatives, stimulated by learning in the field and a strategic and organizational context that rewards cooperation and internal initiative. Top management influences this loop only indirectly, as the architect or designer who structures and shapes the strategic and organizational context, creating a "behavioral environment" (Bartlett and Ghoshal, 1995). This environment may be more or less constructive in generating operational and strategic innovations.

In terms of operational innovations, for example, managers may adopt the practice of management by wandering around production areas and offices, asking questions, and taking an interest in innovations realized and problems for improvement. Imagine the effect that such a leadership style (typical of entrepreneurs such as Steno Marcegaglia and Leonardo Del Vecchio, to name just two) would have. Further, consider the effect of challenging productivity-enhancement projects on the behavioral environment in terms of involvement and mobilization. Examples of such projects are action work-outs, quality circles, and reengineering.

In terms of strategic innovations, a distinction should be drawn between two types of innovations which slot into the strategy of top management. "Induced" innovation, to use Burgelman's term (1991), contributes to the realization of intended strategy. The second type of innovation, if given free rein, is apt to modify the corporate strategy being pursued; Burgelman (1991) calls such initiatives "autonomous." Now, the organizational context may be shaped in such a way as to permit a certain degree of freedom. This may allow some leeway in exploring new business areas beyond the dominant strategy and core competencies of the firm or in utilizing resources for testing and research even when there are no prospects for tangible short-term results.

The greater the freedom of movement assigned to loop 3, the greater the stimulus to unleash creative energy and encourage entrepreneurial behavior. However, disorder may also increase, and resources and energy could dissipate in unrelated directions without tapping potential synergy.

The systemic model illustrated here, which identifies the engines that power the strategy dynamics of the corporate system, highlights fundamental questions that arise in studying the strategic behaviors of organizations. What is the role of top management in shaping corporate strategy? What room is there to maneuver when contending with auto-organizational processes that emerge from the bottom up

(Golinelli, 2000, p. 60); with inertia, typical of variations in the stock of both tangible and intangible resources; with consolidated mental models; and with the challenge of foreseeing the consequences of the decisions taken within the context of dynamic and complex corporate systems? On the basis of the model developed here, the two areas described above intersect in a matrix (Figure 5.7).

The first dimension (the vertical axis) refers to the use of engines 1, 2, and 4. The more intensely loops 4 and 2 work (learning mental models and formulating strategic intentions), the greater the tendency to abandon equilibrium and begin exploring new territory, new business areas, new products, new technologies, and new management systems, and to seize new opportunities.

However, all of this also means running a number of risks: neglecting or underestimating present opportunities, formulating strategic intentions which are impossible to achieve or too far removed from the fundamental competencies of the firm, or creating excessive stress within the organization.

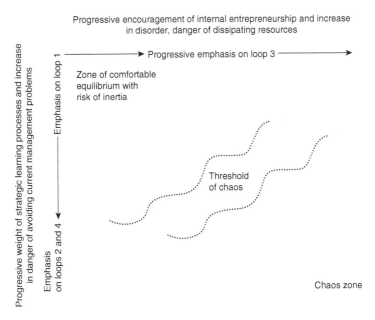

Figure 5.7   Matrix for coordinating engines of the strategy dynamics

On the other hand, management that focuses exclusively on loop 1 risks paralyzing the firm in a comfortable – but potentially dangerous – situation of equilibrium. Equilibrium may become inertia and inability to face the challenges of discontinuity in the organization's environmental context (competitive, social, legal/institutional).

The second dimension (the horizontal axis) pertains to the engine of internal entrepreneurialism and initiative. The fewer restraints and obligations that apply to how loop 3 is used (moving from left to right on the matrix, toward areas of creativity, freedom to experiment, and disorder), the more the organization's strategic behavior is the result of various sources of rationality. This insight comes not only from top management but also from other members of the organization. Therefore, management must decide how much freedom or restraint to apply to loop 3. The objective in this case is to avoid hindering the organization from reaching its inherent potential for innovation and creativity if loop 3 is too restrictive. By the same token, too much freedom of initiative within the organization can give rise to chaos, disorder, and dissipation of resources if loop 3 is allowed to function without instilling the discipline needed to generate innovations.

Our model contributes to explaining how to drive the four strategy engines toward what's called the "threshold of chaos" (Pascale, 1999; Pascale et al., 2000). This area represents a condition – a permeable, intermediate stage between order and disorder – where innovation is produced. As Figure 5.7 shows, in moving toward the threshold of chaos, there are two areas to avoid: on the upper left, pathological equilibrium, where the danger is inertia that paralyzes organizational strategy; on the lower right, where the level of chaos and disorder becomes unbearable.

Innovation cannot arise in a situation or organizational context of comfortable equilibrium, without stimuli and tension to produce innovations which disrupt the status quo. However, neither will we find innovation in chaotic environments where there is a strong thrust toward change and innovation but where this impetus is not channeled constructively. If we take this as a given, the task of the top management of a firm with a consolidated, successful business idea is to introduce elements of disequilibrium, pushing the system toward the threshold of chaos, but taking care not to go beyond it altogether. If, in contrast, the firm is experiencing a serious crisis or strategic disorientation, the task of top management is to introduce elements of equilibrium which serve once again to push the system toward the threshold of chaos. Put another way, this zone is where energies and pressures can be channeled with the aim of realizing the indivisible objectives of recovering productivity and renewing the business idea.

To avoid the opposite dangers of ill-fated equilibrium or pathological chaos, management should have a clear awareness of

1. where the obstacles lie that impede management from guiding the firm along the paths of innovation
2. which aspects of disciplining the behavioral context cannot be abandoned because they are not only compatible with the need to innovate but serve to enact innovative processes

4. Concluding comments

The theoretical contribution of this chapter is a platform for organizing and interpreting literature on strategic management processes in organizations. Through the symbolic language of feedback loops and the underlying logic of dynamic analysis which these loops pattern, this chapter facilitates the reading and comparison of different hypotheses about the mechanisms that can bring about strategic/organizational change. In this sense, the work presented here is an example of how feedback loops can be used to represent and communicate theories on behavior in firms, or social systems in general.

In the strategic management literature, research approaches are gaining ground which are influenced by studies on system dynamics and complexity. The interpretive rationale of these approaches is not mechanistic, and so relationships between circular variables (as opposed to mono-directional ones) are capturing more attention. Nonetheless, the circular nature of the causal model used in many studies is often implicitly enmeshed in narrative theory rather than represented or communicated explicitly and rigorously (Farjoun, 2002).

The work presented here does not offer specific indications in practical terms as to the optimal equilibrium between the various loops or how a firm can reach this equilibrium. However, in terms of applying our model, we do propose a diagnostic tool for strategic behavior in firms. Given that our rationale of representation hinges on the concept of a dynamic, complex system which typically has a capacity for auto-organization in new and unexpected ways, we believe it is interesting to investigate the appropriate dimensions for creating a conceptual space in which we can analyze the strategy dynamics, which represent the tensions, pressures, forces, and processes at play. We do so rather than dwelling on problems of optimization (which have lost relevance in today's prevailing competitive contexts).

A firm's position in the matrix in Figure 5.7 forms the basis for analyzing the trajectory of its strategic behavior from a dynamic point of view. Such analysis focuses on the solidity of this trajectory and examines potential pathological aspects or traps that lie along it, gleaning indications on which retroactive loop must be stepped up, slowed down, or redirected. In addition, this chapter facilitates the metaphoric use of certain concepts which management scholars have borrowed from the research on complexity theory. For example, consider the pathological state of equilibrium represented by the upper-left-hand corner of the matrix in Figure 5.7. We can posit that the more emphasis that firms place on strategy realization processes, to the detriment of learning or entrepreneurial processes, the more a top-down governance approach is adopted, and the greater the risk of entropy (that is, a state of equilibrium lacking utilizable energy)[10] (Vicari, 1991, pp. 95–6). From this perspective, the challenge of guiding the organization toward the threshold of chaos becomes the only route for importing energy into the organization, thereby fueling organizational learning[11] and entrepreneurial processes. As a result, the organization can avoid the entropic decline typical of closed systems (Vicari, 1991, pp. 98–9).

Notes

1. As noted by Mintzberg et al. (1998, pp. 180–2), Quinn can be considered an exponent of the Learning School owing to his emphasis on the incremental component of strategy. However, these authors point out an ambiguity which would place Quinn halfway between the Learning School and the Design School. In some of his work Quinn describes strategy-making as a process in which the CEO has a clear idea of corporate strategy a priori. Incrementalism is the fruit of the implementation effort that must pass through the gradual creation of the political conditions necessary for the strategy to be accepted. Consequently, incrementalism is not so much the outcome of a learning process within the strategy-making process as the effect of the complex governance of the political coalitions present in the firm.

2. Clearly, this second feedback loop, which describes the mechanism of generating and adapting strategic intentions, was not taken into account by Mintzberg. Nonetheless, Mintzberg did consider loop 1 (albeit implicitly) when he explained that emerging strategy takes the form of learning that is triggered by an attempt to realize strategy. Imagine, then, that while strategy is progressively implemented, it produces observable results that become the starting point for in-the-field learning.

3. In referring to this type of emerging strategic initiative, Burgelman (1991) uses the concept of "induced strategic initiatives."

4. In referring to this type of emerging strategic initiative, Burgelman (1991) uses the term "autonomous strategic initiatives."

5. In this chapter, we use a symbolic language based on the distinction between flow variables and level variables to represent economic processes. This view is rooted in two cultural perspectives which provide the background and essential frame of reference for this chapter. The first perspective is the rationale for process representation which hinges on differentiating between flow variables and level variables, the central focus of the system dynamics approach (Forrester, 1961, 1968a, 1968b, 1969, 1971, 1973, 1992). This discipline has a vast repertoire of concepts and operational tools for modeling, simulating, and analyzing the structure/behavior relationship in dynamic systems. The second perspective consists of representing the dynamism of economic processes on the basis of the flow/level dichotomy, which lies at the heart of the Italian economics and management tradition, beginning with Zappa. Zappa asserted that movement is usually represented as a "succession of states" in which we see the accumulation of prior variations (1957, pp. 930–931). However, he suggested that to understand production phenomena fully, it is not enough simply to place a succession of states in a series. Timing and duration must also be defined to describe processes "in a unit of time." Dynamic phenomena can be illustrated by focusing on the distinction between the succession of states (which vary as they accumulate) and processes (defined in a unit of time). This is analogous to a representation based on level variables (which represent the state of a system at a given moment of time, following successive accumulations) and flow variables (which describe the rate of variation of level variables over a given period).

6. The main body of empirical research consists of clinical studies on IBM conducted between 1993 and 2000 using a grounded approach (Glaser and Strauss, 1967). For this study we used open interviews (approximately 20 interviews with managers who held executive positions during this period), analyzed balance sheets, examined procedures and internal documents (memos, emails, manuals), and gathered information published in newspapers, specialist journals, and previous studies. Our analysis of the IBM case served as the starting point for developing subsequent clinical research on case studies, which is currently being conducted with the aim of corroborating the constructs and the relationships between these constructs. In addition, to make our description of the grounded model

more vivid, where plausible we have referred to empirical cases such as that of General Electric, basing our study of this company primarily on secondary sources.

7. From a survey of the literature, we identified a series of broad conceptual categories (for example, the "intended profile of corporate strategy" is linked to Mintzberg's "intended strategy" and to Prahalad and Hamel's "strategic intent," though with subtle differences). These categories were then compared with the constructs and relationships between constructs which emerged in our empirical study.

8. To ensure the effectiveness of the control loop, and to keep it running properly, management can use traditional tools for strategic control or diagnostic control systems (Simons, 1995).

9. As Lucio Stanca recalls, "Gestner told us: 'Don't do any more strategizing. I'll handle strategy with brand managers. You execute.' Before, all of us used to handle strategy. We had gangs of strategists! At IBM Italia alone we had 300–400 strategists. Today we don't do any planning at all!"

10. Through the lens of complexity theory, the notion of equilibrium is tinged with negative connotations, because it is thermodynamic. This equilibrium, in other words, is the static state reached in a closed system when entropy peaks and the ability to generate energy drops to a minimum (Prigogine and Stengers, 1993, pp. 124–130). Thermodynamic equilibrium leads to an inert system, one which inevitably deteriorates (Monod, 1970, p. 187).

11. The literature on organizational learning is useful in understanding the problems relating to governing and designing related processes. Specifically, some papers have opened up particularly significant research areas regarding strategic/organizational change in organizations. For example, Nonaka (1988) addressed order and chaos in organizational learning processes. March (1991) dealt with the problem of striking a balance between exploiting existing knowledge and exploring new territories. Nonaka and Takeuchi (1995) examined the link between producing knowledge within an organization and generating innovation by the organization, and Spender (1996) laid the foundations for the dynamic theory of the firm based on knowledge.

References

Andrews, K. R. (1971). *The Concept of Corporate Strategy*. Homewood, IL: Irwin.

Ansoff, H. I. (1965). *Corporate Strategy*. New York: McGraw-Hill.

——. (1979). *Strategic Management*. London: Macmillan.

Ansoff, H. I. (1984). *Implanting Strategic Management*. Englewood Cliffs, NJ: Prentice-Hall International.

——. (1991). "Critique of Henry Mintzberg's 'The Design School: Reconsidering the Basic Premises of Strategic Management'," *Strategic Management Journal*, 12: 449–61.

Argyris, C. (1982). *Reasoning, Learning, and Action: Individual and Organizational*. San Francisco: Jossey-Bass.

—— and Schon, D. A. (1978). *Organizational Learning: A Theory of Action Perspective*. Reading, MA: Addison-Wesley.

Bartlett, C. A. and Ghoshal, S. (1995). "Rebuilding Behavioral Context: Turn Process Reengineering into People Rejuvenation," *Sloan Management Review*, 37: 23–36.

Bower, J. L. (1970). *Managing the Resource Allocation Process: A Study of Corporate Planning and Investment*. Boston, MA: Harvard University Press.

Burgelman, R. A. (1983a). "A Process Model of Internal Corporate Venturing in the Diversified Major Firms," *Administrative Science Quarterly*, 28: 223–44.

——. (1983b). "Corporate Entrepreneurship and Strategic Management: Insights from a Process Study," *Management Science*, 29: 1349–64.

——. (1983c). "A Model of Interaction of Strategic Behavior, Corporate Context, and the Concept of Strategy," *Academy of Management Review*, 8: 61–70.

——. (1991). "Intraorganizational Ecology of Strategy Making and Organizational Adaptation: Theory and Field Research," *Organization Science*, 2: 239–62.

——. (1994). "Fading Memories: A Process Theory of Strategic Business Exit in Dynamic Environments," *Administrative Science Quarterly*, 39: 24–56.

Coda, V. (1989). *L'orientamento strategico di fondo delle imprese* [Basic Strategic Orientation of Firms]. Turin: UTET.

Farjoun, M. (2002). "Towards an Organic Perspective on Strategy," *Strategic Management Journal*, 23: 561–94.

Forrester, J. W. (1961). *Industrial Dynamics*. Cambridge, MA: Productivity Press.

——. (1968a). *Principles of Systems*. Cambridge, MA: Productivity Press.

——. (1968b). "Market Growth as Influenced by Capital Investment," *Industrial Management Review*, 9: 83–105.

——. (1969). *Urban Dynamics*. Cambridge, MA: Productivity Press.

——. (1971). "Counterintuitive Behaviour of Social Systems," *Technology Review*, 73: 52–68.

——. (1973). *World Dynamics*. Cambridge, MA: Productivity Press.

——. (1992). "Policies, Decisions and Information Sources for Modeling," *European Journal of European Research*, 59: 42–63.

Glaser, B. G. and Strauss, A. L. (1967). *The Discovery of Grounded Theory: Strategies for Qualitative Research*. New York: Aldine de Gruyter.

Golinelli, G. (2000). *L'approccio sistemico al governo d'impresa. L'impresa come sistema vitale* [The Systemic Approach to Corporate Governance: The Firm as a Vital System]. Padua: Cedam.

Hamel, G. and Prahalad, C. K. (1989). "Strategic Intent," *Harvard Business Review*, 67: 63–76.

March, J. G. (1991). "Exploration and Exploitation in Organizational Learning," *Organization Science*, 2: 71–87.

Mintzberg, H. (1978). "Patterns in Strategy Formation," *Management Science*, 24: 934–48.

——. (1979). *The Structuring of Organizations*. Englewood Cliffs, NJ: Prentice-Hall.

——. (1990a). "The Design School: Reconsidering the Basic Premises of Strategic Management," *Strategic Management Journal*, 2: 171–95.

——. (1990b). "Strategy Formation: Ten Schools of Thought," in J. Fredrickson (ed.), *Perspectives on Strategic Management*. New York: Ballinger.

——. (1991). "Learning 1, Planning 0: Reply to Igor Ansoff," *Strategic Management Journal*, 12: 463–66.

——, Ahlstrand, B., and Lampel, J. (1998). *Strategy Safari*. London: Prentice-Hall Europe.

Monod, J. (1970). *Il caso e la necessità* [Chance and Necessity]. Milan: Mondatori.

Nelson, N. N. and Winter, S. G. (1982). *An Evolutionary Theory of Economic Change*. Cambridge, MA: Belknap Press of Harvard University Press.

Noda, J. and Bower, J. L. (1996). "Strategy Making as Iterated Processes of Resource Allocation," *Strategic Management Journal*, 17: 159–92.

Nonaka, I. (1988). "Creating Organizational Order out of Chaos: Self-Renewal in Japanese Firms," *California Management Review*, 30: 57–73.

—— and Takeuchi, H. (1995). *The Knowledge-Creating Company: How Japanese Companies Create the Dynamics of Innovation*. New York: Oxford University Press.

Normann, R. (1977). *Management for Growth*. New York: Wiley.

Pascale, T. R. (1982). Report presented to the Strategic Management Society, October.

——. (1999). "Surfing the Edge of Chaos," *Sloan Management Review*, 40: 47–72.

——, Millemann M., and Gioja, L. (2000). *Surfing the Edge of Chaos*. New York: Crown Business.

Prigogine, I. and Stengers, I. (1993). *La nuova alleanza. Metamorfosi della scienza* [The New Alliance: The Metamorphosis of Science]. Turin: Einaudi.

Quinn, J. B. (1980). *Strategic Change: Logical Incrementalism*. Englewood Cliffs, NJ: Prentice-Hall.

——. (1981). "Formulating Strategy One Step at a Time," *Journal of Business Strategy*, 1: 42–63.

Simons, R. (1995). *Levers of Control*. Boston, MA: Harvard Business School Press.

Spender, J. C. (1996). "Making Knowledge the Basis of a Dynamic Theory of the Firm," *Strategic Management Journal*, 17: 45–62.

Vicari, S. (1991). *L'impresa vivente* [The Living Firm]. Milan: Etas Libri.

Zappa, G. (1957). *Le produzioni* [Production Activities], vol. II. Turin: UTET.

6
Strategy and Communication: The Missing Link

1. Communication and image in business activities

1.1. Defining the problem

A firm communicates simply because it exists – it produces and markets certain products or services and interacts with its myriad audiences. In communicating, it sends and receives information internally and externally. In addition to communications implicit in the firm's culture and daily behavior, there are also explicit communication activities, specifically targeting broad or select publics.

The problem lies in understanding what it means to handle communication activities, in discovering the different options for doing so, and in discriminating between what serves to achieve enduring success and what does not.

In this chapter, we first shed light on the complex role that communication plays (or could play) in business operations. Then, we detail different profiles of this role, according to whether the basic approach to communication problems and activities is oriented toward the short or the long term. Next, we discuss the links that should be established between business strategy and communication. In doing so, we lay the foundations for a classification of the more common anomalies in communication management when somewhere in the corporate system these connections are severed.

How can firms make business strategy the focal point of integrated, incisive management of communications activities? What enables firms to make communication both an activity that is firmly entrenched in business strategy and a powerful lever for implementing this strategy? These are the questions we will attempt to answer in the conclusion to this chapter.

1.2. A model of a well-run business

To clarify the role of communication, we need to think of a well-run business as a dynamic system (Figure 6.1). In such an organization, the nucleus comprises a complex set of tangible and intangible resources organized (1) to produce and sell two kinds of offerings:

- *offerings of goods or services* (2) ultimately earmarked for satisfying *customer needs* (3) to achieve *competitive success* (4)
- *offerings of collaboration with the firm* (5), designed to satisfy the *expectations for mobilizing and enhancing resources* (6) which are or should be provided by the people who control those resources (or claim to do so). The aim is to win legitimacy, trust, credibility, and consensus (7) from various corporate stakeholders (other than customers). In doing so, the firm secures the availability of the resources needed to run the business through a variety of mechanisms (pertaining to authority, contracts or markets, hierarchy, or clan)

The firm's ability to generate sustainable profits (8) is based on competitive success and the consensus of different stakeholders (other than customers). Profits, competitive success, and consensus are key ingredients for fueling, rebuilding, and growing the technological, commercial, financial, organizational, human, and social assets of the firm.

1.3. Role of communication

It is management's responsibility to activate, connect, and maintain the virtuous circles in this model over time. Within this context, communication of all kinds plays a key role (internal and external, commercial and institutional)

- in producing intangibles which enhance the attractiveness of the offering of goods or services to customers or the offering of collaboration to a given stakeholder
- in selling these offerings to interested stakeholders
- in crafting and disseminating a powerful, attractive image (for the company and/or the product). As this image paves the way for

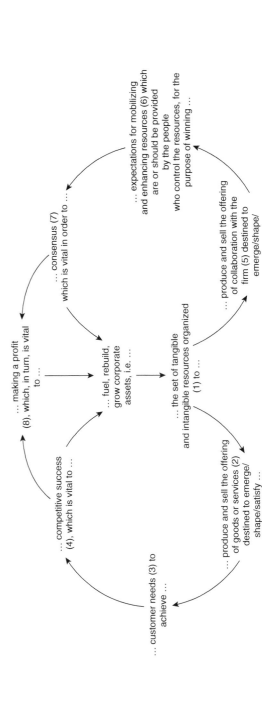

Figure 6.1 The dynamic system of a well-run firm

commercial and social consensus outside the firm, it fuels a positive pressure to work for the functionality and development of the firm

For example, we can observe the productive role of intangible factors of the two offerings (goods/services or collaboration) when communication leverages desires – the need for adventure, elegance, feeling fit, status, and so on – and the offering is perceived as something that can satisfy this need.

Communication in selling ultimately takes the form of direct sales of different kinds, by mail order or through advertisements in newspapers, magazines, and so on. Here selling is purely commercial communication. In other cases, the role of communication can be more accurately described as sales promotion.

When we consider the role of communication in production, we see how it takes on central importance right from the initial phase of designing the offering to present to the market or stakeholders. The sales or promotional role, in contrast, centers on communication as a problem and a process of transferring ideas intended to shape the behavior of the target audience.

1.4. Communication as an investment in corporate image

The role of communication is not linked only to producing and selling a given offering. Communication activity also takes the form of investing in building and disseminating a powerful, attractive image in various ways (Figure 6.2). First, communication can be specifically intended to serve this purpose; second, the messages systematically conveyed and the consensus generated by communication accumulate over time. The corporate image that results may be powerful, persistent, and attractive, depending on a number of factors: the age of the firm (or the product brand or product line in question), the consistency of behaviors and the continuous satisfaction of the targeted publics, the size of these publics, and the intensity of emotion elicited by specific communication events. Examples are potent experiences such as reorganizations. Or, on a completely different level, consider the after-effect on the brand of Alfa Romeo's victories in countless car races from the turn of the century until the early 1950s.

A powerful, attractive image is an intangible asset pivotal to the links which drive corporate development (as illustrated in Figure 6.2).

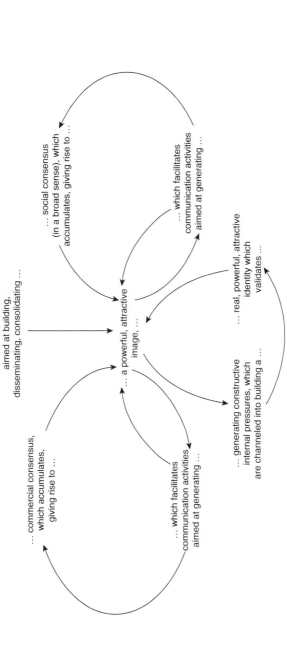

Figure 6.2 Centrality of corporate image in the development process of a firm

But this is true only if management views image as a powerful but delicate instrument for constantly generating new consensus, to be used with forethought, as a constant aim of the firm's investment policy, and as a focal point in an integrated communication system.

2. Basic orientation in the approach to communication problems

2.1. The value of the functionality and long-term development of the firm

In the model of business operations presented above (Figure 6.1), communication plays a key role centering on building and enhancing image (Figure 6.2). This is not spontaneous; rather, it is the expression of an underlying, long-term strategic orientation that takes the functionality and enduring development of the firm as the primary value and subordinates every other value to it.

Functionality becomes apparent in the ability of the firm to perform the interdependent functions of its complex social role in a unified, integrated way. It does so by producing and selling goods and services intended to satisfy human needs, mobilizing and enhancing the resources needed to do business, producing wealth (that is, goods or services with a value consistently higher than the value of the production inputs used), and accumulating the tangible and intangible assets needed to perform these functions and consequently to run and grow the business in the long term.

This last point should be taken above all in a qualitative sense: as the continual improvement of the firm in respect of all of the facets of its complex purpose. Growth in terms of size is advantageous insofar as it bolsters the long-term functionality of the firm, but such growth is driven by qualitative growth. Furthermore, development should be understood as progressive growth in which economic goals (relating to production, competition, profitability, and resource accumulation) are not pursued to the detriment of human and social goals, or vice versa. Economic demands and humanistic concerns are seen as reciprocally functional in a broad, far-sighted vision of the future of the firm and society. The two sets of needs come together synergistically to form a single whole.

The functionality and long-term development of the firm are closely linked concepts: the first cannot be protected in an intensely competitive environment without continual development, which becomes an ideal if it is not constantly oriented toward ensuring the functionality of the firm.

2.2. Communication management from a long-term perspective

With regard to communication problems, a basic strategic orientation like the one described above is transformed into integrated management of myriad communication activities which are mutually coherent over time and which aspire to build and enhance a powerful and attractive corporate image.

The following example clearly shows how essential image is when communication is managed with a long-term orientation. The firm in question treats image as its most precious possession, entrusting it to a special committee. Moreover, this company seeks to protect its image from the harmful effects of a certain degree of deterioration that has affected the "Made in Italy" brand, and it makes sizeable image investments (which differ from advertising investments in the strict sense).

Since opening for business, Flos (a well-known lighting technology firm) has focused on the creation and defense of its image assets. From an organizational standpoint, this special attention to image led the firm to set up an Image Committee. According to Sergio Gandini, head of Flos between 1964 and 1999, "For designers, this committee guaranteed continuity in managerial behavior with respect to initial basic values and allowed managers to shield themselves both from the risk of excessive focus on the product and from policies which were far removed from the basic business approach."

A long-term perspective was also evident in the firm's attitude toward the growing popularity of Made in Italy. In Gandini's words:

We've never interpreted design as a vehicle for advertising an object. In this sense, we believe we are one of a kind with respect to what you call Made in Italy. We're disappointed when Made in Italy is used to camouflage streams of exports with no quality content. In the hopes of boosting exports, the tendency is to assimilate everything under one name, which actually refers to product origin. Made in Italy does not simply say a given product comes from Italy; instead, it reads as a mark of prestigious authentication. So I'd say that there's nothing worse than attributing this label to items which actually have other characteristics.

Flos invests little in advertising in the strict sense, but it allocates around 6 per cent of turnover to promoting corporate image. Publishing catalogs, sponsoring cultural activities, organizing events, and refurbishing showrooms are the main cost items for communication. Later Flos established Flos Consulting, a sister company set up to design the communication strategy for the entire group.

A long-term orientation toward handling communication is also apparent in the impetus to establish a profound, enduring relationship with customers, taking care to satisfy their true interests and avoid betraying their trust.

ARCA, an asset management company, was founded in 1985. At that time, financial institutions were experiencing strong growth in Italy. Disregarding the possibility of gaining a larger share of subscribers through an aggressive communication policy, ARCA opted instead to invest in a campaign focusing more on information than on sales. In addition, the firm decided to compile and publish a quarterly bulletin and send it to all participants in the funds offered by ARCA, "which strives to build a relationship with its investors and the financial markets based on information and knowledge."

At ARCA, this bulletin was credited with cutting the costs of communication with subscribers, institutionalizing customer relations, and remaining faithful to a line of communication based more on objective information than on the power of suggestion. In 1986, ARCA designed a new ad campaign with an accent on education rather than information. This campaign aimed to help savers understand the different savings instruments available on the market and how they worked.

Communication, insofar as it consists of conveying ideas not information, promises something (for example, a higher-quality product, a fulfilling job). In addition, through communication, a company commits to keeping a promise, even far into the future.

When Mulino Bianco was launched, the Barilla team realized that the company's image, albeit an excellent one, could not cover a product that was so different from pasta. So they did not direct their efforts at launching a new brand with an intensive advertising campaign. Instead, they opted to hone technological, production, and distribution competencies to produce a valid offer system that could keep the promise made in the explicit communication.

Today, Mulino Bianco has a solid reputation among its consumers, who consider it an attractive brand. The company remains cautious in deciding whether new products created in its research and marketing facilities can be sold and supported by the Mulino Bianco brand without any risk of brand inconsistency or deterioration.

From the beginning, management was intent on maintaining consistency far into the future: "When we launched [Mulino Bianco] we said that creating a brand was like signing a blank cashier's check that would be paid out over time: with the product, the packaging, the commitment, which had to be consistent with the promises we made to consumers." This long-term orientation in managing communications also emerges in the efforts made from the outset to encourage employees involved in the initiative to identify with the product: "We told the Barilla employees who handled production of baked goods: 'You're Mulino Bianco employees.'"

2.3. Communication from a short-term perspective

Clearly, communication also has to contend with immediate and contingent needs to promote sales and generate consensus. Here, the problem is not neglecting or underestimating these needs but facing them without jeopardizing the corporate image, and continually shoring it up instead.

In many firms, communication is managed in a fragmentary and episodic way, in light of contingent objectives that do not center on a unifying goal which expresses the firm's need for functionality and sustainable development. In other words, communication problems are handled with a near-sighted, short-term orientation, in an opportunistic search for short-lived advantages. As a result, any heritage of credibility accumulated in the past is destroyed, and a blurry, confusing image emerges.

We can clearly see that a short-term orientation is the negation of true strategy, which should instead define the firm's model for interaction with the environment from a long-term perspective. This must be founded on perceived structural changes in the environment, which are irreversible in the short term.

What is lacking in these cases is a business strategy which links all communication activities. But before we examine situations in which this link is missing, we first need a clearer picture of what such a connection should look like.

3. The link between strategy and communication

3.1. The concept of corporate image

The starting point of our analysis is the concept of image. What we mean by image is the perceived identity of the firm – in other words, how the firm represents itself to its publics.

Image is a typical level (or stock) variable that is fed by certain information flows and the personal experiences associated with them. This variable influences the attitudes and behaviors of relevant publics (Figure 6.3). Specifically:

(1) When no communication activity specifically focuses on shaping image, image can be seen as the result of an accumulation of messages conveyed to various publics through the culture and daily operations of the firm. Image is also influenced by the emotions these messages elicit and by evaluations and associations relevant to these messages. Image, in other words, is the product of the more or less positive experiences that different publics have during their relationships with the firm. These experiences transpire at an emotional or rational level, and they gradually accrue in the collective memory.

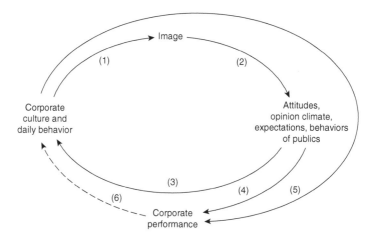

Figure 6.3   Origin and effects of corporate image when no communication activity is conducted with the specific aim of shaping this image

(2) Image, in turn, affects the attitude toward the firm of customers, personnel, shareholders, and other publics in terms of their opinion climate, their expectations, and their behaviors.

(3) All of these variables influence, and often reinforce, the culture and daily behavior of the firm.

(4) and (5), together with these last two factors, determine the competitive, profit, and social aspects of corporate performance.

(6) This performance, in turn, has a return effect on culture and day-to-day managerial behavior, inasmuch as management perceives, interprets, and evaluates performance (an expression of the firm's self-awareness) and reflects on the aims that constitute the *raison d'être* of the firm and its business.

To sum up, then, simply by virtue of its existence, a firm not only communicates (as we said in the beginning) but projects an image, both inwardly and outwardly. This image (be it positive or negative, strong or weak) influences the attitudes and behaviors of various publics and ripples throughout managerial performance and behavior.

3.2. Strategy and communication: how the two should connect

At this point, we slot corporate strategy and explicit communication into the model in Figure 6.3 to grasp the connection between them (Figure 6.4).

(1) Strategy can be regarded, above all, as a vision of the medium- and long-term future of the firm, which matures following some degree of dissatisfaction with corporate performance, and

(2) the firm's essential nature and modus operandi, which are the expression of its true identity (or strategic profile),

(3) and following a recognition of structural changes in the environment (for example, in the lifestyles, tastes, and habits of consumers and in the competitive situation and competitive behaviors).

(4) and (5) The new strategic vision, together with the perceived environmental changes, alters the concept of the "sought-after image,"

(6) and (7) which shifts from the actual image and, with it, forms the basis of corporate communication strategy,

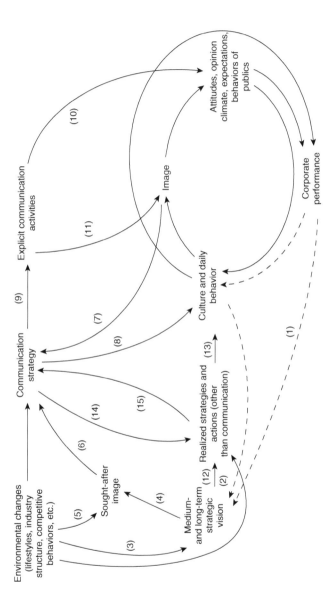

Figure 6.4 Link between corporate strategy and communication

(8) and (9) a strategy aimed at coordinating and integrating all communication activities in a single plan, both implicit in the culture and in daily behavior and explicit,

(10) and (11) with the purpose of modifying the public's attitudes toward the firm and their representation of it.

(12) and (13) The aim of the communication strategy and actions arising from it is to enhance corporate image and the attitudes toward the firm of various publics. This serves little purpose (and even puts the credibility of the firm at risk) unless such a strategy is preceded, accompanied, and followed by continual improvements in the true identity that is expressed in corporate culture and daily behavior. Here lies the need for strategies and actions to realize the medium- and long-term strategic vision in order to inform corporate identity and actual behavior. The aim is to bring these elements into line with the new image that the organization is attempting to project of itself, both internally and externally by means of explicit communication initiatives.

(14) and (15) This primarily involves strategies and actions with the scope of modifying institutional, organizational, and technical structures. The end result of all of this is the creation of the basic implementation conditions for the new strategic direction. Without these conditions, any attempt to re-qualify the firm's image is bound to fail.

4. Strategy and communication: profiles in corporate mediocrity and pathology

4.1. The nature of anomalies found in communication management

We can now detail some of the more common anomalies in communication management. These can be broken down into two categories: (1) a basic strategic orientation focused on the short term and the view that "appearing" should take precedence over "being" and (2) some fault in the management systems and professionalism of the people who handle (or should handle) communication.

In our explanation, we refer to the model in Figure 6.4. The reason is that the anomalies we identify can be illustrated by this model in terms of factors that stop it from functioning – and, more specifically, essential variables or links that are missing.

4.2. A clear strategic vision is lacking

The first type of anomaly consists of structuring and realizing communication plans without a clear idea of the identity of the firm (or its products) to promote inside and outside the firm.

This happens in companies that have a rather weak, ambiguous personality. They hand their communication over to an advertising agency or a public relations firm without establishing an effective, interactive relationship. As a result, the communication plan that emerges is more a reflection of the consultant's work than of the real convictions of management. What follows is that the culture and daily behavior do not match with the image that the communication campaign is trying to promote, and this serves only to augment ambiguity.

A typical example of this is the case of the tractor manufacturer Gruppo SAME Trattori in the early 1980s. This group was officially established in 1979, with the merger of SAME, Lamborghini, and Hurlimann as a single economic entity. The lack of a strong personality was due to a structure modeled on the basis more of fiscal considerations than of synergies and strategic opportunities. The structure of the group "was intended as an attempt to synergize resources and energies of the businesses," but the message did not prove to be a convincing one, because top managers themselves did not share this conviction.

The status of the individual brands was not particularly positive either. Although they were well known in key agricultural markets, the brand image was of a fairly reliable, economical product which was not very technologically advanced. Among all of the parameters, the strongest connotation was a low price. Beyond this, no differentiation was perceived among the various brands in the group.

An initial study was conducted in 1981, and subsequently a communication plan was drawn up with the intention of modifying the situation. This plan was unsuccessful because the relationship between the firm and the advertising agency was not properly established. The agency essentially took on the firm's marketing problems and went so far as to create the personality to attribute to the products in question.

A second survey, carried out in 1984, showed that the campaign had not increased brand awareness but instead had raised the level of confusion among the brands. Management learned from this experience that "we need to ask advertising agencies for a creative way to communicate what the firm has already decided."

4.3. Communication leads to deterioration or "consumption" of the image

Another anomalous situation occurs when brand awareness and prestige are used improperly (either intentionally, for purely tactical reasons, or because of an error in strategic assessment) to promote the sales of a product that is culturally incompatible with the sphere connoted by the brand.

In the early 1980s, Alfa Romeo launched ARNA using the slogan "ARNA, and you're an instant Alfa enthusiast." The new company exploited the heritage of Alfa technology and its sporty image to promote a car which was markedly inferior in terms of technology and performance. There was a strong sense of disorientation in the market as a result of the lack of congruency between explicit communication and the implicit communication of the product features. Inside the company, this episode spurred an exodus of the most competent technicians who were best able to hand down the technological patrimony of Alfa Romeo but who were extremely disillusioned by the ARNA experience.

Nikon has always been known as a camera manufacturer for sophisticated and professional users. In the late 1970s, the firm decided to expand its production line and introduce a mass-market single-lens reflex camera with numerous plastic parts for less sophisticated users. This market segment was growing rapidly, and several other Japanese camera producers had already achieved success. The decision to expand was not an easy one. One Nikon retailer summed up management's concerns succinctly:

> There was tremendous anxiety despite the certainty that the new camera would attract a new segment of young amateur photographers. What would the people think who had used the Nikon F for years, the best of its kind, when they saw the less sophisticated EM model? Maybe that the "mystical Nikon" so carefully cultivated over the years had lost its magical touch. (*Tokyo Keizai Weekly*, 7 July 1979)

This was exactly what happened, and the result was a deterioration of the general strategy. Despite some sales in the low-end segment of the market, Nikon was never able to achieve significant penetration there. In the professional market, Nikon's reputation declined, opening the market to newcomer mass producers.

These examples provide a clear picture of how management can be led to exploit image improperly, overlooking obvious heterogeneity or incompatibility between the brand and a new product. This is probably the result of a desire to cut costs and reduce the time needed for the launch. But image is a delicate resource. When it is consumed or eroded, the negative repercussions affect the relationship of trust and respect with the customer and the motivation of personnel who most identify with the product and the corporate culture.

4.4. The conditions to implement the promised changes are lacking

We see another inconsistent use of communication when, to re-qualify the corporate image, it conveys the message that the firm in question has changed, that it has turned over a new leaf and is moving down the path of better service for customers/users, but the necessary preliminaries are not in place in the organization to implement the desired changes.

The vision of what the firm should be and how it should operate may even be crystal clear. What is missing is the ability to realize this vision. As a result, a gap forms between basic values/objectives inherent in the strategic vision of the future of the firm, as depicted in institutional and commercial communication campaigns, and the values innate to the culture and daily behavior.

After becoming an autonomous entity in 1987, the Ferrovie dello Stato (Italian National Railroad) put together a series of communication campaigns, both internal and external. The message communicated internally ("We're changing, people") immediately served as a driver toward change and an impetus to mobilize energy.

The external communication campaigns promised new functionality and presented an image of future effectiveness and efficiency in supplying rail services. These campaigns centered on attractive and evocative slogans.

Unfortunately, the internal organization and service provision conditions did not improve as promised, and very soon the gap between actual behavior and results, on one hand, and the messages, on the other, gave way to new mistrust and demotivation.

4.5. A communication policy is lacking

Some firms adopt a valid general strategy and express and communicate it internally (through corporate culture and daily behavior) and externally (by means of various explicit communication initiatives). What is lacking, however, is a true communication policy which can effectively coordinate different communication activities, rationalize advertising expenses, and optimize the diffusive and propulsive effects on corporate image.

Although this situation may not be particularly serious in a firm contending with low-level competitive pressures, its effects are felt much more strongly as the organization and the field of action expand and these pressures intensify. The reason is that in such conditions, it becomes more difficult to preserve internal cohesion, to defend current market positions and gain new ones, and to make a reasonable profit. An effective communication policy can be vital to achieving these ends.

One of the leading credit institutions in Italy boasts the highest profit performance and a long tradition of professionalism, coherence, and innovation. All of this has allowed the organization to develop a cohesive internal culture and to sink deep roots in the economic and social fabric of its home region.

This firm's successful strategy reveals a strong personality, expressed through its essential nature and mode of operations in serving its customers, in particular small and medium-sized borrowers. Until today, this institution has not felt the need to create an integrated communication policy to coordinate internal and external, implicit and explicit communication activities addressing its different – and in some cases enormous – publics. Moreover, the communication philosophy of the firm follows the lines of concreteness, sobriety, reserve, and a disinclination to communicate its strategy except in the fragmentary ways associated with corporate operations. Until now, it seems, this approach has worked. However, we can easily foresee that with intensified competitive pressure and the progressive execution of the development strategy in its present fields of business and in new areas, the need for integrated communication management will become more pressing. Management should strive for tighter control of the image projected externally and for greater identification of personnel with the firm and its growth objectives internally.

4.6. Dissonance among types of communication

The lack of a unitary, integrated communication policy may result in more or less serious dissonance among the different types of communication.

Unlike the credit institution described above, the firms that are exposed to this risk do not have a strong, pervasive culture incorporating a well-defined communication philosophy, one which is valid for the entire organization and all of its communication activities. In these firms, the responsibility for corporate communications is usually assigned to various business units. For example, one such unit might be positioned directly under the president or top management and handle the development and management of corporate communications. Another might be part of the Marketing Department and deal with the design and realization of commercial communications. A third might be located in the Human Resources Department and take on internal communications. In groups, commercial communication might be positioned in firms which operate in single business areas, and internal communication in the holding or management companies.

These differences in role and organizational positioning are not necessarily negative. However, they do require coordination of messages and behaviors among the various business units. This must be handled effectively, with appropriate integration mechanisms, such as a cohesive culture, or direct involvement of top management in communication problems. Otherwise dissonant communication results, which may translate into anything from a slight divergence in the message to open contradictions.

At this point, firms in the credit and public service sectors come to mind. In recent years, such organizations have undertaken commercial campaigns which have not resonated with the organizational climate or the feelings of employees or even with messages addressed to them. We might also think of manufacturing firms that emphasize quality and service in their advertising campaigns, without any internal push in this direction. On the contrary, the message conveyed internally might motivate personnel to cut costs and improve efficiency. Instead of fostering quality, this would damage it, and it would be detrimental to service as well.

4.7. A communication policy is lacking or is not implemented

Some firms have a communication policy in addition to a valid business strategy. This may, however, be inadequate in terms of what it entails or how it is implemented.

Some years ago, a large Italian textile group decided to make a size-able investment in communication, with the stated aim of reinforcing the corporate image and thereby gaining greater authority on an institutional level, superior bargaining power with certain key suppliers, and enhanced capacity for market penetration. The long-term strategies were correctly ascertained by management, and communication policy was defined in light of these strategies and after meticulous analysis of the current situation in terms of image with various publics. Externally, the communication process was optimal. Internally, however, management primarily channeled the message down the hierarchical line and underestimated the obstacles and filters that it would encounter. Consequently, the new corporate identity is still far from being assimilated, and the image conveyed through the culture and daily behavior contrasts sharply with the message that was explicitly communicated.

5. Strategy and communication: profiles of excellence

5.1. Summary

After this review of cases of mediocrity or even pathology in communications, we move on to profiles of excellence. In brief, these can be categorized as follows: (1) the strategy is essentially an enterprise development idea which integrates the need for competitiveness and profitability with ethical/social demands (improving personnel, safeguarding the environment, etc.) to form a synergetic whole; (2) the fundamental object of both internal and external communication is the firm's strategy, with its intrinsic unifying force and the power to drive aggregation around the development idea, which constitutes the center of gravity; (3) explicit communication activity hinges on a carefully planned communication strategy which defines priorities and sequences of objectives, messages, publics, and initiatives.

5.2. The strategy of excellent firms

As discussed in Section 2, the strategy of an excellent firm is a business development idea focused on satisfying economic and humanistic needs simultaneously and reciprocally (Figure 6.5). Ultimately, this is a vision of the future of the firm with the power to mobilize resources and energy to satisfy these needs.

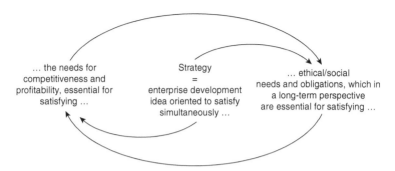

Figure 6.5   Concept of strategy within the framework of an entrepreneurial excellence design

This vision takes the form of

- a challenging goal which can be attained with the steadfast commitment and determination of everyone involved,
- focused on the medium to long term, but with operational implications for the immediate future,
- with an unwavering orientation toward improving customer service, and
- aligned with evolutionary trends in the environment,
- to enhance the technological, commercial, and managerial heritage of the firm over time and
- to open a fruitful path toward learning and development which represents the direction in which to drive the process of accumulating tangible and intangible resources.

A strategic vision with these characteristics not only points the firm in the right direction. It can also be likened to a rich reserve of energy the firm exploits to generate drivers for corporate development. This store can be tapped whenever the firm wishes, simply by communicating the strategic vision in the proper ways (explicitly and implicitly, internally and externally) to the publics which are vital for the firm's development process to advance. Communication, in other words, is what enables a firm to transform the potential energy in a credible strategic vision into a driving force for corporate development.

This analogy with a system for producing and transforming energy is a fitting one. However, it can be misleading unless we remember corporate image, which is both an input and an output of the transformation process in question (see Figure 6.4).

5.3. The communication strategy

The communication strategy should unify and integrate customer and employee needs, the demand for profitability and environmental protection, and so on. Such a strategy translates into events and messages which combine and converge, capturing the public's attention and building consensus around the firm's strategic plan. These events and messages constitute a "hub" around which integrated communication management revolves. In other words, managing communication in an integrated way means that the messages conveyed through events and behaviors are completely consonant with explicit communication. Moreover, campaigns and institutional communication tools reiterate or echo the same messages in communication initiatives specifically targeting one public or another. The exclusive or primary target audience is chosen on a case-by-case basis, according to an order of priority established in a comprehensive communication strategy.

The specific scope of this strategy is to delineate explicit communication initiatives and to coordinate them with other managerial activities aimed at developing the firm. For the most part, every communication initiative is the combination of four elements: the messages to convey, the publics to address, the means or channels to use to reach target publics, and the timing for carrying out a given initiative.

These components must be mutually coherent; when defining them management must not neglect timing objectives, which stem from a plan of action. This plan lists the steps to take in the immediate future and in the short/medium term to move in the desired direction.

Communication strategy is normally built on a number of objectives: *awareness* – modifying the attitudes of certain publics, more or less rapidly (for example, public opinion, institutional investors, unions, environmentalists); *mobilization* – engaging publics such as personnel, the sales network, and major suppliers; *commercial* – undertaking initiatives that target customers or end buyers in some way; *disseminating reputation* – carrying out initiatives to increase recognition of the company or brand in new markets or in areas or countries where the firm is not yet present or is not well known, and so on.

It is extremely important to prioritize these objectives and the various audiences which should be targeted by specific initiatives. The order of priority depends on a number of factors, including how the strategic vision is configured, how far the firm has progressed in realizing this vision, where the forces lie which can hinder or facilitate corporate development, how management diagnoses these forces and their intensity, what financial resources are available, and how quickly management wants to push for corporate development. In any case, analyzing the dynamic cause–effect relationships that bring about the evolution of the corporate system helps simplify the choice of the most appropriate sequence.

5.4. The COM.I.ECO. case

It is useful to look at a concrete case to illustrate the ideas above.

COM.I.ECO. (Committee for Ecological Packaging) is a free association of Italian paper packaging manufacturers founded in 1985. COM.I.ECO.'s mission was to react to declining business in the sector, which continued to lose market share to alternative materials to paper and cardboard in packaging.

The strategy developed by COM.I.ECO. hinged on highlighting the ecological importance of paper and cardboard as packaging, touting them as "biodegradable, recyclable products made from renewable natural resources."

This sector development idea did not jeopardize the country's woodlands in any way, as most of the cellulose used to produce paper came from woods owned by paper companies. For obvious reasons relating to continuity of provisioning, these firms systematically reforested areas where they harvested lumber. However, in pushing for sector growth, paper companies had to contend with a severe shortage of raw materials, a hard-felt problem in Italy owing to the scarcity of wooded areas. As a result, companies could pursue this vision competitively only if they managed to provision the raw materials they needed under advantageous conditions. Furthermore, this need could be satisfied only by promoting paper recycling. Although this was certainly no easy task, recycling was perfectly in line with the necessity of safeguarding the environment in relation to waste disposal: more than 50 percent of solid waste is packaging, which ends up in landfills. So a strategy emerged for firms in the sector which could combine the need to revitalize with the necessity for environmental protection (Figure 6.6).

As a result of its ability to unite these different needs, the COM.I.ECO. strategy had a high level of potential energy that could be converted into a growth driver for the sector. All the committee needed to do was communicate this strategy incisively, building and disseminating the image of paper packaging as an ecological product (Figure 6.7). COM.I.ECO. did so, beginning with raising the consciousness of the public, public administration, environmentalist groups, and so on as regards the need and the civic duty to recycle paper. In doing so, the committee paved the way for initiatives aimed at organizing waste paper collection that mobilized the school/family sector.

PRO-CARTON is an association founded in 1988 among cardboard manufacturers from 12 EU and EFTA countries. After COM.I.ECO.'s positive experience, this association initiated intense communication activity with a strong commercial accent, targeting industrial users of packaging as well as final consumers (to encourage them to opt for products with ecological packaging).

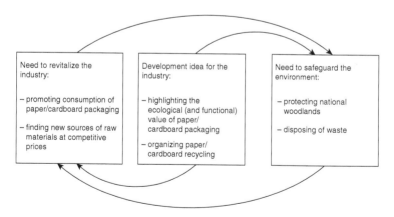

Figure 6.6 COM.I.ECO.: development strategy for the paper/cardboard packaging industry

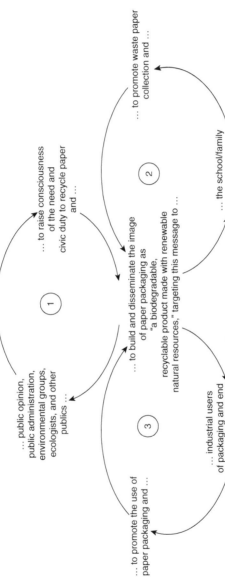

Figure 6.7 COM.I.ECO.: communication strategy

The case described above illustrates a phenomenon of higher-level entrepreneurial activity and a fruitful collaboration among producers in a sector united in the common goal of enhancing their technological heritage in the face of substitute technology and materials. The COM.I.ECO. case fully complies with the profiles of excellence outlined earlier. The only difference is that the development idea at the heart of the strategy encompasses an entire sector rather than a single firm.

It is not hard to find noteworthy examples among individual firms in the extensive literature and countless case studies on entrepreneurial excellence and reorganizations carried out to balance the books as quickly as possible and to invest in getting back on the track of corporate development.

5.5. The Japanese model of excellence

The typical concept of strategy in the top Japanese firms was forged in the difficult years following the Second World War (starting around the mid-1950s) and gradually perfected in later decades. This concept was rooted in the conviction that the prosperity of the firm and the well-being of its workers were one and the same, if only management could obtain whole-hearted collaboration from all workers (not just some) to promote the enduring prosperity of the firm and enable all employees to benefit in terms of improved working and living conditions. All of this would be in keeping with the nation's development needs.

The core of the strategy – what makes it possible to reconcile economic and social needs – is a business development idea, as depicted in Figure 6.8.

- This idea is based on a view of the firm as a community, which engenders in employees a deep-seated sense of membership because they share corporate objectives.
- These objectives ultimately emerge from a challenging plan for achieving new competitive goals in traditional sectors and in new ones.
- This is possible as a result of the contribution of everyone, because all are called on to live the basic values of productivity, quality, and creativity, including the "co-makers of the value chain": suppliers and distributors.

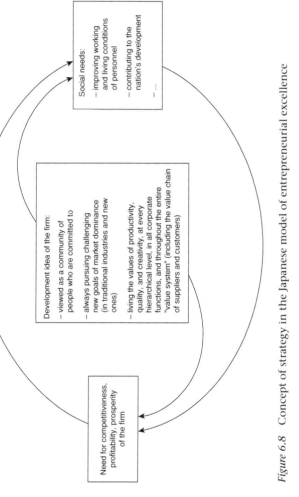

Figure 6.8 Concept of strategy in the Japanese model of entrepreneurial excellence

Here we cannot detail these values beyond the description above. However, we should point out that these cornerstones of the Japanese entrepreneurial ideology are conceived as

- elements of both economic progress and simultaneous human and social progress (accordingly, productivity has nothing to do with Taylorist logic or methods for organizing labor)
- values to live synergistically and not to reconcile with a tradeoff rationale (cost cutting is achieved by improving quality at all levels, not by sacrificing it)
- values that can and must be interpreted at every level of the corporate hierarchy, in all corporate functions, and even outside the firm, among suppliers and distributors who make up the externalized components of the corporate structure
- values which do not readily differentiate between who is more or less important for the success of the firm but instead form the foundations of a highly cohesive corporate culture

A company with a strategy like the one described here inevitably lives on communications that siphon their key messages from this strategy and fuel it at the same time (Figure 6.9). Core stakeholders

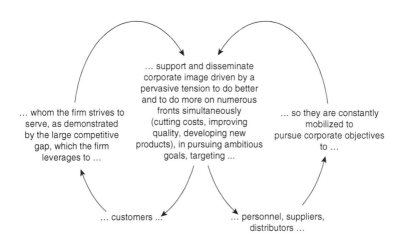

Figure 6.9 Priority objectives and targets in the communications strategy consistent with the Japanese model of excellence

are customers and all personnel, as well as suppliers and distributors who have an deep relationship with the company, as is the norm for the top Japanese companies.

Communication addressed to customers simply leverages the consistent competitive advantages of Japanese companies and the commitment always to do more and to do better in serving customers. Communication directed inside the firm and to co-makers focuses on corporate strategy and the challenging goals that make up this strategy, as well as concrete improvement and progress objectives that serve to achieve these goals.

Communication focused inside the firm and on co-makers calls for a great deal of effort, as we can see from the enormous energy expended to make different systems work: management by consensus; human resources management (recruiting, placement, on-the-job training, evaluation, and so on); union relations, based on frequent meetings at various levels between management and labor representatives (for consultation and decision-making); the system of intense collaboration with production and outsourced distribution; mechanisms for organizational learning (quality circles, suggestion systems, and so forth).

5.6. Strategy and communication in corporate turnarounds

In Italy, numerous turnarounds were carried out in the late 1970s and the early 1980s; this period was an important one for the recognition of the role that communication can play in strategic corporate management. Italian firms experienced the power of integrated communication strategies shaped by the principle of total transparency and directed toward building consensus around a strategy dictated exclusively by the necessity of ensuring the firm's survival. Indeed, the physiology of communication was based mainly on the existence of a valid strategy centered on the pursuit of the well-being of the firm and on the willingness to communicate this strategy (its premises, contents, and consequences) and openly discuss it (in detail, if need be).

No doubt corporate crises facilitated the formation of these two basic preconditions, but fortunately they can be recreated in situations other than when the survival of the firm is endangered. A management team molded by a turnaround comes out of the experience enriched in values and managerial professionalism, and eager to contribute this newfound wealth to other situations.

The turnaround strategy has to address two critical needs: the immediate economic need to balance the books in the short term and the ethical/social need to ensure the survival of the firm (which is a long-term economic need). This ensures that immediate sacrifices are not made in vain but are compensated by other benefits for the people who remain involved in the life of the firm, those who will be involved in the future, and the whole community.

It is not difficult to see how these two needs can be combined. Firms have to center their turnaround strategy on the binominal "efficiency plus development," adopting the guiding principle that the entire process should recover efficiency and free resources. This should be achieved by means of calculated (not indiscriminate) cuts in costs and products/branches showing a loss, with an eye to recovering production investments.

The whole turnaround strategy (and consequently its integral component – the communication strategy) is built around this guiding principle, which represents the central, unifying idea. This guiding principle is the source of key messages that should be communicated to re-establish trust (among customers, suppliers, the financial market, etc.) and to overcome understandable political or union opposition.

We can again turn to the Gruppo SAME Trattori case for an especially interesting example. In the early 1980s, the company was facing a serious crisis. The long-term strategic objective for re-launching the firm was that it should become the technological leader in the sector. This allowed SAME to "talk about re-birth, not only reorganization, and innate to [the strategic objective] was absolutely transparency." One measure included in the recovery plan was job cuts. These short-term sacrifices were essential not only to guarantee the survival of the firm in the immediate future but also to establish a foundation for later development. Management paid special attention to the communication policy from the outset. It was vital to communicate the change in strategy to the people in the company, to the distribution network, and to end users.

The relationship with the union was handled personally by the CEO, with the assistance of the head of personnel. At the same time, the new strategy was transmitted through the corporate hierarchy. When an agreement had been reached, a communication plan was activated that included internal meetings at various levels (where "we constantly hammered home the new corporate objectives"), a later collective meeting with the entire sales force at company head-quarters, then area meetings at which strategic issues and objectives were discussed and absorbed, and finally a large investment in communications targeting the end user.

5.7. Concluding comments

By studying corporate communication activities and determining whether they tie into the general strategy of the firm, we can clearly discern the management style of corporate leaders. This mode of management might

- be more or less rooted in a solid strategy and shaped by transparency and coherence
- use communication mainly for contingent objectives and/or primarily for strategic purposes
- consume image and other intangible resources accumulated in the past or, on the contrary, strive to enhance and enrich them
- be an expression of management more or less aware of its role and of the professional skills necessary to play this role effectively today

Furthermore, analyzing the strategy/communication relationship leads us straight to the heart of problems relating to change and shows us why some firms grow, even quite rapidly, and why others, despite all of their efforts, basically stand still. The former are organizations with a valid strategy that successfully unites economic/corporate needs with ethical/social requirements and obligations and that is apt to generate a constant impetus toward self-realization. This is true, at least, if the objectives and prerequisites of this strategy are properly communicated, along with the results it promises and the commitment it requires. The standstill firms include those which lack a solid strategy or the ability to realize it. These shortcomings are conveyed, as we have seen, in implicit and explicit communication activities disconnected in various ways from each other and from the corporate strategy.

Our conclusions are supported by some empirical evidence and are based on a theoretical foundation which, though solid, is open to additional analytical investigation. In any case, as these conclusions are only the initial results from a fecund field of research, they should be subject to further verification.

Note

Report presented at the conference on "Communication in Corporate Strategy: From the National Market to the Single Market" held at Bocconi University on 18 October 1989. The author wishes to thank Guido Corbetta, Alessandro Cortesi, and Pietro Mazzola from Bocconi's Institute of Management Theory for their help in preparing this report, which is based on empirical evidence and the results of research conducted using the clinical case study methodology.

Part III
Meeting the Challenges to the Entrepreneurial Economy

7
The Role of Ownership in Corporate Restructuring

1. Obstacles to restructuring

A corporate restructuring is a radical transformation. It involves either interrupting certain crisis mechanisms which progressively impoverish the firm, destroying financial resources and technical/industrial and commercial assets, or stabilizing the crisis by sustaining a constant level of losses. These mechanisms must be replaced with drivers that develop financial resources and allow the accumulation of experience and knowledge, which are critical to success in the competitive arena.

Accomplishing a corporate restructuring is extremely challenging because the process generally meets with strong resistance, usually from stakeholders who (rightly or wrongly) feel threatened by the prospect of restructuring and prefer the alternative: survival without economic sustainability.

First and foremost, restructuring is unpopular with the representatives of owners and management who risk losing their positions and who may also have reason to fear derivative suits by their successors. Second, opposition to restructuring comes from union leaders who cannot (or will not) conceive of securing workers' interests beyond the rigid logic of defending civil rights. Banks and credit institutions also resist restructuring processes when they refuse to provide their financial backing yet are willing to finance a chronic crisis. Finally, the conservative block forms a united front with political groups and forces that work toward a progressive politicization of economic life and that profit from controlling failing companies.

Naturally, these interests tend to materialize behind the smokescreen of unrealistic recovery plans. Opponents to the restructuring can also exploit social tensions generated by the crisis and conveniently channel them through anyone who shows little inclination to collaborate.

The more solid the coalition of interests that opposes change, the more essential a resolute, united front becomes to pursue the restructuring. The "welfarism party" must be countered by "corporate renewal party." Crisis management which hinges on shrewdly maneuvering different forces at play and manipulating political/ social pressures must be replaced with management based on clear and accurate information, in-depth analysis and constructive debate, and increased responsibility taken by stakeholders, according to the role each plays.

2. A precondition to restructuring processes: a responsible ownership structure

For the "renewal party" to succeed, someone with persistence and resolve has to take the lead on the restructuring strategy. Obviously, this "someone" can be none other than the people at the top of the corporate hierarchy, because institutional responsibility for strategic leadership of the firm rests here.

However, to assemble an executive team fit for duty which endures over time, a solid and responsible ownership structure is needed, one capable of correctly interpreting its role in terms of choosing top management and covering losses and recapitalizing the firm.

There have been cases of self-motivated managers of firms in crisis taking it upon themselves to reorganize their companies, despite counterproductive interference from the owners. To do so, however, management must break away from ownership, not only by relying on alternative sources of power but also by cutting financial ties. Clearly such circumstances are rare, especially in firms experiencing a crisis, which normally means negative cash flows.

Therefore, solid and responsible ownership is a prerequisite for restructuring. If this is lacking, what other center of gravity can pull together the primary resources needed to activate the process (both management and finances)? How can a firm attract competent managers? How can these managers be effectively held accountable for the goals of the restructuring? How can the firm win the confidence of third-party lenders?

Private ownership is not solid if, for example, it does not have the resources needed to recapitalize the firm once losses have been covered. By the same token, government ownership is not responsible if it is made up of individuals and groups who couple fund allocation with undue interference in management, creating a burden for the firm and taking away responsibility from management. Fund allocation should, instead, be contingent on management taking specific steps toward recovery. Another example: ownership is neither solid nor responsible if it consists of a consortium of banks lacking internal cohesion, reluctant to take on their ownership role, and anxious to hide or defer major losses on non-performing loans.

In these and similar circumstances, restructuring ownership is indispensable to reorganizing a firm. In private firms and groups, depending on the specific circumstances, this could mean turning out discredited owners and making way for new partners with the necessary resources and credit; writing off past losses from corporate accounts on previous owners, and in some cases lenders as well; converting severance funds into equity, and so forth. In the case of state-owned enterprises, the problem is different. Restructuring ownership involves counteracting the tendency to privatize the public sector. This can be done by effectively giving responsibility to members of the government ownership structure and ensuring that decision-making processes are handled properly, in particular as regards nominating the heads of state holding companies and funding these entities. Specifically on this last point, it is critical that financial problems are framed not in generic terms but with reference to the specific requirements of recovering losses and re-launching production in individual holding companies.

In any case, it is not the intention here to explore what it means to restructure ownership in concrete terms. The aim is to come to a better understanding of the role of ownership in reorganizing firms. A clearer notion of this role is extremely useful in understanding both the reasons so many crisis situations persist and the concrete need for restructuring ownership.

3. The ownership role: (a) providing the tension for recovery

From what was stated above regarding obstacles to corporate recovery it is clear that restructuring processes are not spontaneous;

instead, they are the result of determination and deliberate actions. This means that if management does not provide a stimulus to the recovery process, or does not judiciously channel this momentum, reorganizing the firm will be an arduous task.

The question is: Who can give such a stimulus? The obvious answer is lenders, provided they approve financing for restructuring objectives, monitor the use of resources to this end, and penalize failure to achieve these objectives.

Specifically, one determinant is the behavior of parties who confer funds in the form of equity. If these parties are always willing to cover losses and reconstitute capital under any circumstances, without ever questioning, if not the very survival of the firm, at least the continued existence of certain business units, a stimulus to recovery is highly unlikely. Nor can the stimulus be generated by parties who provide funds in the form of loan capital, because they will feel protected from the risk of default by the debtor. Not even the actions of managers with every good intention to pursue restructuring would create the needed stimulus, because they would not have the support of owners and would have to contend with the latter's willingness to bear any loss and to guarantee the survival of the firm whatever the cost.

Such behavior by ownership can be found in the sphere of state-owned enterprises. Among private companies different pathological situations may arise in which owners cannot or will not risk additional capital. Far from providing a stimulus to achieve recovery objectives, owners either take no action or exploit the potential of political/social pressure generated by the corporate firm to reap benefits that have nothing to do with the prospect for recovery.

Owners who, instead, give impetus to recovery objectives are defending their own capital in the firm. They show confidence in the possibility of recovery by risking their own savings. They carefully choose competent managers who feel responsible for the resources entrusted to them and who act accordingly.

This physiological model of behavior by owners should represent the paradigm in the sphere of private enterprise and should to some extent be applicable to government ownership as well. At any rate, this is true if we embrace the notion that any discussion of the social role of a state-owned enterprise is distorted and meaningless unless the minimum requirements are met for the efficient and effective management of the firm in question.

4. The ownership role: (b) governing managers in charge of restructuring

The stimulus to achieve recovery goals provided by a healthy ownership structure is highly motivational for corporate executives, whose dependence on owners is naturally accentuated in crisis situations. Via executive management, in turn, this impetus proliferates throughout the corporate hierarchy to the lower levels, motivating the whole organization to recover economically and recuperate competitively.

For this model to work, corporate executives must be chosen carefully; they must be given results-based compensation, and they must be monitored effectively by means of simple, timely controls.

This is where another critical role of owners comes into play, that of supervising managers who are charged with reorganizing the firm. This role is a complex and sensitive one, even in cases where there is not a clear and complete separation between ownership and management. When owners who do not run their company represent controlling capital, the problems they face in interacting with owner/managers are similar to the conflicts that arise when there is a total separation between the governing body and management. What is more, substantially similar difficulties emerge between owner/managers and non-owners/managers, where the former tend to delegate a great deal to the latter.

Whatever the case may be, to play their role well, owners' representatives must display a generous dose of professionalism by implementing and monitoring appropriate operational mechanisms, such as recruitment, selection, placement, assessment, and compensation of managers, as well as handling information on and supervision of their performance.

This need for professionalism is perhaps more acutely felt in firms that require restructuring, given that the supervision of managers under such circumstances is a particularly delicate task. Owners must be able to distinguish competent managers from those who have contributed to creating or consolidating the crisis. In addition, owners need to renew the management team to equip the firm with managers with adequate skills to deal with the complexity of the problems that restructuring entails. Finally, owners should minimize the possibility of making mistakes in choosing and evaluating managers, because crisis situations often tolerate little or no margin of error.

5. The ownership role: (c) recapitalizing the firm

A responsible ownership structure not only provides a stimulus to recovery and deals effectively with problems pertaining to corporate executives. Such ownership is also capable of thoroughly understanding and fulfilling the need to reconstitute equity capital.

The reconstituted equity capital required for a firm undergoing restructuring can be broken down as follows:

1. the total negative net worth accumulated by past management (uncovered operating losses less share capital and reserves, both disclosed and hidden)
2. losses to be incurred before reaching breakeven
3. the minimum amount of share capital required by law
4. the minimum amount of equity capital that third-party lenders (banks and suppliers) deem necessary for granting the firm the credit and confidence it needs

Negative net worth accumulated by past management measures the immediate need for unsecured loans, which in some cases may be covered in the terms of credit of third-party lenders. Future losses to be incurred before reaching breakeven also represent a need for unsecured loans, albeit diluted over time, which owners must take into account when undertaking restructuring.

The other three factors represent a need for financing in the form of equity, which may be gradually introduced over time. The minimum share capital required by law obviously does not satisfy this need, except in the case of very small firms. The minimum equity capital resources needed to get a loan depends on the assessment of third-party lenders, who take various factors into consideration, including the parameters normally used to quantify the level of indebtedness of the potential borrower, the perceived risk of the entrepreneurial restructuring initiative, and the guarantees offered.

This is one way to evaluate the need for risk capital. There is another line of reasoning that shrewd and mindful owners should follow when assessing this need. They must consider the complexity of the actions called for in the restructuring plan and the ability of management to carry out these actions. Clearly, if the recovery goals can be achieved by making relatively simple moves (price maneuvers, marginal product variations, etc.), no particular problems will arise. If, instead, complex processes must be activated (innovation, conflict resolution, etc.), owners must realistically evaluate whether current management is up to the task and, if not, the time it would take to upgrade these resources. If breakeven seems too distant a goal given the current skill level of available managers, this distance must be shortened, raising equity to an appropriate level. If this is not done, owners risk getting caught up in a spiral of losses and debts and chasing after a continually climbing breakeven point without ever reaching it.

Correctly identifying the exact resources needed to offset deficits and recapitalize the firm is the key to a successful restructuring. If this is not done, effectively making management responsible is impossible, and the relationships between ownership, management, and third-party lenders will be shaped by an underlying lack of clarity, allowing the spokespeople of groups holding power to adopt behavior which may not be conducive to achieving the objectives of the restructuring. Moreover, equity capital resources may be more theoretical than actual, and if they are inadequate the chances for recovery may be jeopardized from the outset. Unsecured loans may be used illegitimately for investments in risk capital, and capital increases may be justified by misleading considerations which give priority to the need for financial recovery and ignore the fact that economic recovery should logically come first (in the sense that economic recovery is a logical starting point in drawing up a comprehensive restructuring plan).

A solid and responsible ownership structure calls for a clear and detailed description of the requirements for re-establishing equity capital. But obviously this is not all. Such an ownership structure is also distinguished by the ability to (1) evaluate correctly the expected benefit/cost ratio of the restructuring from a private or public investor's perspective, as the case may be; (2) negotiate skillfully with representatives of the old leadership, with third-party lenders, and with public powers and unions to optimize the relationships with all of these parties; and (3) meet relative financial deadlines punctually after the investment decision has been made.

6. Concluding remarks

If we compare the role of ownership profiled above with what we know about common behavior in the business world, the divergence between the two is astounding. Here we are referring above all to facts and behaviors seen in large state-owned groups and private firms in crisis any time massive capital increases become inevitable because of urgent and escalating corporate losses. On the basis of the information available to an outside observer, at least, the impression emerges that the reality is the antithesis of the optimum situation. Rather than providing a stimulus for restructuring, on occasion ownership seems to strive solely for survival. Instances of choosing the wrong managers and punishing and demoting competent ones are too numerous to count. Capital increases are regularly surrounded by a fundamental lack of clarity regarding the real situation of individual organizations in crisis, the complex needs around re-establishing equity capital resources, and the prospects for recovery.

Beyond the usual comments, true as they may be, on the lack of honesty and professionalism which underlies this type of behavior, it is important to emphasize that in certain circumstances it is far easier and less risky to manage an extended crisis than to restructure. After all, the first means leaving things to follow their natural course, and the second calls for obstinate resistance. Only by starting from this basic assertion can we formulate provisions and initiatives that invigorate and encourage what we call the "corporate renewal party," empowering it to overcome the "crisis party."

The crisis situation among small and medium-sized private groups is different, provided they do not come to insolvency procedures or serious bailout initiatives. Here, too, the behavior of owners is not what one would hope in most cases. But the reason for this is the abnormal situation that emerges. The role of owner can no longer be taken on by the old corporate leadership, which has been discredited and lacks the necessary financial resources on one hand, and on the other is rejected by lenders.

These pathological phenomena only serve as proof that even fairly well-articulated legislation is not enough to counteract the forces of the crisis. A law intended to promote corporate recovery can do so only in conjunction with initiatives of a very different kind aimed at re-launching production. These initiatives, in turn, cannot be realized unless all entrepreneurial potential is tapped – potential which fortunately is in abundant supply in several countries. Until we eliminate the countless forms of repression of this potential and support its realization (in compliance with an established set of rules of economic play), we have no reason to expect that a law on corporate restructuring alone can solve the problem.

8
The Relationship between the Firm and Its Workforce: Prospects for Change

Today a change is needed in labor relations in the firm in terms of greater involvement and collaboration of the workforce as a whole. To some extent this change is already underway. However, its actualization calls for a transformation in the fundamental conception of the firm – why and how it exists and operates. This is, succinctly put, the purpose of this chapter, which first describes the model of labor relations that has predominated until today in Italy and the dynamics that have led to its destabilization. The chapter then focuses on the community view of the firm, and it concludes with a discussion of what can be done in Italy to drive the diffusion of this conception.

1. The antagonistic conception of the relationship between the firm and its workforce

The labor relations model applied in most Italian firms is based on the conviction that the relationship between the firm and its workforce is intrinsically conflict-ridden and that collective negotiations are the way to solve this conflict. The unadulterated version of this model draws a definite distinction between the roles of management and of the workforce, placing the two in direct opposition. The proper functioning of the firm pertains to management alone. Workers, for the most part, take no interest; they simply perform the duties set down in their contracts and, when these expire, demand proportionate improvements in work and pay conditions. Union disputes and negotiations have objectives that are largely detached from business strategy and are defined with an orientation more toward the past than the future (Nacamulli et al., 1986, p. 51; Ambrosini, 1989, p. 7).

In this model, moreover, the majority of workers have little or no sense of membership in the firm. It could not be otherwise, given that ownership of the firm is identified with ownership of the firm's capital. Furthermore, management is seen as being commissioned to act on the owners' behalf – in other words, to achieve the highest possible profit wholly to the benefit of the owners themselves.

This antagonistic conception of the relationship between the firm and its workforce is clearly rooted in liberal fundamentalism on one end of the spectrum and radical Marxism on the other. The former is wedded to the idea of an entrepreneur/owner, an undisputed commander-in-chief of his or her company, which is run solely for personal interest; the latter holds that class struggle is the only path to up-ending the power structure in the productive sphere and in society as a whole.

Interesting to note is that the distinguishing features of this conflictual conception (including the sense of detachment from the firm's mission and objectives) can be found in every area in which the method of collective negotiations is implemented, including state-controlled enterprises, local government administrations, and not-for-profit organizations. In other words, this conception also exists outside the field of action of private economic ventures, in contexts where there is not or should not be a commander/owner who pursues anything other than the interests of the economy and society for the general public. But this affirmation only confirms what was stated above regarding the origins of the antagonistic model of labor relations, molded by a vision of society divided into opposing classes (capitalists/employers and workers). In this perspective, class solidarity cuts across production contexts, whether in the private or public sector, in market or non-market economies, in profit or non-profit organizations.

Class solidarity impedes the process of formulating and sharing the corporate mission and common goals, which are the focal point for creating convergence between management and the workforce as a whole in an organization. This impediment may even exist in organizations that operate in the public sector and have clear shared missions of momentous social import. Class solidarity, in other words, obstructs the creation of "organizational solidarity," which is what makes the community model of the firm work (see Dore, 1987, esp. the introduction to the Italian edition, by M. Salvati).

The antagonistic view of the firm, moreover, does not affect labor relations alone. This conception more broadly encompasses relationships with anyone who acts as an advocate for humanistic or ethical/social issues, such as respecting and protecting the environment, improving workers' standard of living, creating employment opportunities, and promoting development in local areas. The antagonistic view, in other words, is based on the idea that economic/business needs (for efficiency, profitability, and competitiveness) inevitably conflict with those of an ethical/social nature. What is more, this conflict can be resolved only within a framework of zero-sum games, systematically favoring either this or that need to the detriment of others, or by seeking some sort of a compromise.

The antagonistic view does not even entertain the possibility that entrepreneurial creativity can be leveraged to devise far-reaching projects with long-term benefits that far outweigh immediate sacrifices. This would be a synergistic way to bring together different needs which appear to conflict only from a near-sighted, short-term perspective.

The diffusion path of the antagonistic view of the firm should not be surprising. The dominant model historically rationalized in Western capitalist societies does not depict a firm as especially attentive to ethical/social appeals or as capable of taking them on and coming up with entrepreneurially valid answers. In any case, we cannot help but think that in Italy, the dissemination of the antagonistic view of the firm is also evidence of a deep-seated and widespread lack of organizational culture. This is the reason behind the inability to do the following:

- grasp the organizational phenomenon in all of its complexity
- look beyond the short term to understand the needs, and all of their interconnections, that organizations contend with
- fully conceptualize the complex role that organizations are called on to play in society
- unleash the full potential for entrepreneurial innovation that exists in organizations and in the economic system

2. The crisis of the antagonistic view of the firm

Whatever the case may be, we must be aware that the antagonistic view of the firm is undergoing a crisis, one which will most likely intensify in the future, irrespective of the preferred approach to solving the conflict between economic/business needs and ethical/social ones. Firms that follow the logic of producing the highest possible profits (albeit in keeping with the letter of the laws in force) come up against problems of consensus which sooner or later impede the implementation of business strategy. If, in contrast, firms adopt the principle of giving priority to social concerns over economic ones (as was the case in the past with state-controlled enterprises), the role of profit and economic sustainability inevitability fades to the point of vanishing completely. On one hand, mounting social pressures on the business world no longer leave room for behaviors or choices that are not based on a profound understanding of these same forces. Firms must be able to dialogue constructively, to reorient, and to incorporate these social pressures into strategic company planning. On the other hand, the intensity of competitive pressures means firms must keep raising the bar in terms of competition and income, leaving no chance of survival for firms which lack this drive.

A compromise to harmonize different needs at play does not represent a viable solution either. Such approaches may well secure relative social amity, but they cannot bring about the mobilization of willpower and energy required to face today's competition.

Although there is no doubt as to the crisis of the antagonistic view of the firm, it is not nearly as clear how this situation can be rectified definitively and comprehensively, except in cases in which the very survival of the firm is in question. Let us explain. Reflecting on company reorganizations, which were highly concentrated from the late 1970s to the first half of the 1980s, we can plainly see that these experiences involved trying yet intense collaboration between management and workers. During these processes, everyone had to come to terms with the hard facts and reach an agreement on the actions to implement to recover efficiency and re-launch growth. These ordeals have undoubtedly shaken up the model for regulating labor relations described above, but they have not yet caused it to collapse entirely, except in firms that actually endured these events (and even here, perhaps not permanently). The question, then, is how to disengage definitively from the antagonistic conception of the firm and labor relations without going through the trauma of a crisis severe enough to jeopardize the survival of the firm. Put another way, the challenge is to develop collective learning processes that lead to a drastic and lasting transformation of the behaviors of management and its stakeholders before disaster strikes that proves fatal to the firm.

Before addressing this issue, however, we should take a closer look at the paradigm of collaboration in labor relations, shaped by the experience of outstanding Japanese and Western firms.

3. The collaborative view of the firm

The paradigm of collaboration in labor relations can be briefly described as follows. The prosperity of the firm and the well-being of its workers are an indivisible binominal; that is, one cannot exist without the other. The reason is that for the firm to be able truly to serve its customers and prevail over the competition while realizing consistent profit margins, personnel must be willing to step up and take responsibility for the firm's problems. However, this willingness cannot come about if employees are not, or do not feel themselves to be, the focus of the attention and the concerns of management. Personnel must have the clear perception that working for the prosperity of the firm means simultaneously working for their personal well-being, that of their families, and that of the wider community to which they belong.

This last statement has obvious implications in terms of profit allocation. The priority here is guaranteeing the functionality and sustainable growth of the firm. In other words, profit must fuel the accumulation of the tangible and intangible capital needed to optimize the firm's competitiveness and its ability to respond to the expectations of various stakeholders, beginning with its employees. In terms of the view of the firm we are discussing here, this is like depicting profit as an essential end-means qualified by the fact that it stems from the competitive and cohesive capacity of the firm, and it serves first and foremost to sustain this capacity.

Again, according to the collaborative view of the firm and labor relations, at the heart of the strategy lies a challenging vision of long-term company growth, conjoining and conciliating economic/business and ethical/social needs in a non-zero-sum game that proves highly remunerative. This "vision," while clearly indicating the direction in which the firm is heading, likewise drives constantly toward its own realization. This is practicable as long as the firm adequately communicates this vision – its contents and its assumptions, the results it promises and the commitment it requires.

The critical components of the collaborative model of the firm are transparency, relationships based on reciprocal trust, constructive dialogue to share the corporate strategy, and active participation in implementing it. Most importantly, all members of the organization are called on to contribute to developing company know-how (be it technological, commercial, or managerial) and to embrace certain fundamental values of the firm such as productivity, quality, and creativity. The crucial point is this: the collaborative model of the firm engenders a permanent mobilization of all of the energy inside the organization to achieve challenging long-term goals. (Outside energy is also tapped among players who are co-managers of a superordinate strategic plan: suppliers, distributors, and partners.)

The corporate values mentioned above are carefully and thoroughly elaborated in order to become pervasive – that is, shared by everyone and interpreted for every role at every level in the organization. In contrast, a corporate culture that develops within the context of an antagonistic view of the firm and labor relations is typically based on values that do not pertain to all members of the organization but are instead restricted to certain areas. Such values lead to discrimination and contrast between employers and employees, between areas of excellence and mediocrity, between recognized business areas and those dominated by a hegemonic culture (Coda, 1989, para. 12).

4. Transitioning from an antagonistic to a collaborative view of the firm

From the discussion above it is clear that the transition from an antagonistic view of the firm and of labor relations to a collaborative one involves an actual cultural revolution. Thus, such a conversion is not easily achieved, especially if a firm is not in the midst of a particularly serious crisis. This is true even if the antagonistic conception in its purest form is undoubtedly less common now than it was 15 years ago. Simply consider in today's entrepreneurial world the wide recognition given to the critical role of human resources in the current competitive context. This context compels all firms to improve simultaneously in terms of quality, costs, service, the rate of new product releases, and the ability to adapt to manifold and mutable customer needs, with everything that this entails in terms of flexibility (of product range, of volume, of delivery times, and so on). The unions, for their part, at one time took no interest in corporate balance sheets, for fear of becoming "trapped" in the rationale of the counterparty. Now they seem to realize that effectively safeguarding workers must go hand in hand with the proper functioning of the firm, and they acknowledge the firm's need for competitiveness and economic sustainability. Despite the undeniable progress, it remains a long road to the decisive and comprehensive establishment of the collaborative model of the firm described above.

What is lacking, first and foremost, is sufficient general knowledge of this model. Progress has been made in the debate surrounding profit and ethics in business, to which notables from the world of culture and economics have added their voices, and about which they are still having their say. In light of this, we are struck by the effort it takes to cast off the idea of economic needs as the antithesis of humanistic ones. Profit is praised one minute and reviled the next. Still today there are only a few isolated calls to shift the debate onto the much more serious and fruitful terrain of the "quality of profit." Meanings of an ethical or social nature are defined with no regard to the complexity of economic reality or the problems of corporate governance. These ethical/social reasons are factitiously contrasted with what are claimed to be economic reasons (or the firm's *raison d'être*, as someone has put it), which are defined in the abstract. However, there is not the slightest inkling of the radical distinction between a short-term economic orientation, which threatens and sacrifices the prospects for the firm's sustainable growth, and a long-term economic orientation. To sum up, then, too little has been done in Italy to elaborate, share, and spread a serious entrepreneurial and managerial ideology that takes into account the conditions for sustainable functionality of firms and, above all, the multifaceted, interconnected functions that all firms are called on to perform – functions which, taken together, delineate the complex role firms play in society (Figure 8.1).

Such conceptions of the role of the firm, and more generally the role of any production organization, are for the most part reductive

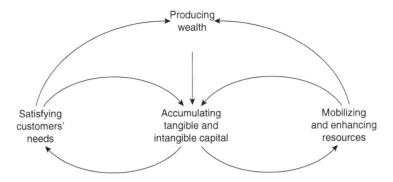

Figure 8.1   The role of the firm in society

and incomplete. These views underscore the economic function of the firm one minute and this or that "social function" the next. None of these views acknowledges that no single function shown in Figure 8.1 can be carried out at an acceptable performance level if the others are overlooked or without a unitary strategy that encompasses all of the functions in question and trains the attention of management on each as it relates to the others. It is precisely this unitary strategy that is key to a firm's functionality and long-term growth. The essence of such a strategy is a creative, forward-looking synthesis of myriad differentiated needs – economic/business and ethical/social – none of which can be considered secondary in importance or be sacrificed for the sake of the others. The elaboration of a business ideology requires an awareness of the complexity and richness of the contents of the firm's role but that a distinction be made between social expectations that are legitimately addressed to the firm and demands that are potentially detrimental to it. The latter are incompatible with the basic requirement underlying the firm's *raison d'être*: the economic satisfaction of human needs. Generally speaking, the thrust of such demands does not promote respect for or enhancement of any type of resource (human, financial, environmental, infrastructural, or otherwise). On the other hand, it is crucial to reject a purely economic view of the firm in which the pursuit of efficiency precludes respect for the people who do the work rather than striving to better these human resources and every other resource the firm puts to use.

All of this derives from the principle of systematic unity or consonance, which forms the foundation for the lasting functionality of any organization. Indeed, far from running counter to ethical meanings, this principle represents a key point of convergence between ethics and Management Theory.

Excogitating and disseminating a company ideology that adequately addresses the demands of the day and is capable of advancing the search for a basic convergence between economic/business needs and ethical/social needs – this is no doubt a compulsory step on the path that leads beyond the antagonistic conception of the firm and labor relations. Nonetheless, it would be naïve to believe that simply sharing knowledge of the collaborative model of the firm is enough to overcome resistance to it, which would come from no small number of people. In the world of entrepreneurs and unions, the model's opponents fear curtailment of freedom of economic initiative or, at the opposite end of the spectrum, entrapment in the business rationale. Either would lead to a loss of power resulting from the antagonism between the firm and its workers.

The truth is that the collaborative model does not entail a restriction on the freedom of endeavor, but a re-orientation in exercising that freedom, in the direction indicated by the search for sustainable profitability. Furthermore, the model does not involve entrapping workers or their representatives in a business rationale that is distorted by a myopic view of the interests of owners. Instead, the active and constructive contribution of workers is engaged to establish a long-term business logic, one that can secure levels of employment and bolster standards of living for workers and the population at large.

Adopting this viewpoint also means recognizing any type of firm or production organization as a preferred place for seeking and achieving continual growth in productivity,[1] which is indispensable to constantly responding better to the needs of the customer/user. This growth also generates resources required for the investments needed to satisfy the demands of workers and other stakeholders and to further increase productivity (Figure 8.2).

Espousing the collaborative view of the organization and its growth means shifting the focus of attention of the stakeholders:

- from issues pertaining to the distribution of wealth to the production of wealth
- from large-scale solidarity across classes to the same across organizations
- from managing current operations to managing growth

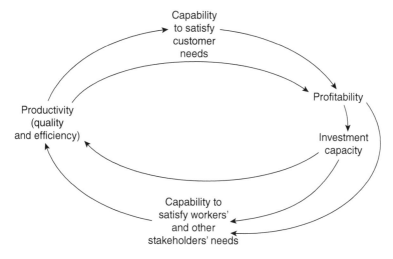

Figure 8.2 Typical virtuous loops driving a firm's long-term development

At this point, what can be done in concrete terms to promote and accelerate the cultural and behavioral changes that all of this requires? Could structural modifications be useful? Examples might be those regulated in EU Directive V on the structure of public companies, which in some cases provides for worker representation in the governance body. In addition to such legislative reforms, would a radical overhaul of the system of union relations be useful? This means a move toward intense collaboration and continuous dialogue between management and union representatives in terms of constant verification of the convergence between company growth and workers' well-being, in particular ex ante. Or is the right path to elaborate and disseminate participatory organizational strategy? This would mean maximizing the potentialities and involvement of all actors/parties in improving the functionality of the firm.

Addressing such complex issues here is impossible; in fact, doing so would go beyond the scope of this chapter.[2] Nonetheless, we can assert that all of the paths described above (and still more) are useful and necessary to prompt firms in Italy to leave antagonistic models behind and move toward a collaborative one. We believe such paths are effective to the extent that the decision to embark on them (1) comes from awareness that the conceptions of labor relations which currently predominate have had their day and must be radically overhauled in the direction of the collaborative view and (2) goes hand in hand with the progressive growth of stakeholders at a cultural level, in particular with regard to the ability to distinguish strategies and behaviors oriented toward sustainable development from narrow opportunistic ones.

The first point means that any alteration in institutional or organizational structure must not shift the focus from the heart of the problem, which is and remains radically to transform the way labor relations are understood and experienced in the firm. Reforming the structure of the firm, which involves qualified worker representatives becoming members of certain corporate bodies, can contribute to establishing a basic strategic orientation toward the long term. However, in no way does such a reform ensure that this will actually occur or that a management style will be adopted which is based on respect for and advancement of all workers.

A change in the system of union relations, as outlined above, is not only useful but essential to realizing the collaborative model. This model requires that various aspects of labor negotiations must be seen from a different perspective, with an eye to promoting the workers' interests and firm growth at the same time, without sacrificing the latter for the former. But, in addition to the problematic nature of this kind of change, no one system of union relations exists which can guarantee that all workers become the focus of the attention and the regard of management so that they, in turn, become capable of taking on the problems of the organization.

As regards participatory business strategies, these serve little purpose if they are not an authentic expression of a different way of managing the firm, aimed at igniting and fueling the virtuous circuits illustrated above (see Figure 8.2).

To sum up, although maneuvering institutional and organizational variables is useful if not indispensable, this cannot lead us to forget that the problem of disseminating the collaborative model of the firm is essentially about

- changing the mentality and values of management and of the firm's various stakeholders
- developing entrepreneurship and managerial professionalism capable of creating motivating work environments in which all people feel respected and appreciated and can be proud of their work and their organization

- growing professionally at all levels and in every function of the organization

What we should take away from all of this is that to overcome antagonistic models of labor relations, judicious use of training is critical. This lever should be activated on the initiative of firms, entrepreneurial associations, union organizations, and bodies and institutions offering training, and should target specific people, objectives, and contents on a case-by-case basis. However, the point of convergence should be promoting and disseminating progressive cultural growth among all stakeholders so that they hone their ability to distinguish between what enhances and what hinders growth in firms and in society and behave responsibly.

Notes

1. "Productivity of any production entity – be it an organization or part of an organization, a local or national economic system – should be understood here as the value of the output produced by a unit of work or capital. Clearly, productivity in this sense increases if the quality of output improves (where there is a customer/user) and/or enhances the efficiency by which output is obtained" (Porter, 1990, p. 6).
2. On the topic of designing the institutional and organizational structures of the firm in total compliance with a community view of the firm, see the work of Carlo Masini (1960, 1962).

References

Ambrosini, M. (1989). *Non solo autonomi. Risorse umane e relazioni di lavoro nell'impresa che cambia* [Not Just Independent Workers: Human Resources and Labor Relations in Changing Organizations]. Milano: Vita e Pensiero.

Coda, V. (1989). *L'orientamento strategico dell'impresa* [Strategic Orientation in the Firm]. Turin: UTET.

Dore, R. (1987). *Taking Japan Seriously: A Confucian Perspective on Leading Economic Issues.* Stanford, CA: Stanford University Press. Published in Italian as *Bisogna prendere sul serio il Giappone, Saggio sulla varietà dei capitalismi*, with an introduction by M. Salvati. Bologna: Il Mulino, 1990.

Masini, C. (1960). *L'organizzazione del lavoro nell'impresa* [Organizing Work in the Firm]. Milano: Giuffrè.

——. (1962). *L'azienda di produzione comunità economico sociale* [The Production Concern as a Socio-economic Community]. Milan: Giuffrè.

Nacamulli, R. D. C., Costa, G., and Manzolini, L. (1986). *La razionalità contrattata. Imprese, sindacati, e contesto economico* [Negotiated Rationality: Firms, Unions, and the Economic Context]. Bologna: Il Mulino.

Porter, M. (1990). *The Competitive Advantage of Nations.* London: Macmillan.

9
Ethical Codes and Market Culture

1. Defining the problem

There is growing awareness of the enormous damage inflicted on the economy by behaviors driven by corruption and the allocation of appointments on the basis of a spoils-sharing system rather than a desire to serve the good of the business world and the country. Furthermore, the public has realized the hardships caused by actions that have jeopardized entire production sectors.[1] This awareness brings into sharp focus the need to change direction. We must immediately begin the work of rebuilding a healthy economy, one based on new rules established to prevent the re-emergence of past pathologies.

Within this context, consensus is growing in support of the proposal to adopt standards of behavior which realign corporate action with the principles of propriety and transparency. Such standards would apply to large public and private groups, business associations, professionals directly implicated in corruption phenomena (such as bookkeepers and auditors), and the public administration.

Though this idea is still at a germinal stage, certain business groups and associations have taken preliminary steps toward its realization. Nevertheless, the general impression is that entrepreneurs in Italy are still a long way from a clear understanding of what codes of ethics entail and of the effects to be expected from them. This is true despite the fact that many multinationals introduced such codes long ago.

This being the case, it is essential that we explore the issue of codes of ethics in the business world (and public bodies and agencies as well). We must ask how the introduction of these standards can help cure the grave ailments that afflict the economy. Is it reasonable to anticipate a serious and effective drive in a new direction, finally to build the modernization process which the country so desperately needs on solid foundations? Or can we expect only an irrelevant contribution or, worse still, one manipulated in such a way as to ensure that everything follows the same old rules?

The answer to these questions is: It depends. Obviously, it depends on the content of codes of ethics. But that is not all. Most importantly, it depends on the true intentions of the people who decide to establish such codes, the moral motivation that drives them, and the deep-seated conviction of their own free economy values.[2] These are what form the basis for the constituent norms of the code. But even these are not enough. In a world permeated by values which are the very antithesis of an ethical code, any such standards we attempt to set can be effective only if we include a valid strategy for changing corporate culture. Establishing and applying an ethical code is only one of a number of measures this strategy should implement in following a carefully laid-out plan to transform the current situation radically.

In this chapter, we discuss the issues pertaining to codes of ethics in the following order. First, we attempt to come to a better understanding of pathological phenomena that destroy the functionality of firms and markets. These are the very problems that codes of ethics ought to help prevent. Next, we discuss what these codes actually are. Finally, we look at the conditions for the effective implementation of codes of conduct.

2. A sick economy

The pathological phenomena which are central to our discussion can be grouped into two broad, interrelated categories:

- systematic spoils-sharing – in other words, allocation of appointments to state-owned agencies and companies
- pervasive corruption, which has taken root in the relationships between the public and private spheres

The spoils-sharing practices (described in detail below) represent economic crimes which the criminal courts may not be able to prosecute directly, even though these phenomena are no less serious than corruption involving public/private relationships. As a result of spoils-sharing, the vast aggregation of state agencies and companies has been bent to the will of political parties. This seriously jeopardizes the functionality of these organizations and compromises the full realization of their production missions, which often serve the economy of entire systems/areas, regions, or the country as a whole.

To realize how serious these phenomena are, consider their impact on organizations that make up the National Health System (local health units, health centers, and public hospitals; Sorci, 1992). Consider also the effect of spoils-sharing and corruption on the functionality of local administrations and the firms that fall under their control, the system of state ownership in businesses (encompassing firms that are vital to economic and civil advancement), and so on. Spoils-sharing practices involve assigning loyal party members to serve as executives and to hold key subordinate positions in organizations. These appointees are then expected to act as agents of the party apparatus that put them where they are and to grant requests for "favors." Such favors may involve hiring or promoting members of a given party or political movement; favoring ties with certain suppliers, regardless of an objective evaluation of how these suppliers fare with respect to pertinent competitive variables (quality, price, service, etc.); funding parties or political representatives; and so on.

Clearly, in such cases, instead of acting like administrators and managers by shouldering responsibility for implicit business interests, political appointees behave like agents of political movements or representatives. The resulting damage to businesses and the economy as a whole comes not only from cost increases incurred from granting favors but more importantly from the consequent loss of corporate functionality. Depending on the circumstances, this may mean low-quality public services, delayed or cancelled execution of public works, the transformation of production concerns into simple salary suppliers, and so forth. In other words, acquiescing to requests for favors from political agents is detrimental to the functionality of the firms in question and seriously undermines the basic rules of good management and corporate organization. These rules include activating competitive mechanisms among suppliers; hiring only as many people as the company needs, and only those with the skill sets required to perform specific tasks; giving promotions and rewards on the basis of merit, as demonstrated by a job well done and positive results achieved; and so forth.

Closely associated with spoils-system practices (although radically different in nature) are corruption phenomena pertaining to ties between the public and private spheres. We are referring here to a wide variety of circumstances, including bidding on contracts to supply public companies or execute public works; purchasing real estate by public agencies (social security or welfare institutions or other); allocating to one local administration or another government subsidies (including EU funding) used to move forward with works that have already been contracted; issuing authorizations for land fills, quarries, and the like; managing price control systems (as with pharmaceuticals); and illicit lobbying, with the aim of deferring or amending government regulations to benefit one group or another.

In these cases, too, the damage to the economy is caused not only by resources being diverted from production activities into the coffers of political parties or the pockets of politicians and public officials. The more severe economic damage arises from several negative repercussions: the fact that beneficial market mechanisms are not allowed to take full effect, resulting in cost increases, inefficiency, and the obstruction of innovative processes; the severe setbacks experienced in key sectors such as urban/industrial waste recycling; the impediments thrown up to business development in regions, areas/systems, and production sectors; and the waste or underutilization of resources (human, financial, environmental, and infrastructural). To sum up, on one hand entrepreneurial potential is left untapped, and on the other corrupt businesspeople are free to exploit the absence of an efficient financial market and to slip through the cracks in the system. In some ways, this system is crippled by an excess of regulations; in others, it is lacking in market regulations and institutional norms that serve to promote production and systematic development.

3. Ethical codes: what they are and what purpose they serve

Now we explore the content of codes of ethics and what they mean specifically in terms of the pathologies described above. We use the expression "ethical code" in a broad sense, encompassing any official corporate document drawn up in any form that contains

- a list of the values which underpin the culture of the firm (e.g., product quality, customer service, respect and appreciation for every employee)
- and/or a declaration of responsibility toward each category of stakeholder (customers, workers, the local/national community, shareholders) to whom the firm is morally obligated
- and/or a more or less detailed blueprint of corporate policies or directives as regards corporate ethics (or ethical business behavior)
- and/or a description of the regulations or standards of behavior which all workers (or those at certain levels) must uphold to put the firm's ethics policies into action

Codes of ethics as outlined above are obviously documents that take a variety of forms and dimensions depending on whether they place emphasis on general values (or guiding principles) or contain more specific directives. Such codes may seek to clarify corporate identity from an ethical standpoint rather than detailing the ensuing employee standards of behavior.

Consequently, the contents of codes of ethics can be represented on a matrix constructed as follows: on one axis, the constituent directives ranked from general to specific; on the other axis, directives classed as corporate policy statements or individual duties of employees (see the statements in Figure 9.1). In any case, codes of ethics, be they more or less clear and complete, tend to define what the firm means by "ethical business conduct," that is, how the firm defines integrity and propriety in conducting business.

The contents of codes of ethics, whatever they may be, can reflect the deep-seated convictions of top management; however, in some cases there may not be strong consensus among management supporting the values underlying these codes.

Codes can exist in firms with a long-standing, consolidated tradition of honest, upstanding behavior or, on the contrary, in corporate circumstances contaminated by more or less rampant corruption and spoils-sharing. At this point, it is clear that the purpose of the ethical code varies according to the situation, as we can easily see in Figure 9.2.

	INDIVIDUAL DUTIES OF EMPLOYEES	CORPORATE POLICY STATEMENTS
GENERAL DIRECTIVES	I ask everyone in the GE Community to make a personal commitment to follow our Code of Conduct: • Obey the laws and norms that apply to our business conduct everywhere in the world. • Be honest, upstanding, and trustworthy in all activities and relationships as a member of GE. (General Electric, 1993) The firm expects its employees to avoid any activity, interest, or association that may potentially interfere with responsibilities or evaluations undertaken for the firm or its customers. (Morgan Stanley, 1993)	• Integrity is the rock on which we build our business success. ... The search for competitive excellence begins and ends with our commitment to ethical business conduct. (General Electric, 1993) • As intense as the competition may become, and as high as the stakes may rise, GE will only compete by legitimate and ethical means. (General Electric, 1993) • The purpose of corporate communication is the truth, conveyed in an effective and persuasive fashion. (Caterpillar Tractor, 1985)
SPECIFIC	• Knowledge or influence deriving from membership in the firm should not be used to further personal interests. (Morgan Stanley, 1993) • Employees are prohibited from impelling the firm to buy products or services from family members or from firms in which family members have significant or controlling interest, except with explicit authorization after an open examination of the pertinent facts. (Morgan Stanley, 1993)	• Particular care must be taken to avoid practices that seek to increase sales by means other than the correct commercialization efforts based on the quality of the project, production, price, and service. (Caterpillar Tractor, 1985) • In our advertising, and in every other form of public communication, we will avoid not only falsehoods, but also exaggerations and excessive assertions. (Caterpillar Tractor, 1985)

Figure 9.1   Examples of the content of ethical codes

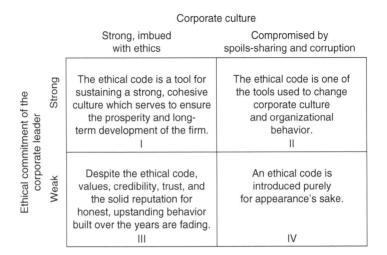

Figure 9.2   The different uses of ethical codes in corporations

The contents of the ethical code are crucial for clearly specifying what is good and bad in organizational behavior, in particular as regards the ethical issues a firm may face at a given moment in time. Figure 9.3 provides examples of regulations consisting of unequivocal directives that are the antithesis of those followed by countless firms involved in spoils-sharing and corruption. These norms regulate human resource management, competitive conduct, relationships with suppliers, transparency in accounting, and relations with the political sphere.

At this point, as we reflect on their content, what becomes apparent is the role codes of ethics play in firms in terms of clarifying how they do business. It is true that certain standards of behavior, such as those described in Figure 9.3, could be considered a sort of "corporate statute," equivalent to a law (a point we take up again at the end of this chapter). However, the fact remains that only codes of ethics, as expressions of a voluntary and autonomous desire for self-regulation, can be so specific (in defining right and wrong, proper and improper behavior), as no legal norm reasonably can. Such codes can focus on particular circumstances pertaining to a specific firm operating in given sectors in certain countries. In addition, such codes can

Human Resource Management

Personnel shall be recruited, selected, hired, and promoted on the sole basis of an objective assessment of qualifications needed for the position in question, without discrimination on the basis of religious beliefs, gender, membership in political parties or movements, etc.

Only those positions will be filled which are truly productive or necessary in order to achieve approved corporate objectives.

All employees must have a clear understanding of the purpose of their work and their business unit, and are expected to perform their work efficiently and well.

All employees must be asked to exercise their skills to the fullest and be given the opportunity to do so. This includes the ability to generate ideas and suggestions for innovating and improving the firm.

Competitive Behavior and Supplier Relations

Fair competition is vitally important for the market economy to function properly.

Commercial success must be pursued by making every effort to achieve a defendable competitive advantage, excluding any practice that may violate the rules of fair competition. In dealing with public or private customers, our firm will employ only commercial practices grounded in the utmost ethical rigor. We will never attempt to promote the sale of our products by paying bribes, or granting favors, gifts, and the

like. We will choose our suppliers, and purchase our materials and services of all kinds solely and exclusively on the basis of an objective assessment of quality, price, delivery capacity, service, and maintain sources for provisioning that meet our company's needs.

Transparency in Accounting and Financial Statements

The language used on financial statements is the universal business language. Anyone who uses our corporate financial statements (investors, lenders, and other interested parties) has the right to truthful information.

Our firm's total transparency in accounting is founded on valid, accurate, and complete basic information regarding data recorded on our books. All employees involved in producing, processing, and recording this information are responsible for the transparency of corporate accounts and financial statements.

Every entry in our accounting records must be an exact reflection of what is described in the support documentation. No information shall be concealed by management or independent auditors.

Any employee who discovers any possible omission, falsification, or negligence in accounting data or the documentation on which such data is founded must report this information.

Relations with the Political Sphere

Our firm will not grant favors or make contributions of any kind to political parties, movements or associations, or representatives of similar organizations.

Figure 9.3 Standards of behavior more directly linked to pathologies which emerge in firms involved in spoils-sharing or corruption

Source: Adapted from *Caterpillar: A Code of Worldwide Business Conduct and Operating Principles*, 1985.

be continuously updated, taking into account previously neglected issues that may come to the fore at a given point in time. Codes of ethics, moreover, can be written using corporate language which is readily understood by company employees. Such codes interpret and individualize the content of certain legal regulations into the firm's own corporate language; they serve to ensure the full respect for the law by the firm and all of its personnel.

But to grasp more firmly the difference in weight, in regulatory terms, of codes of ethics and of laws, we must remember that the former are organizational instruments expressly created to consolidate an ethically inspired corporate culture or to transform a corporate culture that has lost touch with the principles of propriety and transparency (see Figure 9.2, Boxes I and II). This is why it is nonsensical to assert that codes of ethics serve no purpose because relevant laws are already in place and firms must simply respect them. On the contrary, where conditions exist that guarantee the effective application of codes of ethics, they can also serve to prevent laws from being broken.

4. Conditions for effective ethical codes

Anyone in the field of business management, whether scholar or practitioner, knows very well that the documents that formally delineate corporate structure are one thing, but the rules and behavioral models that constitute how the organization really works are quite another.

The size of the gap between the organization "on paper" and the organization "in practice" can vary. In well-run firms, changes made to the formal organization serve either to strengthen and secure present positive behavior models or to modify current models to bring the real organization into line with the ideal one. Clearly, the decision to introduce an ethical code may be taken for either of these two reasons (assuming no intentional manipulation is involved). No particular problems arise in adopting a code when doing so simply means formalizing an unwritten standard of behavior which has been in effect for some time, one which has already permeated a strong, cohesive corporate culture. However, the effectiveness of the code – that is, whether it is actually respected by members of the organization – is a different matter.

The question is a complex one (as is generally true with problems involving changing the culture or the consolidated modus operandi of an organization) that warrants study on a case-by-case basis. It can be said, in any case, that an effective code can come only in the wake of a valid strategy for organizational change. As a result, normally, myriad levers are used, only one of which is a carefully composed code of conduct.

Here is a list of basic conditions for effectiveness which must not be neglected.

(1) The effectiveness of an ethical code in preventing violations of its constituent standards of conduct depends on how ethically driven corporate leadership is. Also essential is managers' commitment to spending their energy, intelligence, and creativity to convey and instill an ethical impetus in all members of the organization, to encourage each individual to embrace the spirit and the letter of the code. Given these key conditions for effectiveness, it is clear that no ethical code can even be brought to the discussion table in firms that are intricately involved in spoils-sharing and corruption unless a radical alteration of the culture and behavior of top management takes place first.

(2) The more successful the firm is in doing the following, the more effective the ethical code will be: communicating what's good and what's bad clearly and incisively in terms of both values and general principles, and how to apply them to concrete problems; making explicit the transition from stating corporate policy to identifying the individual duties that ensue, whenever this transition is not immediately evident; and focusing on pertinent ethical issues that arise at a specific moment in time.

(3) Establishing an ethical code may be seen as a way of preventing constituent norms from being violated. However, this viewpoint makes no sense unless organizational procedures intended to minimize or eliminate the risk of such violations are simultaneously or previously adopted. For example, it would be wrong to issue a ban on payments to political parties or representatives without carefully charting courses of action that divert or completely cut off the routes that have been used in the past to pay off politicians. Action must be taken regarding the procedures for making third-party payments which end up being funneled into the party system, and mechanisms

must be put in place to establish which illicit funds are tapped to make these payments. Inertia on these fronts would have repercussions for the credibility of corporate leaders and any ethical code they might issue. On the other hand, taking effective measures on these matters would send a powerful message as to the sincere intention to change direction, giving a completely different meaning to the decision to establish a self-regulating code.

(4) In firms in which destructive spoils-sharing practices are rampant and political agents have not lost their power to pressure their key appointees, the problem is removing these people from their positions. What's more, the firm must send an incontrovertible message to all personnel by taking decisive action against anti-corporate behavior, demonstrating that it will no longer be tolerated. Unless all of this is done, the establishment of an ethical code will be reduced to an unrealistic move or one made purely for appearance's sake.

(5) To be effective, codes of ethics must be incorporated into an organizational mechanism designed specifically to delineate

- tasks and responsibilities pertaining to the code of conduct, with special focus on procedures for communicating and preserving/ updating the code, provisions for counseling (on questions of interpretation and application), timely notification of violations (or risks of violations), and locking the code into other operational mechanisms (see point 6 below)
- positioning within the organizational structure of the committee responsible for the above

(6) To guarantee effectiveness in preventing code violations, the organizational mechanism mentioned above must be combined with other operational mechanisms, in particular those pertaining to

- human resource management (selection, job assignments, training, evaluations, rewards/penalties, etc.)
- inspection and control, which should be refocused in light of the need to prevent violations of the ethical code which may not be addressed by the internal auditing procedures currently in place

(7) In firms that are either victims of party-related "occupation" or accomplices to corruption, the effectiveness of codes of ethics can be

greatly reinforced in an environment in which corporate stakeholders have high expectations, hold management to exacting ethical standards, and are fully aware of what this means in concrete terms. This awareness is critical; it ensures that these expectations do not ultimately materialize in the form of sterile moralizing campaigns, which do nothing to affect corruption phenomena and can be leveraged by firms to serve ulterior motives and interests, seriously jeopardizing corporate functionality and development.

To make the environmental context evolve in this direction, it is worthwhile reopening the debate on the corporate statute. This should not be seen as conflicting with the workers' statute but as a definition of fundamental values, approaches, and applicable norms of ethically unassailable conduct shared by all stakeholders.

This statute can be drawn up for all firms (private or public, for-profit or not-for-profit) with a production mission entrusted to fully responsible and totally autonomous governance and management bodies within an explicit framework of "rules of play." The long-term functionality of a firm is based on principles, values, and standards of behavior that are, for the most part, shared by all firms. The statute in question, in this sense, should acknowledge norms of good management, such as those listed in Figure 9.3, as well as basic underlying principles. These include corporate autonomy, the responsibility of management and the parties who assign managerial posts, economic sustainability, and transparency (cf. Coda, 1988, §18; 1993).

A statute created along the lines described above should be the object of a social pact which expresses a steadfast, shared desire to turn over a new leaf. Such a statute represents a pact among stakeholders, both those with central and those with peripheral roles, at a sector and territorial level, in the public as well as the private sphere.

Notes

Report presented at the ISVI (Istituto per i Valori d'Impresa) Workshop entitled "Codes of Ethics and the Market Culture" at Mediocredito Lombardo in Milan on 5 November 1993. The author wishes to thank U. Lago, S. Bertolini, M. Molteni, R. Castoldi, and G. Corbetta for their help in conducting the research for this chapter.

1. Consider here industries which depend on central or local government decisions (for authorizations, financing, etc.).

2. This term is used with the same meaning it has in the Enciclica *Centesimus Annus* (1991) by Pope John Paul II, §42.

References

Caterpillar Tractor (1985). *A Code of the Worldwide Business Conduct and Operating Principles*.

Coda, V. (1988). *L'orientamento strategico dell'impresa* [Strategic Orientation of the Firm]. Turin: UTET.

———. (1993). "Sui principi costitutivi di un'economia sana e sulle linee di intervento per promuoverne la diffusione" [On the Principles and Policies of a Healthy Economy and the Lines of Action for Promoting its Dissemination] (1993). In AA.VV., *Economia e criminalità* [Economy and Criminality]. Rome: House of Representatives.

General Electric (1993). *Integrity: The Spirit and the Letter of Our Commitment. Guide to Our Policies*.

John Paul II (1991). *Centesimus Annus*.

Morgan Stanley (1993). *Code of Conduct*.

Sorci, V. C. (1992). "Dall'assistenzialismo allo sviluppo" [From Welfarism to Development], *Azienda pubblica* [The Public Firm], 3.

10

In Support of a Free and Responsible Entrepreneurial Economy

In this chapter, we address how to bring together the countless job seekers who are motivated to work and the many unsatisfied needs in society today. Clearly, this problem challenges the role of entrepreneurs. The essence of entrepreneurialism is devising and realizing economically viable ways to merge needs and resources. We can take this issue as an invitation to further our understanding of the following questions: What exactly is this entrepreneurialism which we so badly need? What are the spheres of entrepreneurial commitment and responsibility? What conditions are required for entrepreneurialism to grow and expand?

Before delving into these questions, we ought to be aware of the decline that the Italian economic system experienced for three decades, beginning in the early 1960s. We should also discuss the recent transition phase the economy has embarked on, which is far from reaching a conclusion. Laying the groundwork for our discussion in this way will give us a clearer vision of the radical and contrasting transformation processes needed (which are to some extent underway) to modernize the country and free all of its potential to serve the common good.

1. An overview

Over a period of at least 30 years (until 1992), Italy experienced a downward economic spiral (though not without sporadic upturns). This led the country further and further away from the liberal economy model outlined by the Magisterium of the Catholic Church in its social encyclicals, in particular *Mater et Magistra* (Pope John Paul II, 1991) and the *Centesimus Annus* (Pope John XXIII, 1961), the latter of which asserts with conviction that "the economic world is the creation of the personal initiatives of individual citizens" and the action of public powers involves "by its very nature, orientation, encouragement, and integration."

During these three decades, the public sphere of the economy expanded considerably; worse still, power became concentrated in the hands of political parties. These parties increasingly interfered in economic life, abusing the welfare state and promoting political patronage, often under the guise of solidarity. Little or no respect was shown for the autonomy of the organizations which gradually fell prey to party control or for freedom or responsibility, efficiency or professionalism, the values which underpin the proper functioning of any production system.

The ripple effects of all of this were felt in countless areas: unproductive public spending; the national deficit; the tax burden; the deterioration of public services; delayed execution or cancellation of vital public works; widespread corruption in relations between the business world, the public administration, and politicians; and regulation of public economic activity, which introduced serious obstacles to freedom of initiative while doing nothing to guarantee more comprehensive protection of the health of the country's citizens, the territory, or consumer interests (Porter, 1990, p. 697). In addition, no clear rules were established in key sectors such as the financial market, broadcasting, telecommunications, or waste disposal/recycling (McKinsey, 1994). Passive attitudes became entrenched in the minds of broad swathes of the population – passivity that is the very negation of any spirit of initiative or sense of personal responsibility. Overall, the country was losing its ability to compete.

The old consociative regime that spawned all of this found itself in increasingly dire straits as a result of the spiraling damage to public finance. Italy was also further distancing itself from the rest of the European Union, while having to respect commitments deriving from membership in that body.[1] Added to this were the blows dealt by referendums, the electoral success of various political movements, and the actions of the magistrates investigating the "Clean Hands" scandal. Yet the old regime continued to cling to power until the April 1992 elections. These gave us a parliament which set up a government that finally began to address the problems of reorganizing the country.

Since then, a long, laborious transition phase has begun, leading toward a new order, which for the most part remains to be discovered and constructed. The following are some of the first crucial steps taken in the direction of radically transforming the economy: an agreement on labor costs deactivated automatic inflation mechanisms; large public firms were converted into joint-stock companies; reorganization and privatization processes were set in motion; firms were reorganized and divestments made; fiscal deregulation was attempted; a slow, ponderous trek began toward active labor market policies, in keeping with EU guidelines (Commission of the European Community, 1994, p. 52); and Finance Acts tentatively affected public spending (not only public revenue).

This new chapter opened in 1992, marked by extreme levels of turbulence, instability, and uncertainty about the future. The country has been exposed to the acutely perilous risks of the initiatives and behaviors of a group of executives who have not abandoned their past habits: corruption is far from being eradicated; old spoils-sharing practices are still in use; politicians intrude on the operations of public organizations; total incompetents (passed off as "experts") are nominated to posts in the public economic sphere; and obstacles are thrown up on the path to privatization.

By their very nature, problems associated with any transition are extremely complex and difficult to manage. Although some upstanding people have come to the fore in positions of responsibility, the process of generating a new executive class is not yet underway. New leaders must be capable of dealing with the problems facing the country, and they must distinguish themselves from their predecessors in terms of competencies and dedication to the common good (Ostellino, 1995).

This is the very brief overview for the present chapter, which aims to contribute to a clearer understanding of the transformation of our economic system in the direction of a free and responsible entrepreneurial economy. To achieve this aim, we must now clarify the concept of "entrepreneurialism."

2. The pathways to an entrepreneurial economy

In essence, entrepreneurialism is the ability to invent and realize production systems which focus on satisfying three kinds of requirements effectively and simultaneously:

- the demands of customers, the end users of a firm's products/services
- the expectations of various stakeholders who provide the resources required for production
- the need for a financial equilibrium which is self-fueling, and as such self-sustaining over time without depending on subsidies to compensate for inefficiencies or management errors (Coda, 1991)

The paths to entrepreneurialism outlined above lead to value creation across the board. The resulting production system generates value for the following parties simultaneously:

- customers, who are offered a product system characterized by a ratio of perceived value to asking price which progressively increases
- workers, who see the production system as a sort of gymnasium where they can learn, train, realize their potential, and hone valuable skills for the labor market
- shareholders, who see the value of their stock increase
- distributors and suppliers, who see themselves as part of a winning business strategy which will enhance the value of their firms
- the general public: the firm acts responsibly toward the public, embracing the values of a market economy, of environmental protection, and of increasing the value of work and savings; as such, the firm is a source of widespread well-being

Again, the paths toward entrepreneurialism lead to growth in productivity and development, where productivity and development are inseparable concepts. Productivity – that is, the value of output (or value added) per unit of labor or unit of capital – is the fundamental guiding value in an entrepreneurial economy. Boosting productivity means offering the customer more quality more efficiently. This makes additional resources available that can be channeled to

- enhance levels of consumer satisfaction and loyalty
- respond more fully to expectations pertaining to protecting and enhancing jobs, savings, and the environment
- develop new products or services, new markets, and new business areas

Depending on the circumstances, we can increase productivity in a number of ways: by divesting activities that are not directly linked to our core business; by focusing on the production mission of the firm; by reorganizing the firm; by repositioning the firm in new market segments (customer groups/types of needs); by updating technology; by moving the organization toward models that successfully engage all employees, holding each of them personally accountable; and by more fully integrating different corporate functions.

Growth in productivity may call for sacrifices, even major ones, in terms of jobs. But without a strong, steadfast commitment to boost productivity, there can be no development and no new jobs. So these sacrifices are acceptable, and they make sense if the point is to revitalize firms and pave the way for investments destined to bear fruit in the future, including the creation of new employment opportunities.[2]

But for development to occur, growth in productivity is not enough. Entrepreneurialism is needed whose cultural heritage embodies the value of development. This kind of entrepreneurialism must not only reorganize, redirect, and consolidate existing businesses effectively but also conceive and realize new initiatives, according to a prudent yet challenging development plan.[3]

Mature entrepreneurialism, rich in content, capable of creating value across the board and uniting productivity and development, is certainly not a dominant feature of Italy's business culture. However, we must promote entrepreneurialism that meets these standards, enlightening the community as to its merits and thereby creating a social climate that values this business approach. But this is not the appropriate forum for discussing how this can be achieved. First, we must realize that the paths to entrepreneurialism mapped out above do not pertain to the business world alone; they are relevant to any production organization, profit or non-profit, public or private, operating in a market or non-market context. This key point calls for serious reflection to grasp all of its implications, in particular those relating to organizations and production concerns of all kinds which fall into the public sphere.

3. Entrepreneurship in the public sector

Creating value for the customer; promoting personnel; achieving a self-sustaining financial equilibrium, responsibly and autonomously; spurring growth in productivity to free up resources to invest in a future that meets the expectations of a serene and civil existence – these concepts and values may seem revolutionary with reference to the different levels of the public administration, local governments, state universities, local public health units, and so on. Yet they are entirely valid and completely applicable in all of these areas.

Exposing production concerns in the public sphere to entrepreneurial values and approaches means unleashing a vast potential for growth in productivity and development. This would be enormously beneficial in terms of balancing public finance, improving public services, re-launching investments and accumulating public funds, boosting economic growth and moving toward a more civilized country.

In essence, two paths can be followed to achieve all of this (and a few painstaking steps have already been taken):

- transferring production concerns from the public to the private economic sphere by privatizing public organizations and outsourcing production activities
- applying business models to the production organizations that are to remain in the public sphere (Coda, 1994)

Privatization is a critical juncture in the process of liberating the economy. Privatization relieves the state of burdensome responsibilities which absorbed massive resources in the past, and it drastically reduces the spectrum of activities in which political patronage and improper exploitation can occur. Privatization also frees up resources that can be applied to cutting the public deficit and investing in production. In addition, it releases the public entities involved from restrictions on their strategic potential and operational capacity; introduces new investment opportunities in a financial market in dire need of them; and, if properly managed, allows the country's level of economic democracy to rise.

However, privatization processes also give rise to a series of complex problems regarding ownership structure and appropriate procedures for guaranteeing transparency, evaluation, regulating natural monopolies, promoting competition, and so on. Fully achieving the benefits expected from privatization is contingent on addressing and solving these problems.

Outsourcing production activities involves entrusting them to private firms. Outsourcing contracts may differ from concession schemes or conventions. In any case, it is crucial that the private firms which emerge and prosper from these contract relationships do not become parasites thriving on the dysfunctions of the public sector through perverse collusive relationships. These private enterprises, instead, should be encouraged to innovate and pursue growth in productivity not only in their own interests but also to the benefit of customers. To ensure that this happens, the validity of the relationships between public and private sectors must be ascertained, and if necessary these relationships should be re-molded with an eye to promoting productivity and encouraging investments.

Last comes the complex process of applying business models to the production organizations destined to remain in the public sphere. This calls for redesigning the regulatory framework applied to the public sector and the institutional structure of its constituent production units. In addition, organizational mechanisms must be implemented similar to those used to run a business, in particular in relation to information and oversight. Most important of all, competent leaders are essential. The entire process essentially entails filling the wide cultural gap between an organizational unit structured simply to provide services/pay related expenses and an autonomous entity responsible for

- satisfying the final users of its services
- motivating its personnel to act accordingly
- balancing its books without depending on government subsidies
- planning and investing for the future, on the basis of an independent capacity to generate savings and obtain financing

It is vital to promote entrepreneurial principles of efficiency and effectiveness in national and local administrations, and more generally speaking in all production organizations that fall in the public domain, accelerating the processes described above (privatization, application of business models, and outsourcing production activities). All of this serves to re-launch organizations that are currently under state control and to inject the public apparatus with renewed efficiency. As an entity that produces, saves, and invests, the state itself becomes a driver for development. In addition, the state and the public administration can once again take on their true role as guides, regulators, and guarantors of an economic system based on decentralized decision-making and built on the cornerstones of responsibility and freedom of initiative. Now we will describe this role and explain the main lines of action it should follow.

4. Conditions for entrepreneurial development

How well a market economy works depends on the extent to which it is truly free and responsible. In such an economy,

- obstacles are systematically identified and removed which may hinder the freedom of economic initiative by individuals or associations, profit or non-profit organizations
- rules are designed, introduced, and enforced which promote the exercise of this freedom in a responsible way
- the production system is permeated by the entrepreneurial values and practices mentioned above at a national and a local level

But who is to take responsibility for all of this? Whose job is it to define and create the conditions that facilitate the emergence of the entrepreneurial potential that abounds in Italy? And who should promote entrepreneurial development at a local level in the constituent system-areas of this country, areas that often represent a wealth of untapped potential and resources which are not adequately exploited, if at all?

Clearly, the answer is a "system guide" who contends with economy policy at the national and local levels. From an organizational perspective, this could be considered a meta-entrepreneurial role (or higher-level entrepreneurial role). Put another way, rather than directly dealing with production and development problems (except for production organizations and investments that remain within the public sphere), whoever took on this role would address two fundamental challenges which must be faced first:

- formulating and disseminating a long-term vision of system-wide development (at the national and local levels)
- defining and implementing a context which favors the realization of this vision through the initiatives and actions of individual citizens, existing firms, new firms, and non-profit organizations (both present and future).

The first challenge is clearly a strategic one. Just as clear are its entrepreneurial implications, given that it requires an ability to bring together needs to be satisfied and resources to be exploited. This must be done at an aggregate level, with a thorough understanding of the problems facing the sector and the macroeconomic context. The second problem can be compared to the complexities of defining an organizational environment in which myriad organizations and individuals make their own choices and assume different behaviors. These groups and individuals are variously linked to an intricate network of collaborative and competitive relationships.

Given the above, we now explore the lines of action that this meta-entrepreneurial actor should take.

At a national level, top priority for rapid action goes to

1. liberalization/deregulation in order to
   - reduce or simplify bureaucratic requirements for business initiatives (for instance, creating a new firm or obtaining a permit to open or expand a chemical plant)
   - simplify and streamline the regulatory system (for example, tax laws)
   - eliminate obstacles that prevent market entry or growth for firms (in sectors such as retail distribution, power production, multimedia communication)
   - expand the freedom of choice for firms (consider removing restrictions on opening hours/days for retail stores, for instance) (McKinsey Global Institute, 1994)
2. efficient and transparent regulations aimed at allowing
   - privatization of public utilities
   - the full functionality of the financial market, bringing it in line with the strict standards of transparency of the most advanced stock markets
   - the launch of new sectors (such as pension funds and waste recycling) and the opening of new areas for entrepreneurial

initiatives and responsibility, including for private non-profit firms (for example, in the field of conservation and enhancement of our cultural, artistic, and archeological heritage; education; basic social services) (Silva, 1995)
- revival of the building sector
- an even more flexible job market, through the widespread use of new employment contracts (for example, temporary or part-time jobs or apprenticeships)
- environmental protection, within the context of sector/area development

Subsequently, we need to focus our attention on the question of how to promote a profound cultural transformation in light of three key objectives:

1. to counteract passive or demanding attitudes (expectations of a secure job in the public administration or in the industrial plant of a large enterprise) and instead promote auto-entrepreneurial attitudes and behaviors, with full awareness of the momentous changes currently underway and the opportunities these changes offer
2. to nurture a social climate which holds innovative entrepreneurialism in high regard, whatever the cultural origins (capitalistic or cooperative, private or public, inside a large organization or independent), provided the end result of this entrepreneurialism is to create value across the board, capably combining productivity and development
3. to raise the bar for economic leaders, specifically those people who govern and run firms and business organizations of all kinds, business associations, trade unions, chambers of commerce, and so on

To pursue the first objective, age-old practices linked to abusing the welfare state and promoting political patronage must be definitively done away with. Also, major commitment and creativity are needed in pursuing active labor market policies in keeping with EU guidelines.[4]

The second objective is also vital. A social climate must emerge that places high value on innovative entrepreneurialism capable of driving progress and promoting respect. This provides fertile terrain for propagating business values, advancing entrepreneurial vocations, and activating social control mechanisms that encourage genuine respect for and continual fine-tuning of the rules of a market economy. Furthermore, this climate cannot come about without a steadfast commitment to disseminate a healthy business culture throughout all social levels and spheres.

But how can we value what we do not know? Without an underlying economic culture, how can we recognize an innovative business: one that produces wealth and well-being as a result of its competitive capacity and cohesion; a business that enhances the value of work, savings, and environmental resources; a business that constantly strives to provide customers with higher quality and greater efficiency? How can we distinguish such a business from one that exploits any and all occasions to make a profit, without considering the negative repercussions that this opportunistic behavior might have on long-term development and profitability?

This call to disseminate a business culture among all citizens should come as no surprise. Simply consider that a key enterprise represents a precious asset not only for its shareholders but also for society at large. In various ways we are all stakeholders: as consumers, as employees, as shareholders, as providers of funds for the banking system (which, in turn, finances business), as members of the local community who are interested in the production facilities of the firm, as citizens of a country which is becoming increasingly integrated in the international economy, who must be acutely aware that their well-being, and that of their children, depends on the vitality of the national production system, and that a true democracy and a free responsible economy are one and the same.

Last but not least important is the objective of raising the bar for the quality of our economic leaders. This obviously includes politicians who have the power to appoint a multitude of key economic positions (ministers, economic authorities, economic parliamentary commissions, and myriad bodies and agencies headed by government appointees).

The economic system and businesses in general need prudent and responsible owners, independent and competent administrators, honest and principled managers to achieve high standards of performance (in terms of competition, finance, and employment).

How can these basic subjective conditions be realized to foster the functionality and development of organizations and the system as a whole? The problem is a complex one, and the solution involves

- the functionality of markets and respect for valid rules underpinning a free economy (rules of competition, transparency, ethics in business relationships, autonomy and responsibility, accountability of administrators and managers, merit-based promotions, and so on)
- a higher level of culture and economic information among citizens, to cultivate the ability to differentiate between good and bad administrators, well-run and poorly run firms
- the efficiency of systems for preventing and penalizing behaviors associated with corruption and spoils-sharing
- the different processes described above (privatization and corporatization, liberalization and regulation), which mark the path to modernization for Italy

What we have discussed so far applies to the role of economic policy at a national level. But what about at a local level – specifically, districts and system-areas, which are the basic economic units to be governed within the framework of a higher level of entrepreneurialism? At this point, various issues come into play: intense cooperation, constructive dialogue, and the capacity for systemic thought by players who are responsible for guiding and developing the economy at a local level. Here we refer to chambers of commerce, local authorities (of the city, province, and so on), business associations, local banks, local trade unions, and so forth. What should these parties do? They should set up a roundtable and meet regularly. The following items should be on the agenda:

- coming up with a shared vision of long-term development for the system-area that responds to the need to exploit present and future resources
- translating this vision into one or more priority projects
- identifying the obstacles to pursuing the shared development plan and the conditions that would facilitate the realization of that plan
- removing the obstacles and creating the conditions in the preceding point, in accordance with a specific plan of action, calling

into play various parties and assigning them responsibility for the progress of the priority projects (regional, ministerial, community authorities, and so on)
• monitoring the progress of projects

All of this can be extremely challenging and complex to achieve, to the point of seeming utopian. Yet this is a path which must be mapped out and followed with determination. Developing an entrepreneurial economy is a process that will encounter opportunities along with obstacles (social/cultural, infrastructural, and so forth) – and very different ones as well, even within the same province. For this reason, different action is required from one system-area to another.[5]

Admittedly, this chapter focuses more on the challenge of transitioning our economy and less on the employment problems we are facing, in particular in Europe and in Italy. But, on reflection, this choice is a response to the need to identify the structural causes for poor employment performance in our country and to eradicate them. We must follow the routes that lead to developing a free economy which serves the common good, in keeping with the path marked out by the Magisterium of the Catholic Church in the papal encyclicals cited above, and more recently in a document released in 1994 by the Italian Bishops' Conference, "Democrazia economica, sviluppo e bene comune" [Economic Democracy, Development, and the Common Good].

Notes

1. For example, consider the EU regulations that have progressively blocked moves to use public funds to recapitalize organizations operating at a loss, thereby triggering the collapse of firms in crisis and the system of state ownership (Dini, 1995).
2. Compare the proposal for "a sort of European social pact" formulated by the Commission of the European Community (1994, p. 51).
3. The work of Brunetti and Camuffo on Marzotto (1994) provides a wealth of ideas and inspiration in this regard.
4. Important examples of active labor market policies are those which pertain to job orientation, community work, self-employment, paths for professional re-training, for mobile workers and/or the Extraordinary Wages Guarantee Fund, and public/private partnerships (GEPI, 1994).
5. An enlightening example is the Verbano/Cusio/Ossola district (SDA Bocconi, 1984).

References

Brunetti, G. and Camuffo, A. (1994). *Marzotto: Continuità e sviluppo* [Marzotto: Continuity and Development]. Milan: Isedi.

Coda, V. (1991). *Impresa e sistema economico fra efficienza ed equità* [The Firm and the Economic System: Efficiency to Equity]. Milan: NED.

———. (1994). "Impresa, mercato e liberazione dell'economia" [The Firm, the Market, and the Free Economy], in L. Majocchi and M. Vitale (eds.), *Per una nuova cuitura di mercato* [In Support of a New Market Culture]. Milan: Il Sole.

Commission of the European Community (1994). *Crescita, competitività, occupazione* [Growth, Competitiveness, and Employment]. Milan: Il Saggiatore.

Dini, L. (1995). Speech at the convention held in Milan at Assolombarda on 27 March on "Le privatizzazioni per lo sviluppo del paese e dell'imprenditorialità" [Privatization for the Development of the Country and Entrepreneurialism].

GEPI (1994). *La GEPI e le politiche attive del lavoro* [Agency for the Management of Industrial Shareholdings and Active Labor Policies]. Rome: GEPI.

Italian Bishops' Conference (1994). "Democrazia economica, sviluppo e bene comune" [Economic Democracy, Development, and the Common Good], *La Società*, 4: 591–622.

McKinsey (1994). *Employment in Developed Countries: Italy.*

McKinsey Global Institute (1994). *Employment Performance.* Washington, DC: McKinsey Global Institute.

Ostellino, P. (1995). "Seconda classe" [Second Class], *Corriere della sera*, 23 March.

Porter, M. E. (1990). *The Competitive Advantage of Nations.* London: Macmillan.

SDA Bocconi (1984). "Per un recupero della imprenditorialità nel VCO (Verbano/Cusio/Ossola). Cause della crisi e ipotesi di soluzione" [Recovering Entrepreneurialism in the VCO Area: Causes of the Crisis and Possible Solutions] *Novara*, periodical of the provincial administration, Special Issue.

Silva, F. (1995). "Vi sono rimedi per l'alta disoccupazione?" [Are There Any Solutions to the Problem of High Unemployment?]. LIUC Papers, Economy and Business Series 3, no. 18.

Index